[TMP **III**]
VOLUME

Foreword

Ken Harman Hashimoto

CURATOR & GALLERIST

You'd assume that after a decade of doing this annual exhibition, I'd be pretty darn tired of the Moleskine Project. Over these past ten years I've curated quite a few group shows, many of which have toured or reappeared year after year and I'll be the first to say that even the most successful group shows tend to fizzle out eventually.

Now of course that's not because these shows don't have the potential to soldier on, but rather it's simply because our artists (and myself as a curator) are usually more interested in pushing forward and exploring new ideas, rather than looking backward and revisiting older concepts.

And yet here we are, more than ten years after we first unveiled Rod Luff's Moleskine Project solo show in San Francisco and the exhibition is still going strong… if not bigger and better than ever before.

I firmly believe that one reason for the incredible lasting power of this dynamic group show is because the exhibition format itself. The intrinsic and inherent nature of a blank sketchbook is to encourage the user to continue on and to fill each subsequent page. It's a challenge, a call to arms, and for the select few artists who are actually able to finish their book from start to finish, a badge of honor when it's done.

Anyone who's cracked open a Moleskine knows that writing, drawing, sketching, or jotting on the first page is simply the start… once you're in the swing of it the real challenge is attempting to make sure that each following page is better than the last. That's the challenge you sign up for when you first slide off that black rubber band off the smooth leather cover and open the book to Page One.

As a gallerist, making sure each exhibition is better than the last is my curatorial challenge. Encouraging myself and my artists to push better and bigger each time is why this show is just as fresh and exciting this year as it was ten years ago.

It's for this very reason that the show has travelled beyond San Francisco to London, to New York City, to Honolulu.

It's because of this boundless creative pursuit that this exhibition will soon make its forthcoming museum debut at the Mesa Arts Center in Arizona in October 2022.

It's because of this drive, this desire to not just fill each page but to grow with each page that you're holding this book in your hands today.

I hope you enjoy the many wonderful works of art found within this book and hope the latest edition of our ongoing show inspires you to fill a Moleskine sketchbook of your own.

Introduction

Rod Luff

For the past decade the Moleskine Project has paid tribute to the art of the sketchbook, the backbone of creativity for many artists. Early in my career, I used to take my sketchbook with me to practice, study and jot down immediate ideas, many years later this practice hasn't changed for me as a working professional. The immediacy of a sketchbook allows artists such as myself to generate ideas and images quickly, which can then be taken by others to a fully rendered final product in a commercial setting. Simultaneously I also use my sketchbook for creative growth and exploration when pursuing my personal or fine art work.

The Moleskine Project exhibits other artists who too employ this medium throughout a multitude of disciplines from fine art to illustration to tattoos to comics to concept art and beyond. Artists like Aaron Li-Hill have even gone beyond the two dimensional surface by cutting and carving into the book itself, adding a third dimension of shadows and depth.

Several artists have defied tradition by wholly rendering their pages in oil paint, a medium uncommonly associated with sketchbook paper. Throughout these pages you'll find work across a broad spectrum ranging from the gestural lines of Conrad Roset to the incredibly detailed and surreal worlds depicted in Jeremy Enecio's graphite drawings.

There's something for everyone in these exhibitions and books, taken from a variety of art styles, media and professions. It's inspiring to me as one of the curators of this show to witness just how much creativity and personal expression can be contained within the humble pages of a sketchbook. I would like to thank Ken Harman Hashimoto for developing this into what it is today, as well as the hard work of the Spoke Art crew who make it a reality year after year. And a huge thanks to all the amazing artists that have lended their time and skills to this special and unique project!

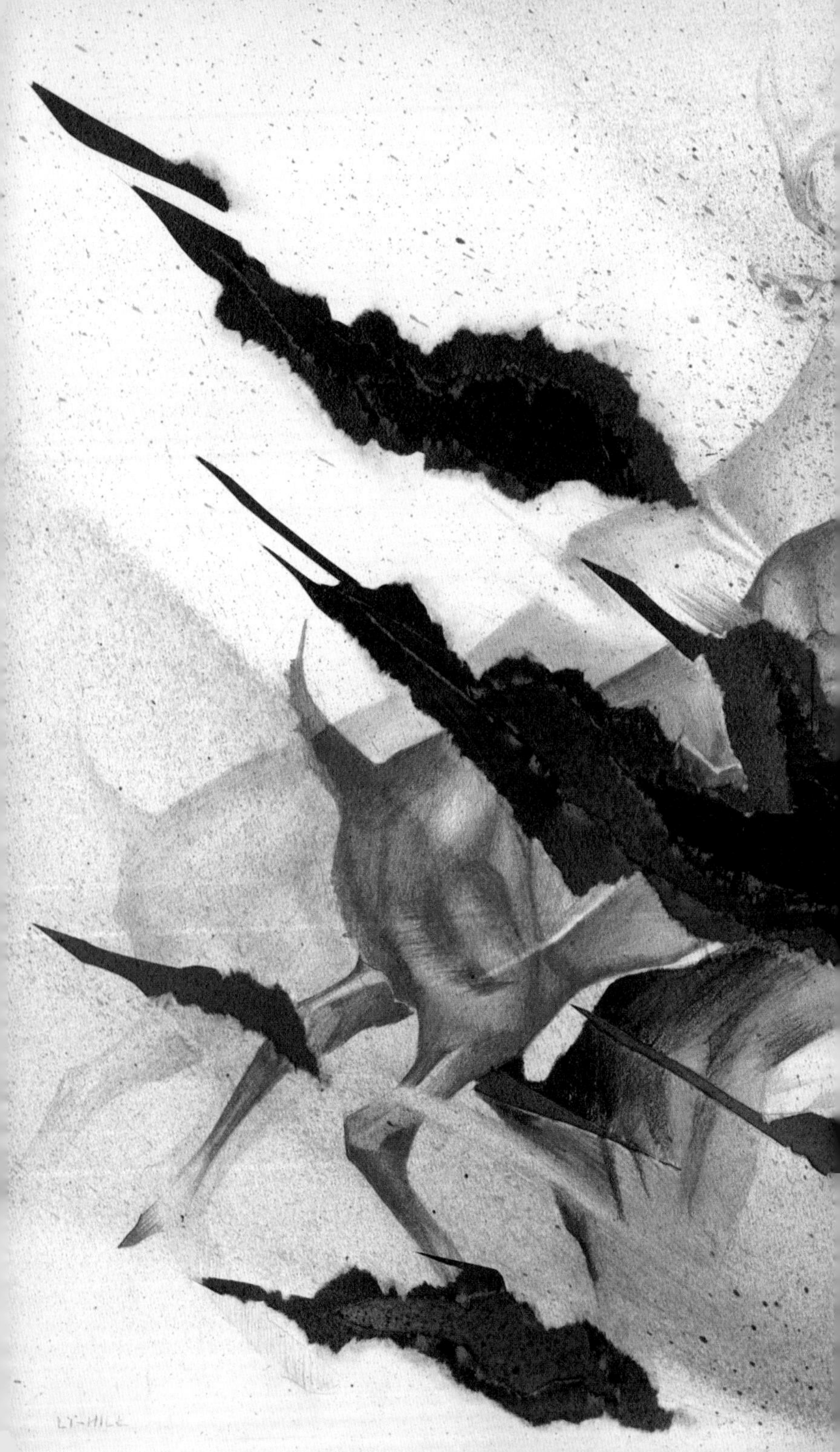

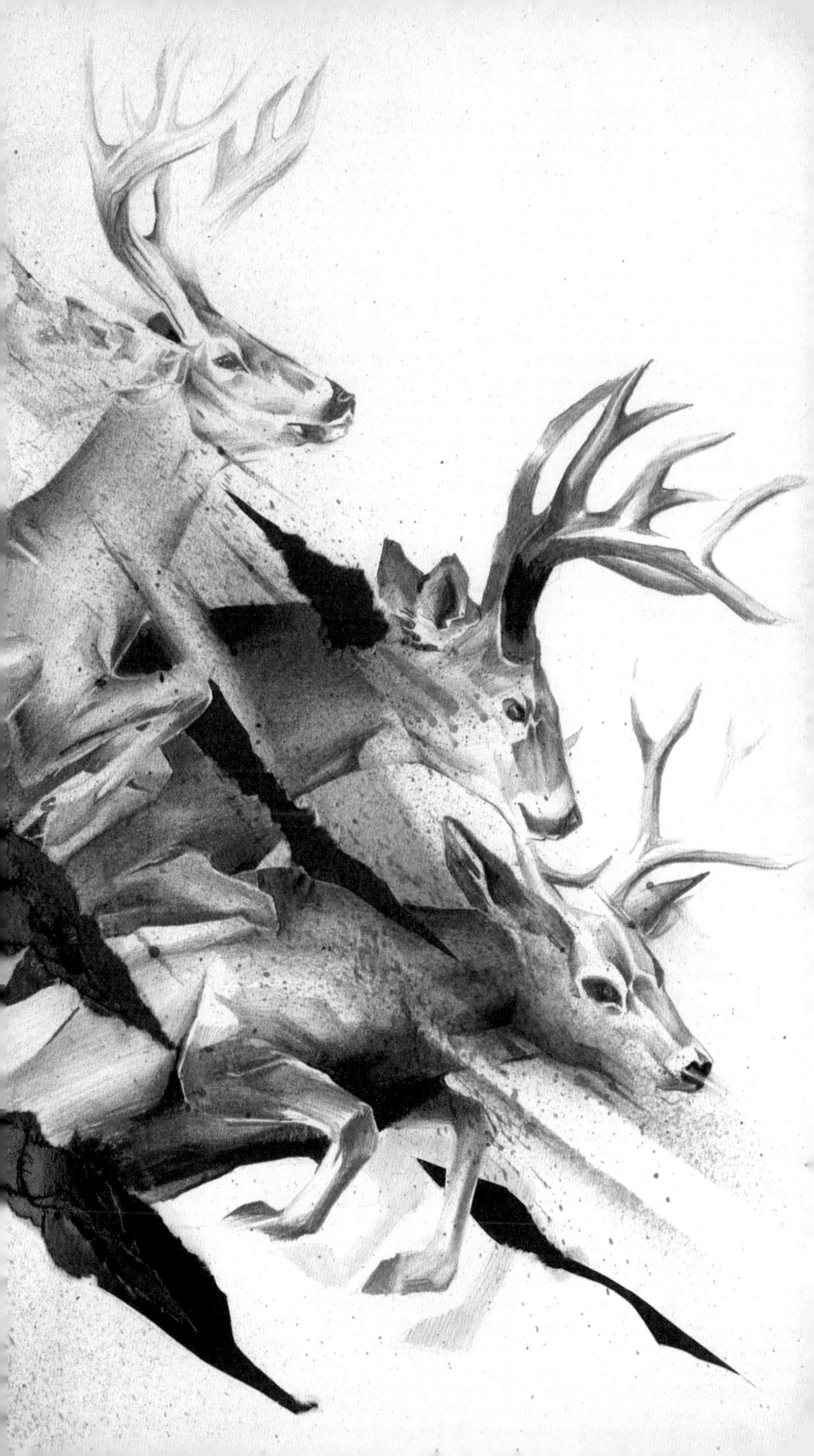

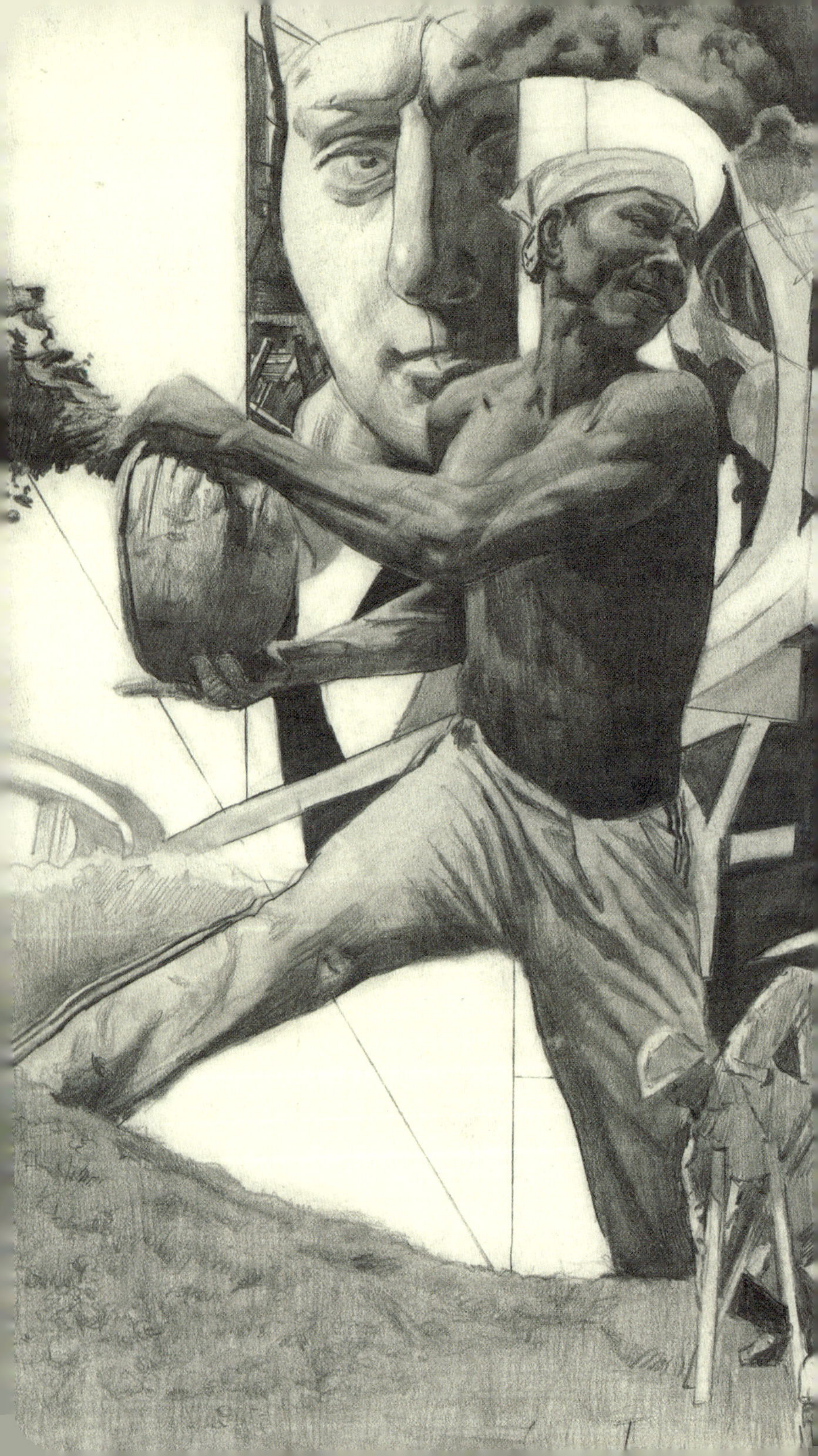

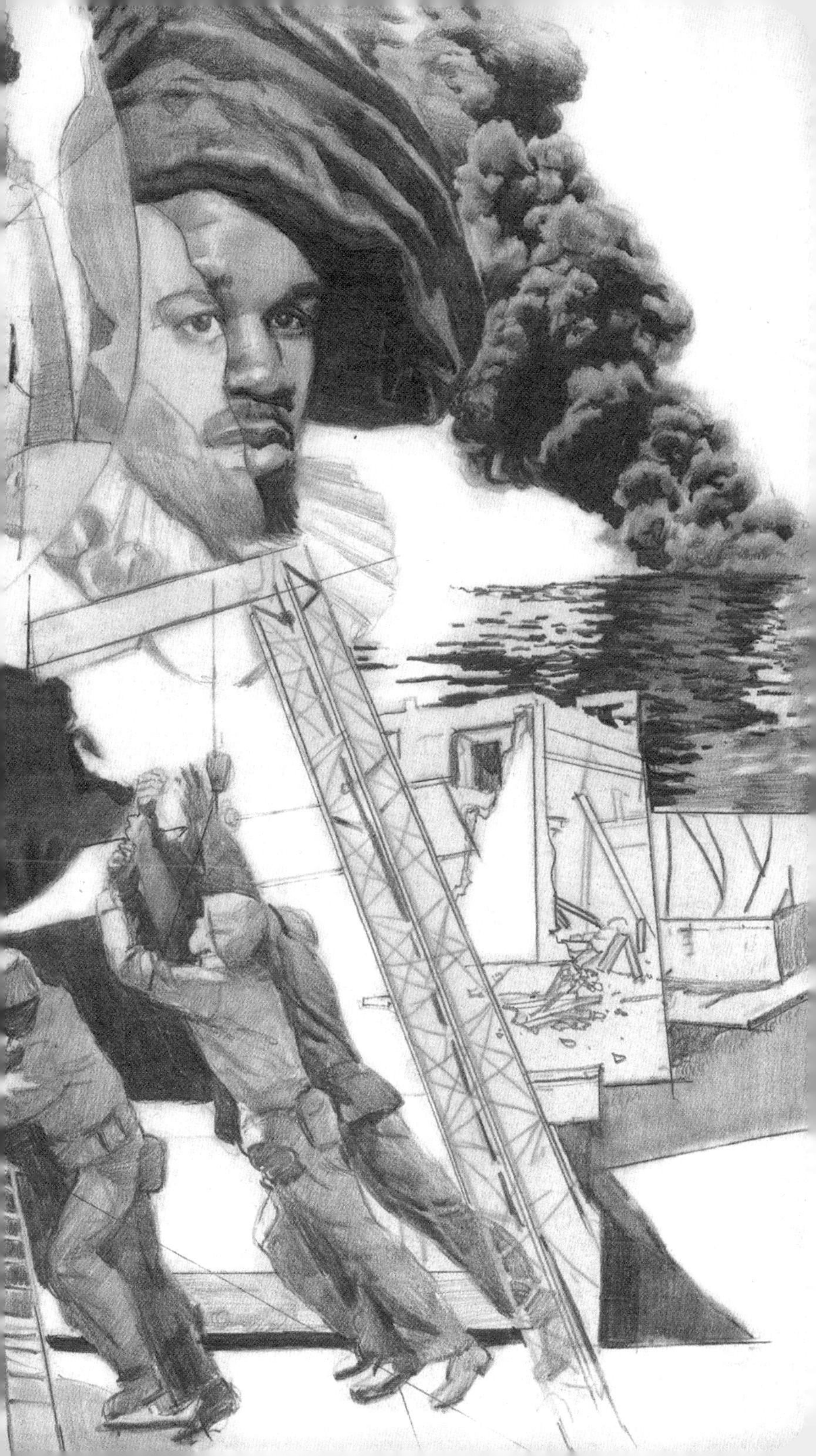

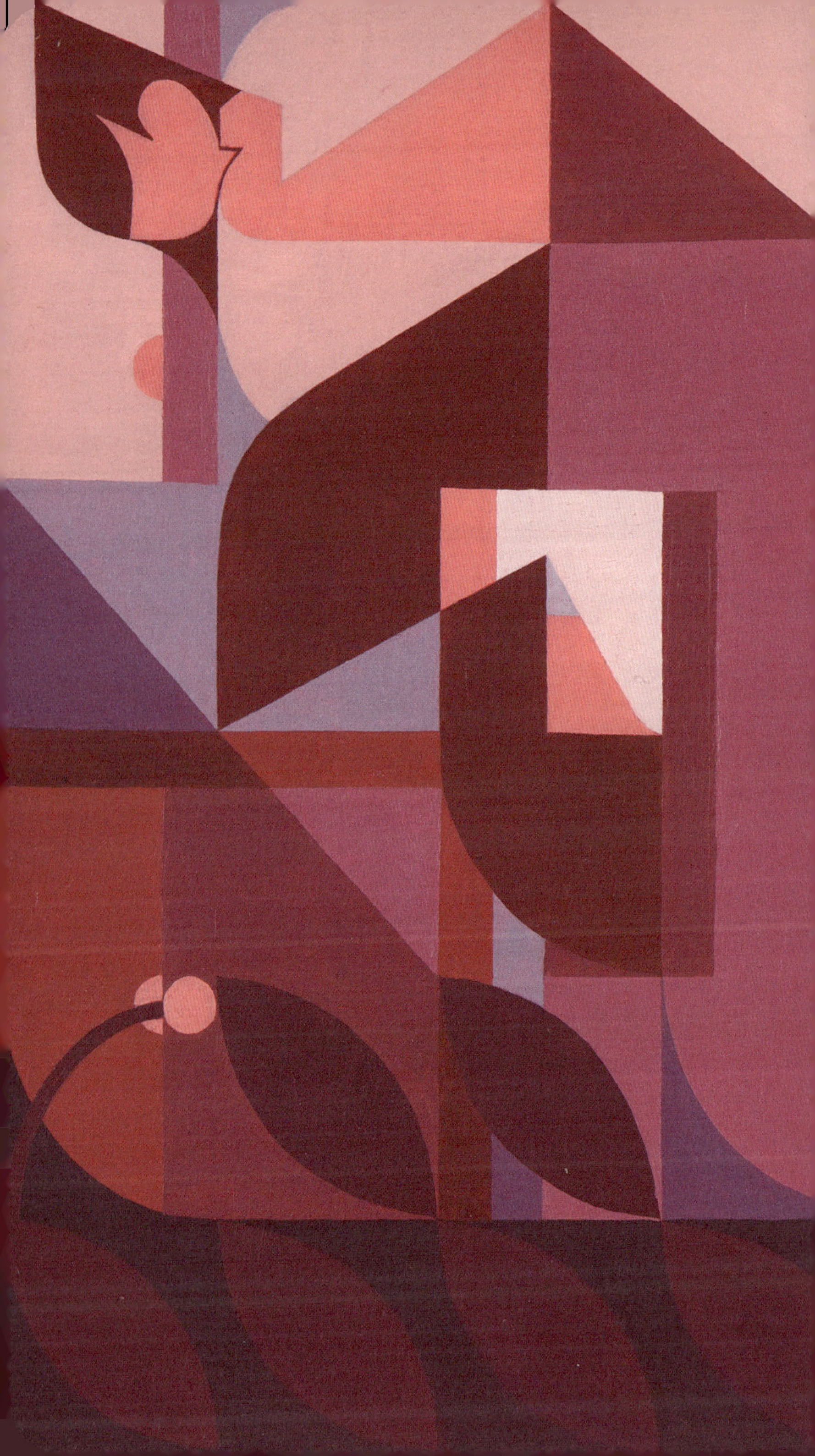

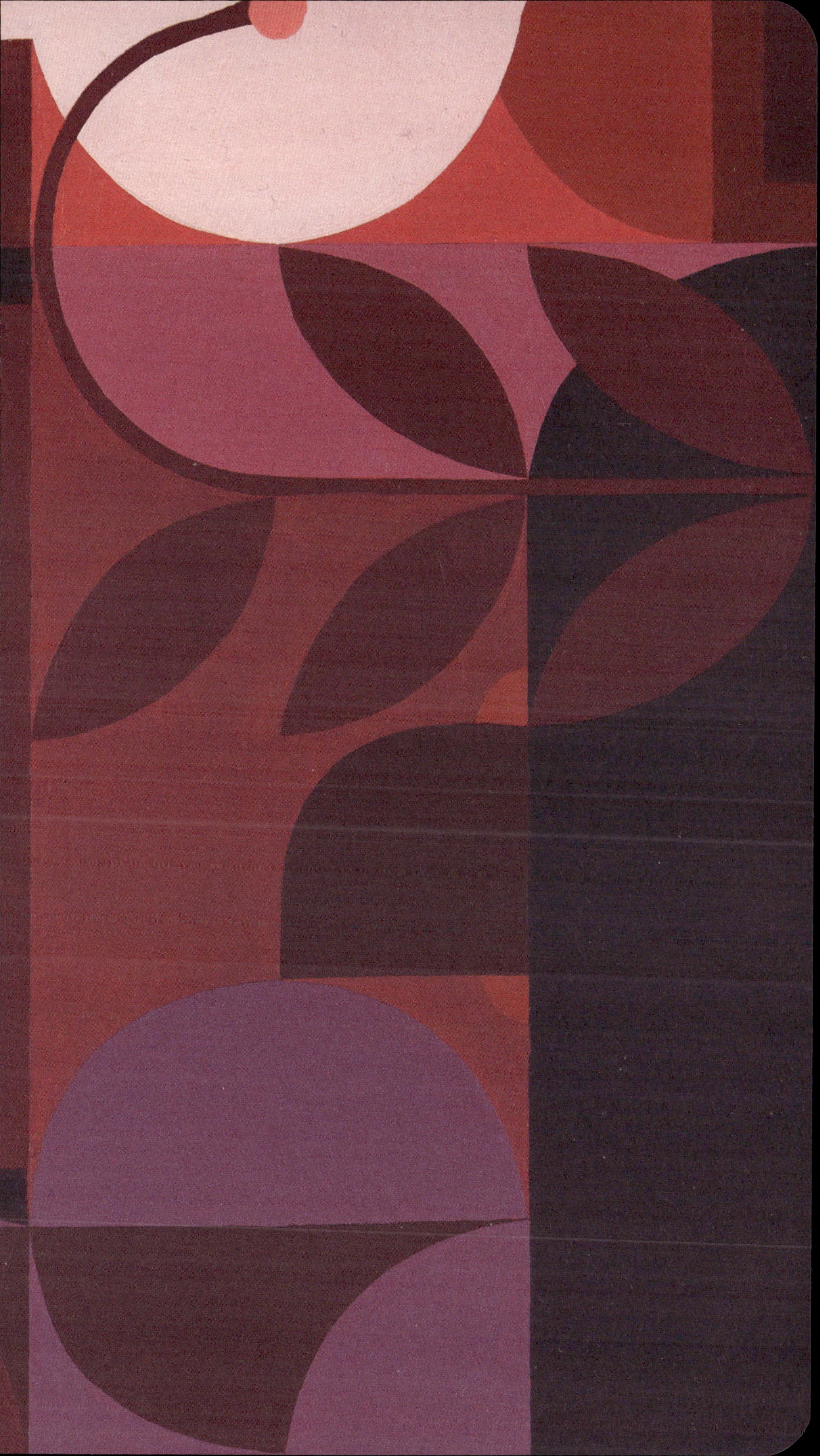

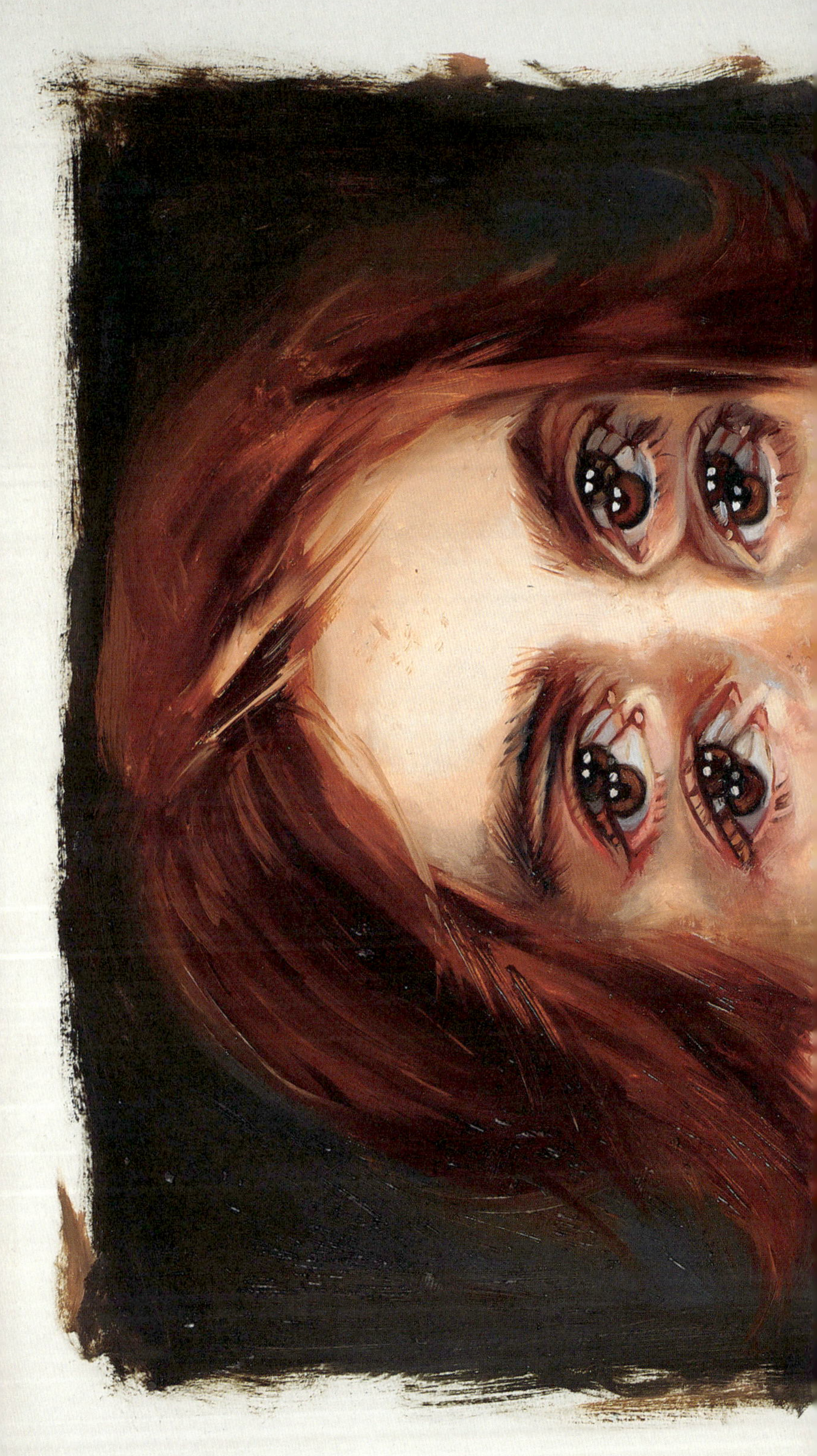

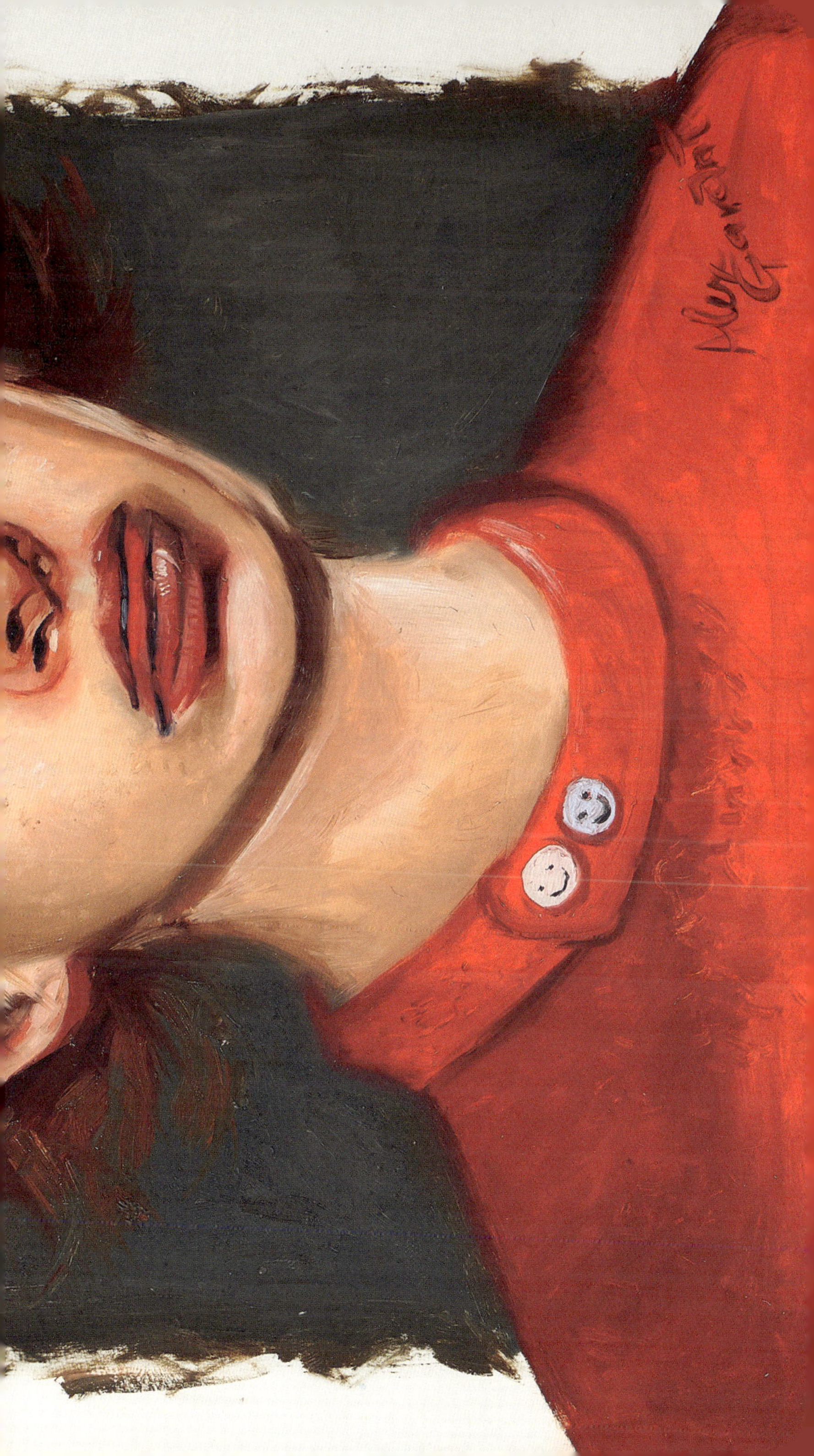

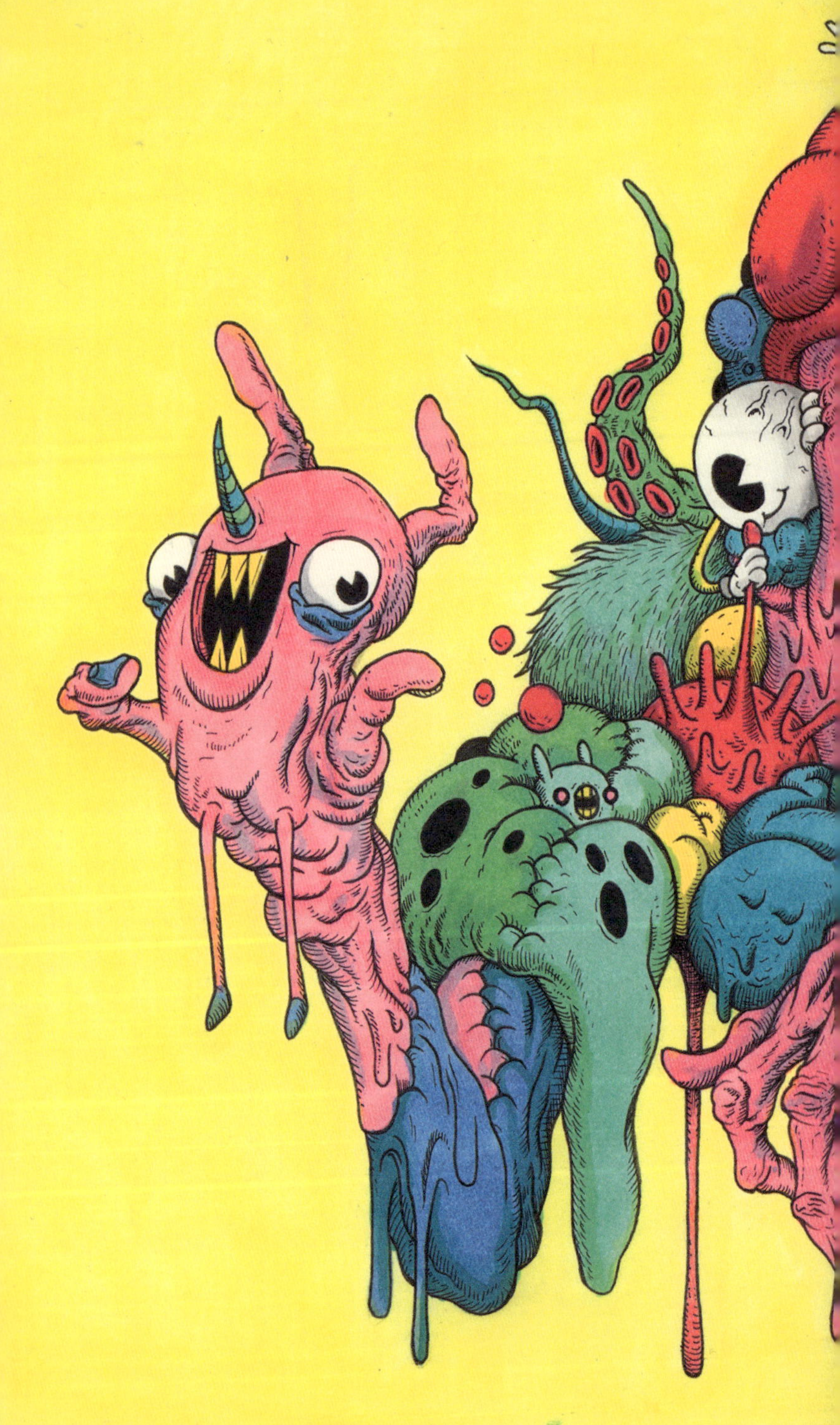

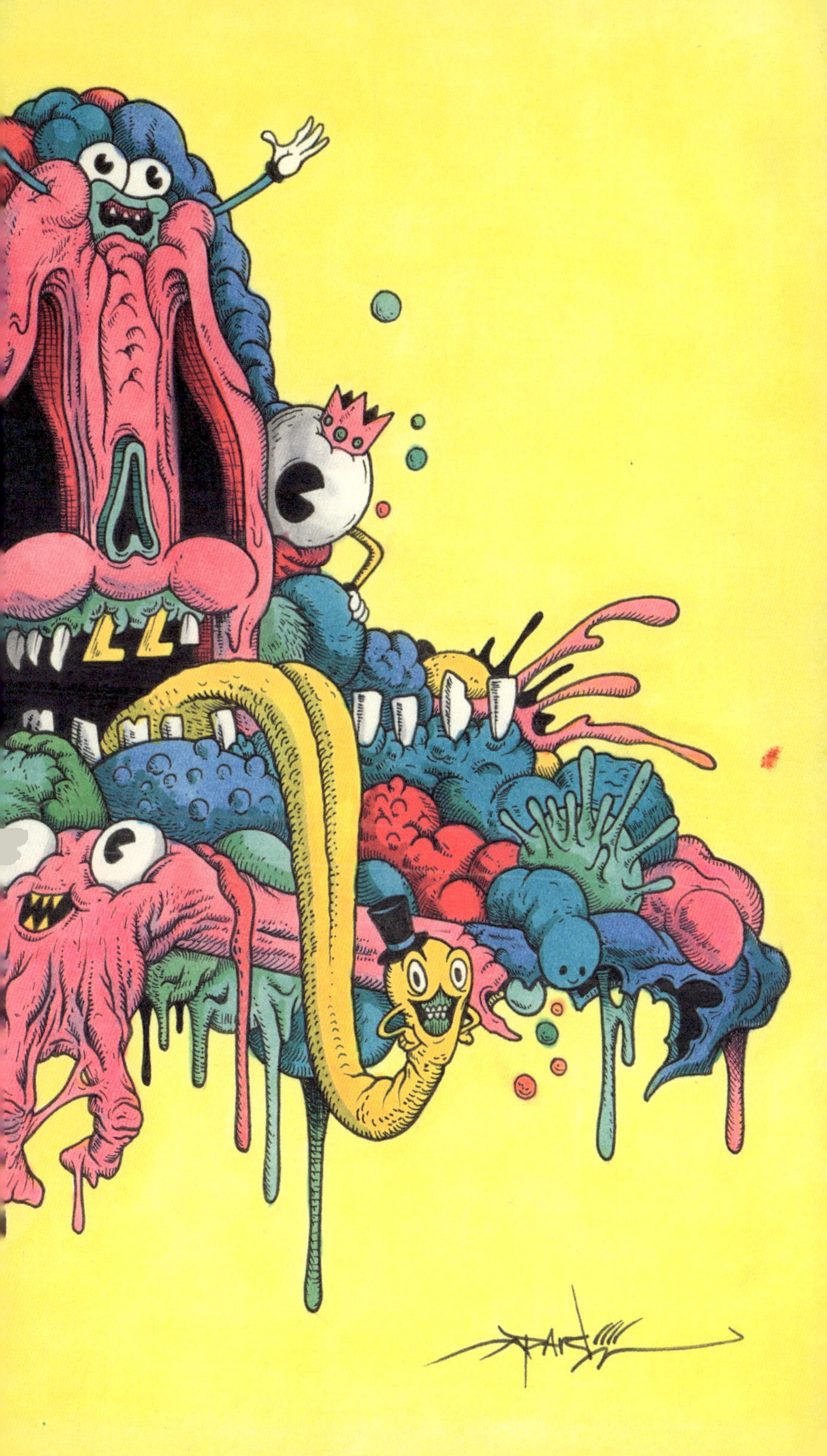

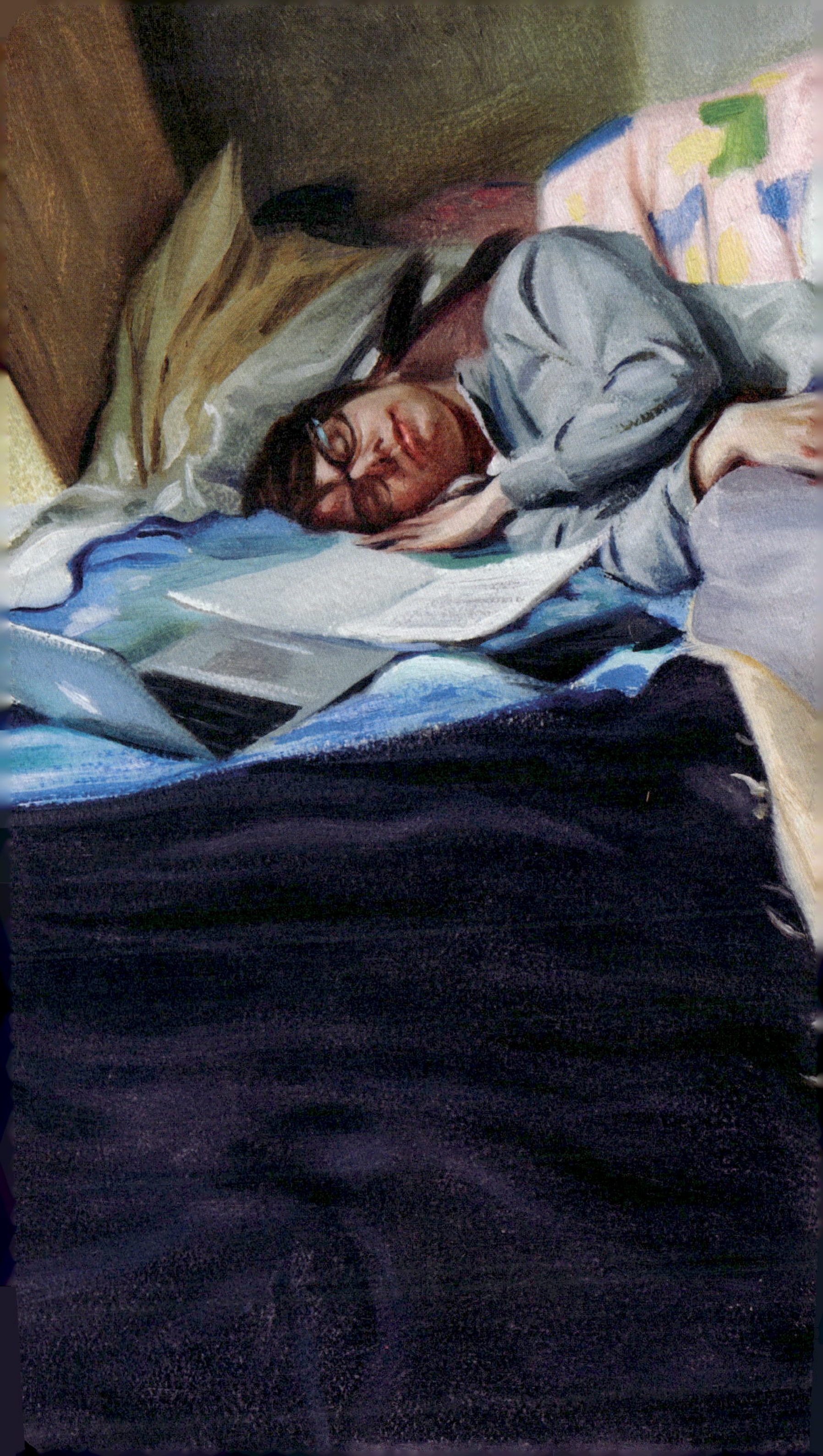

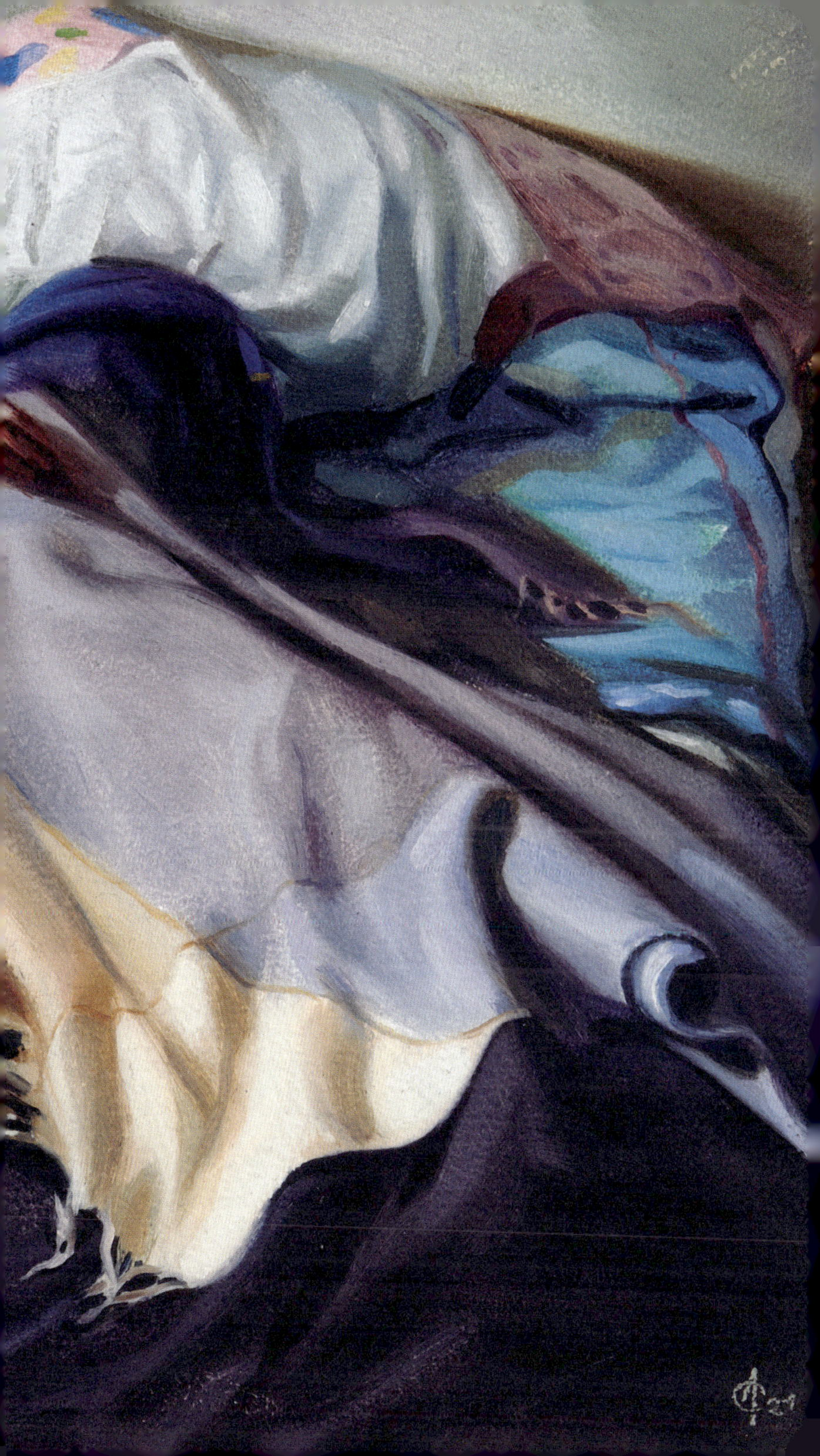

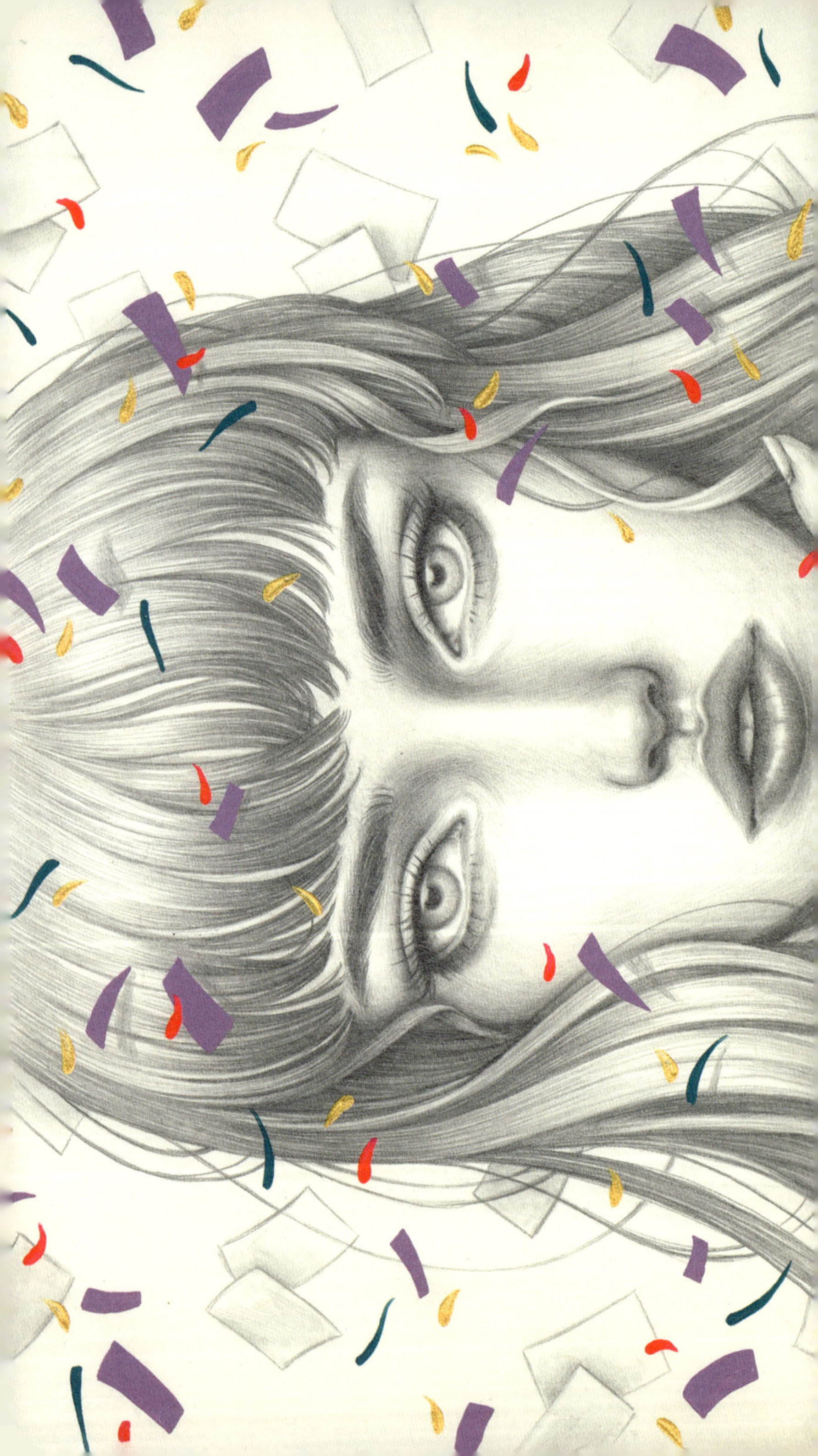

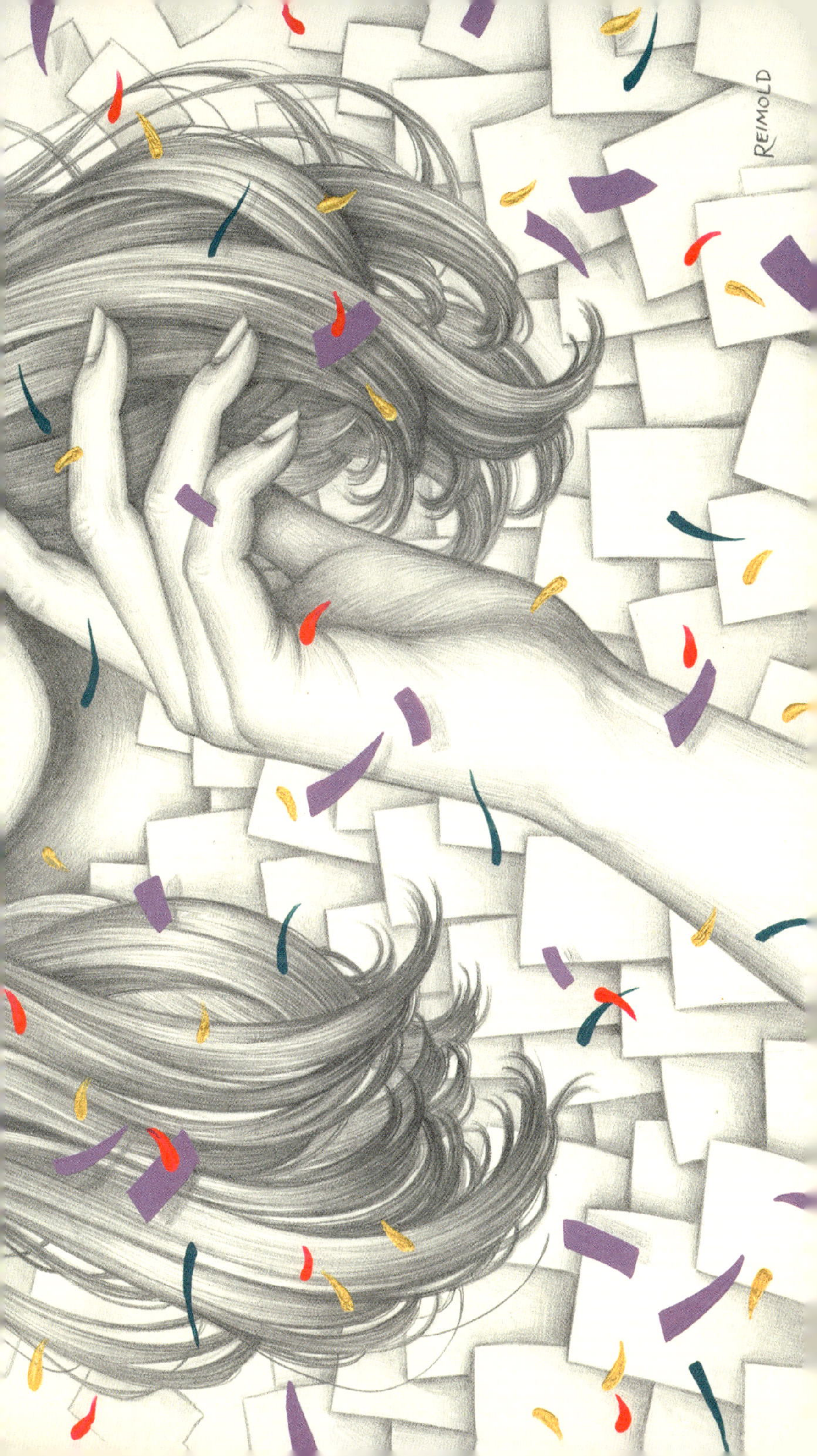
REIMOLD

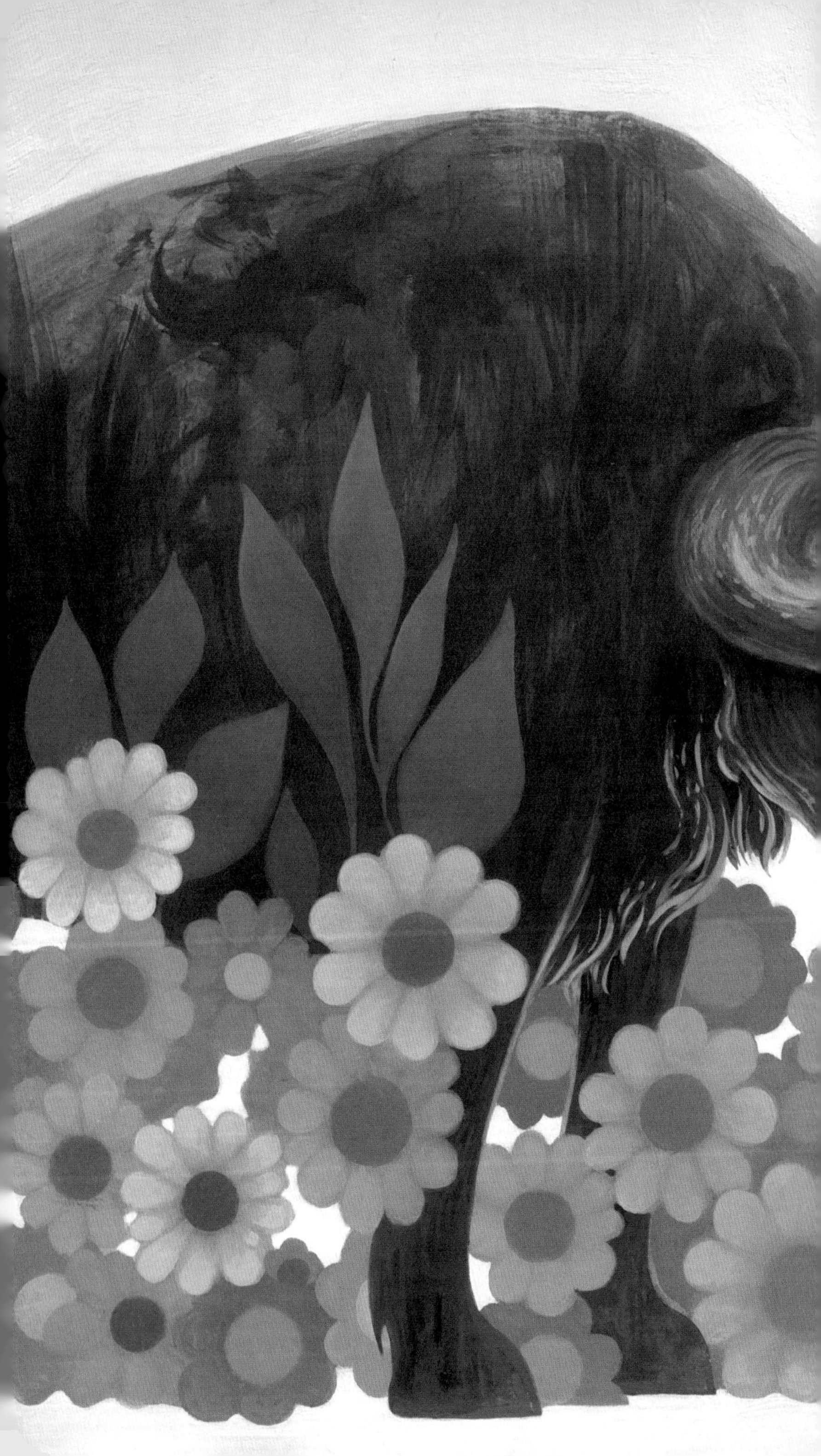

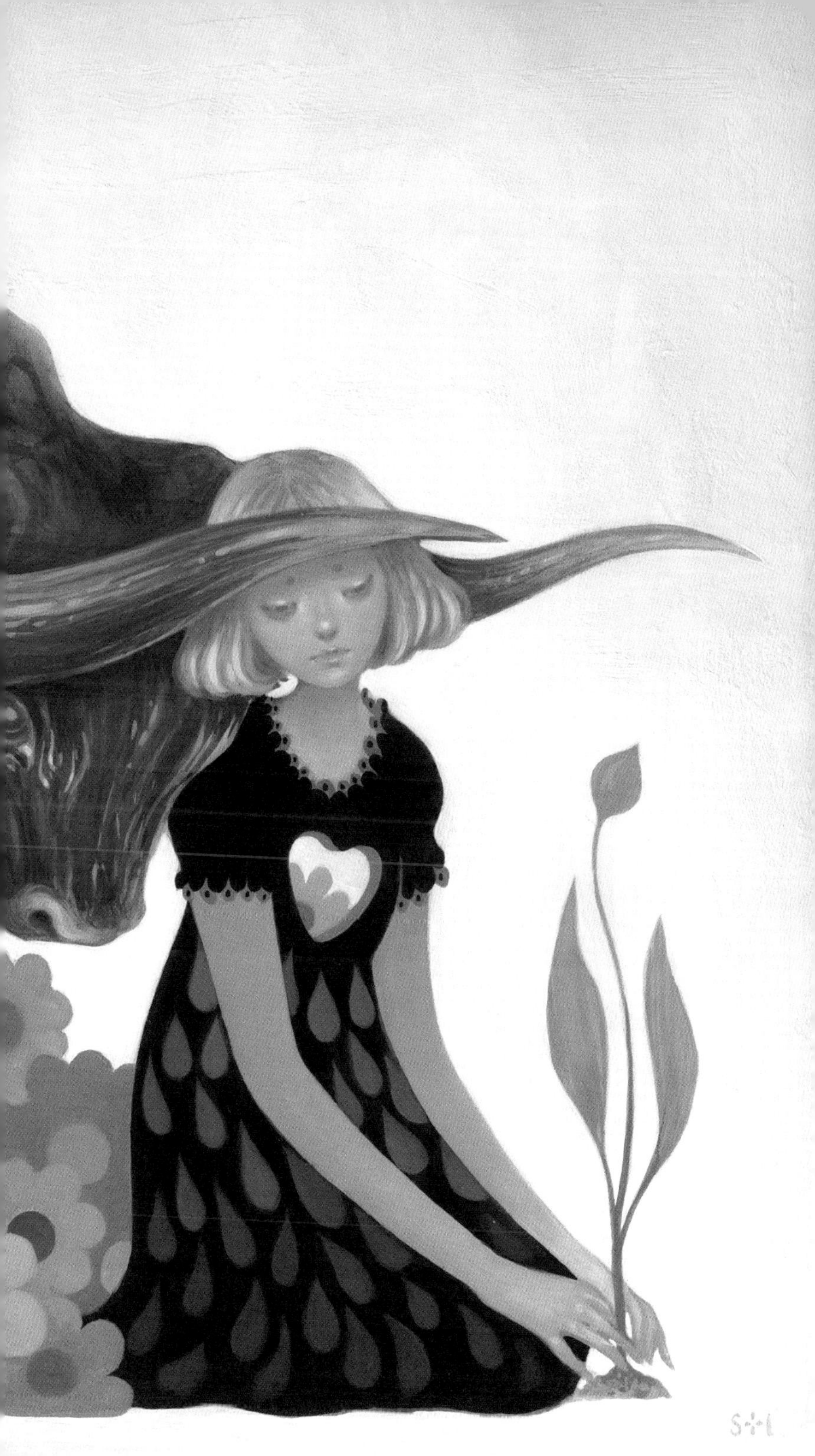

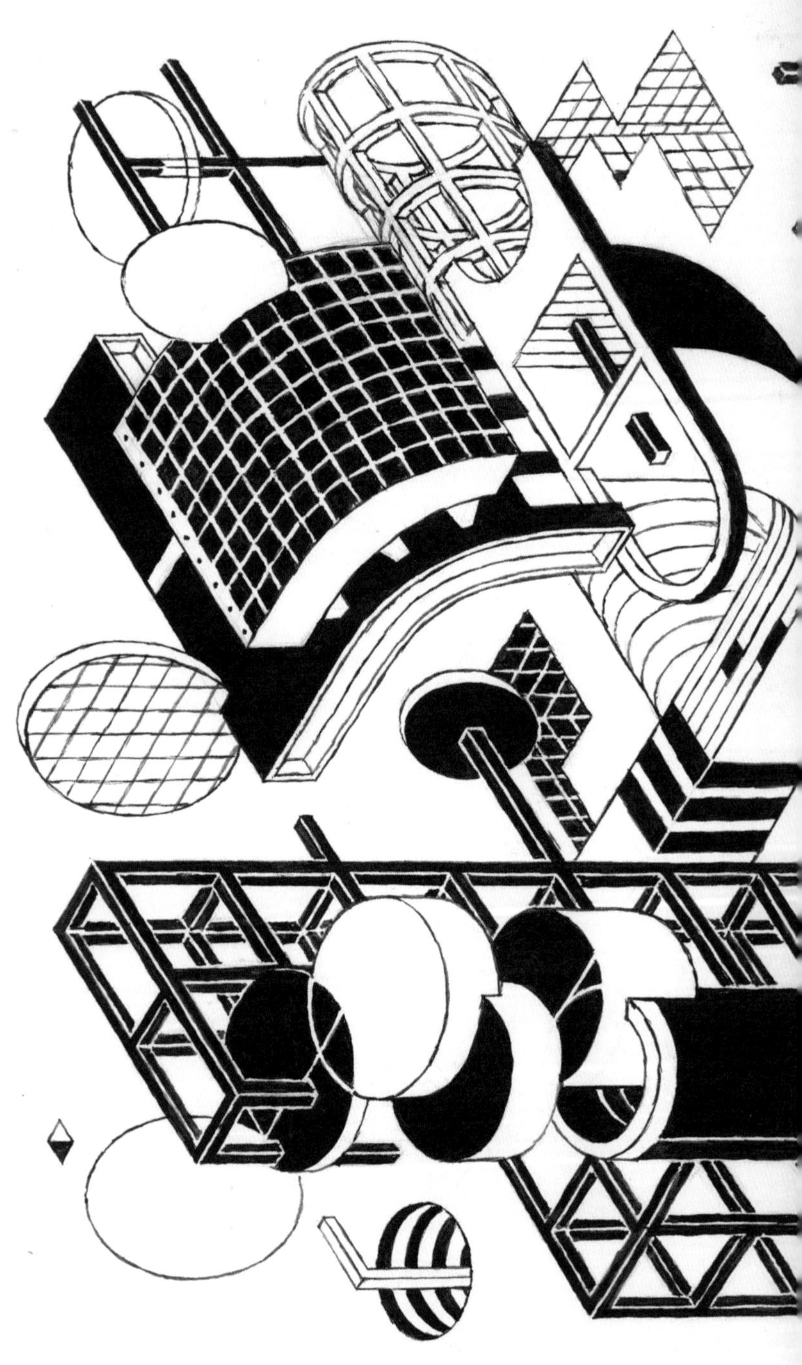

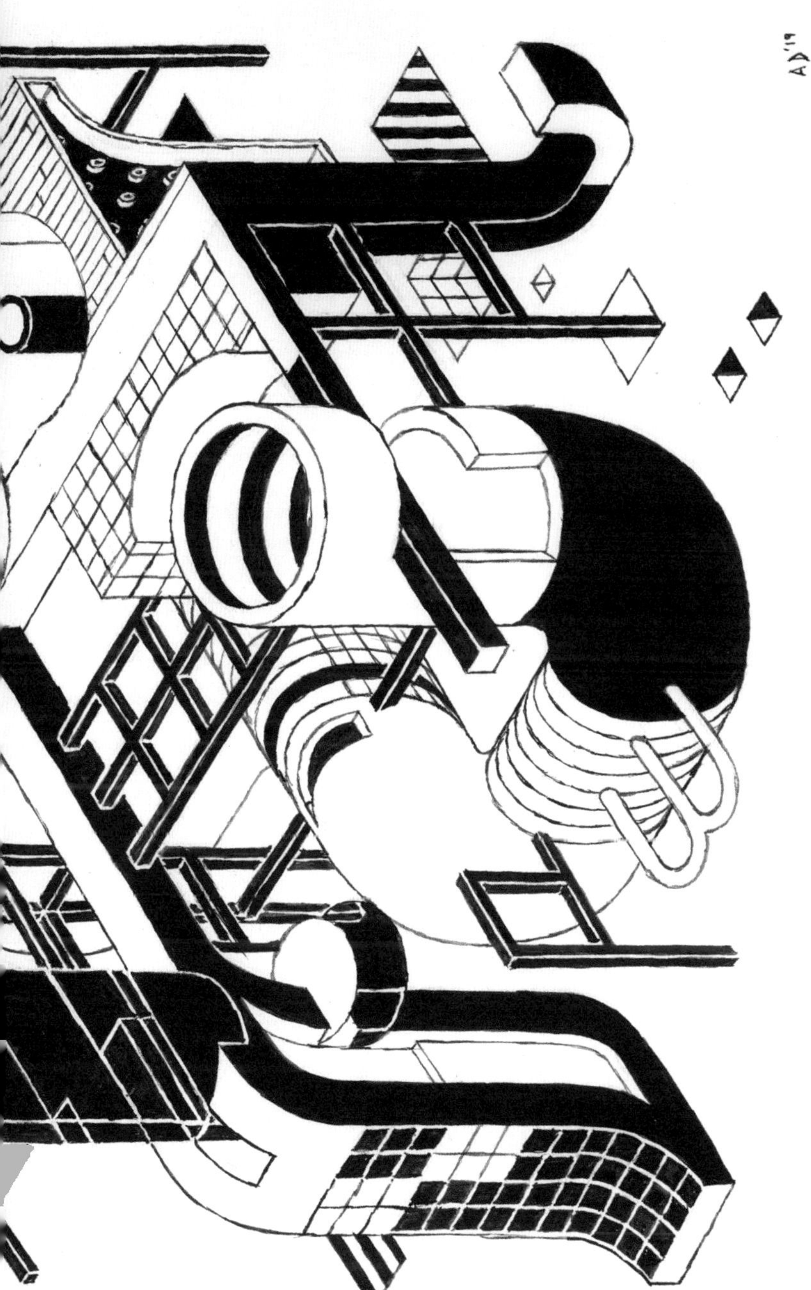

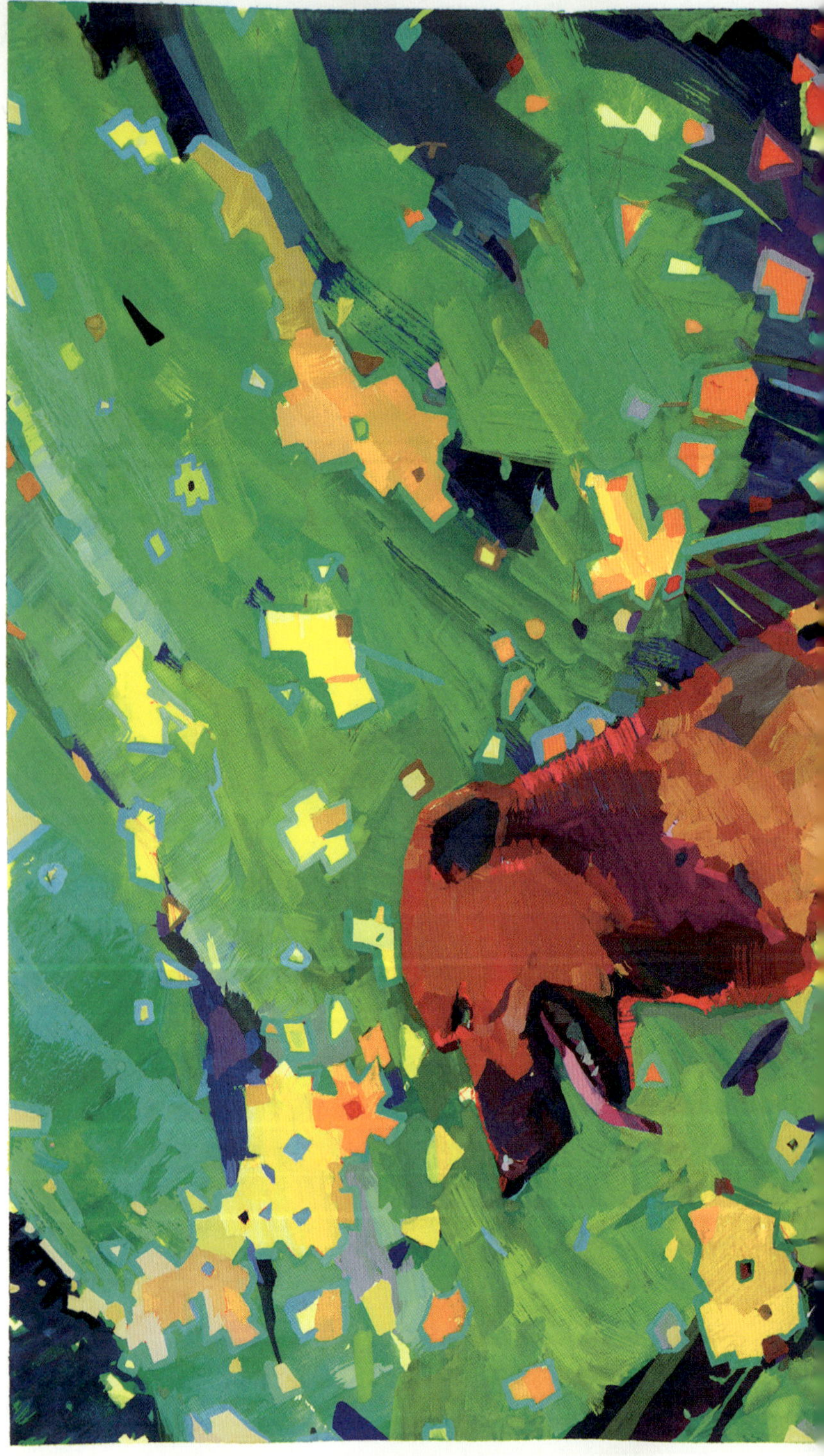

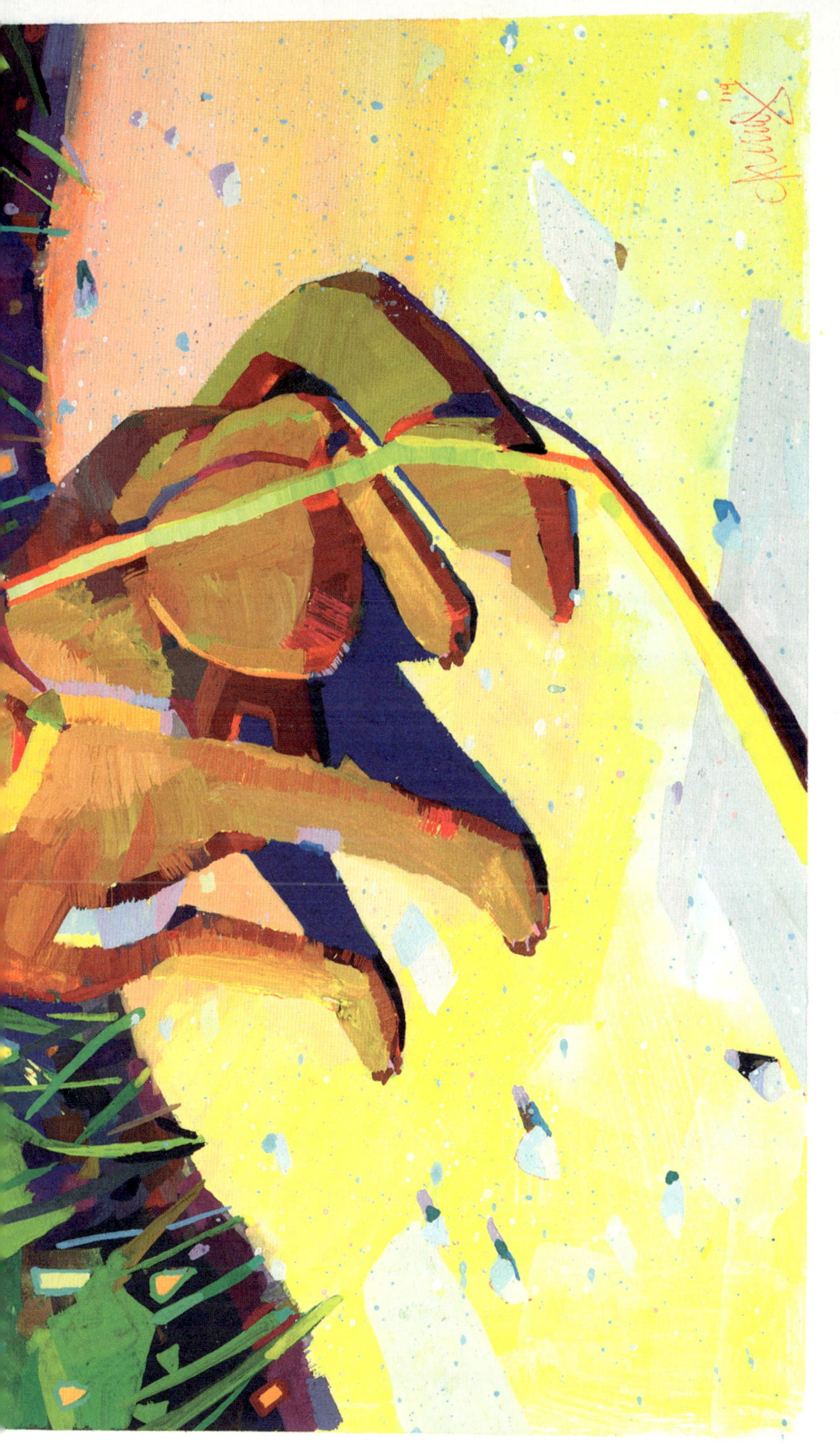

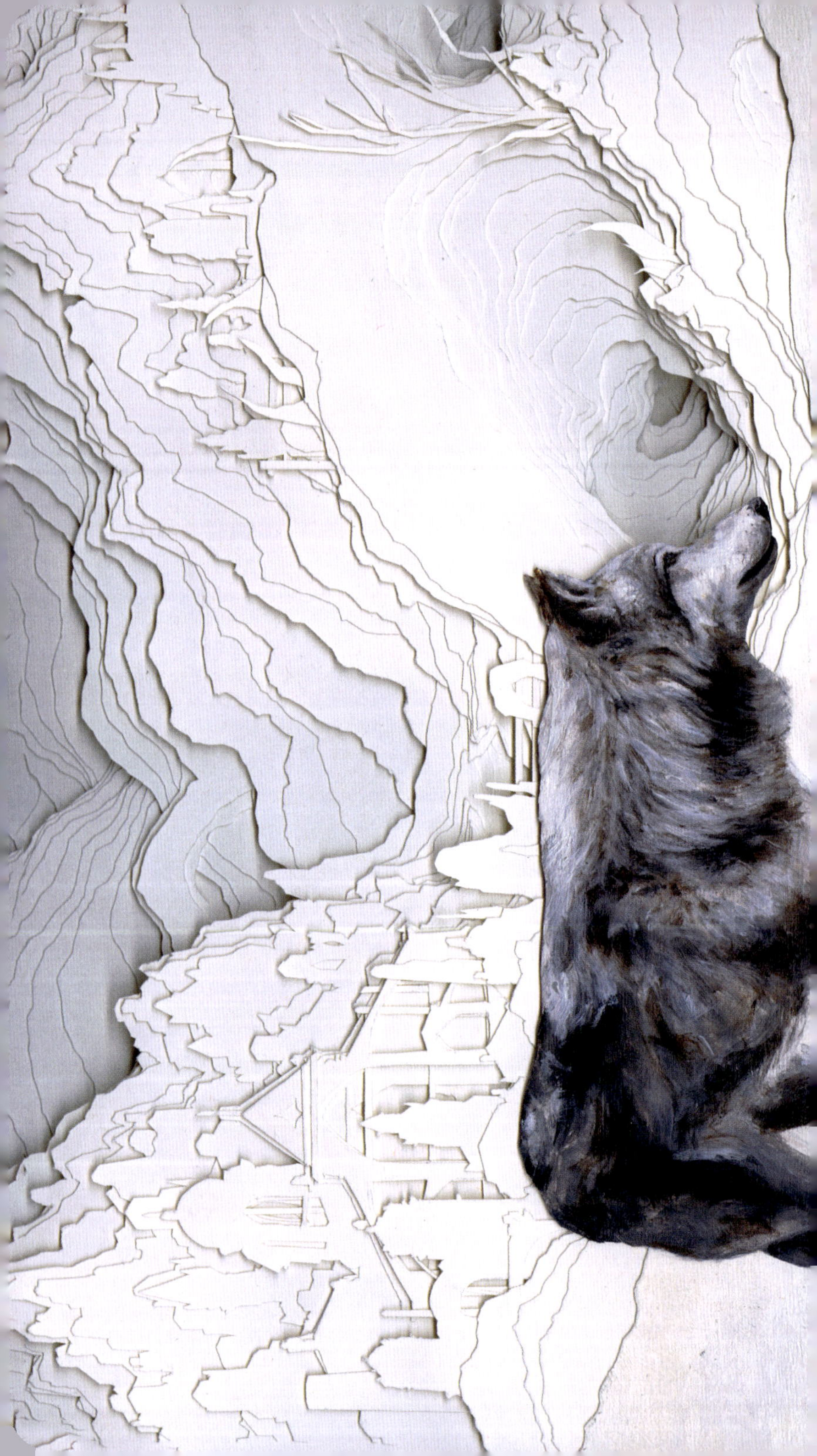

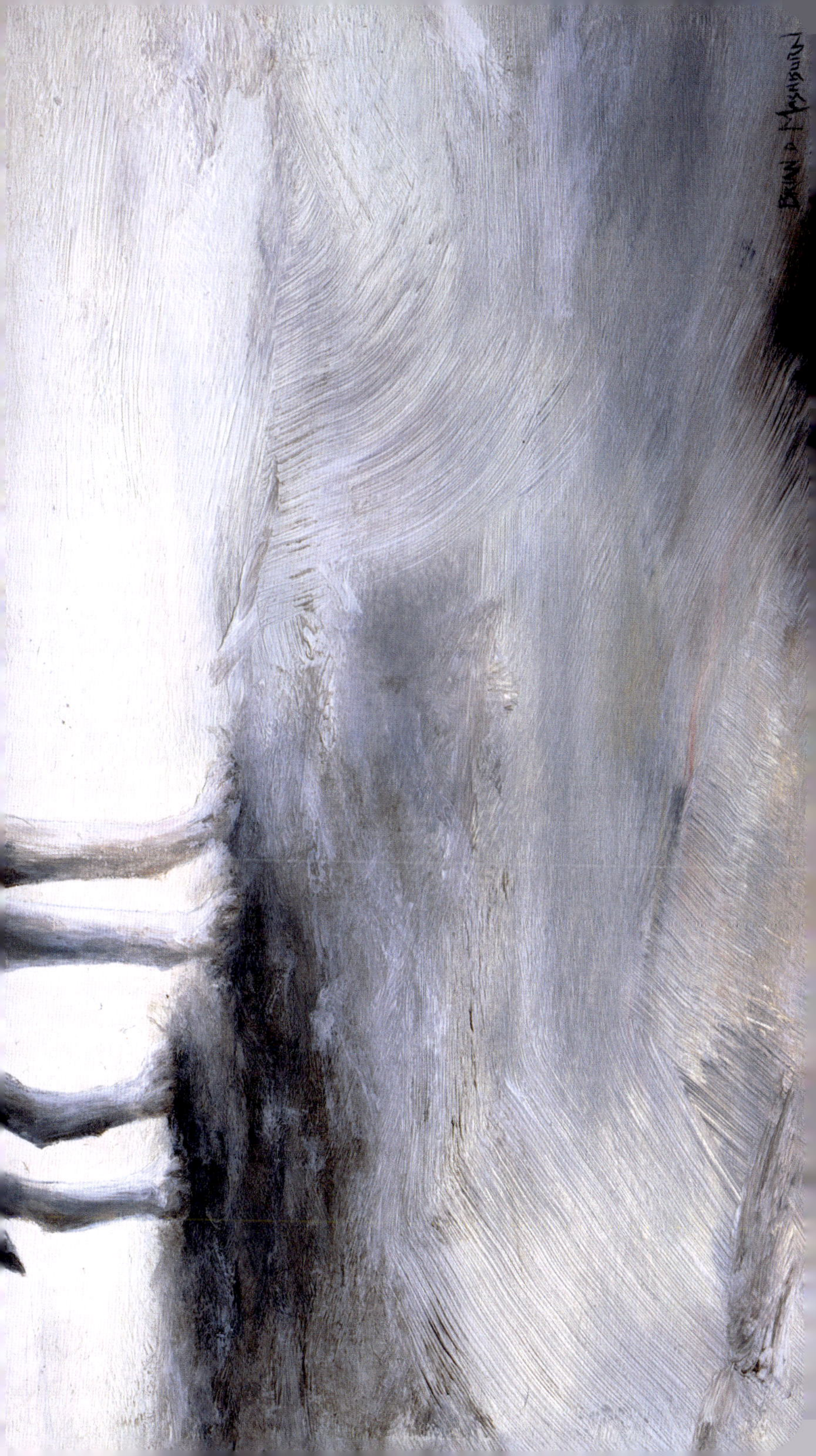

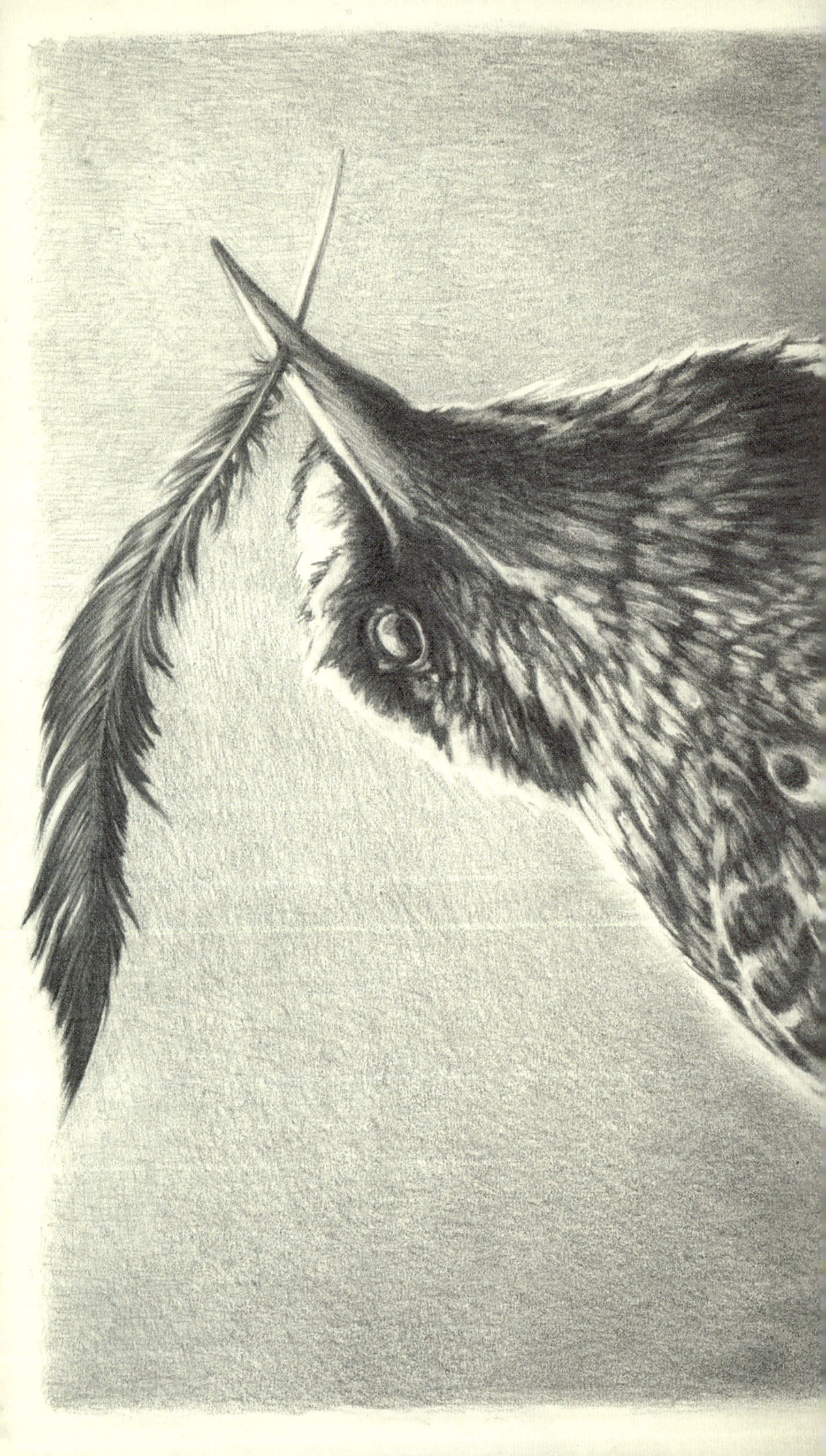

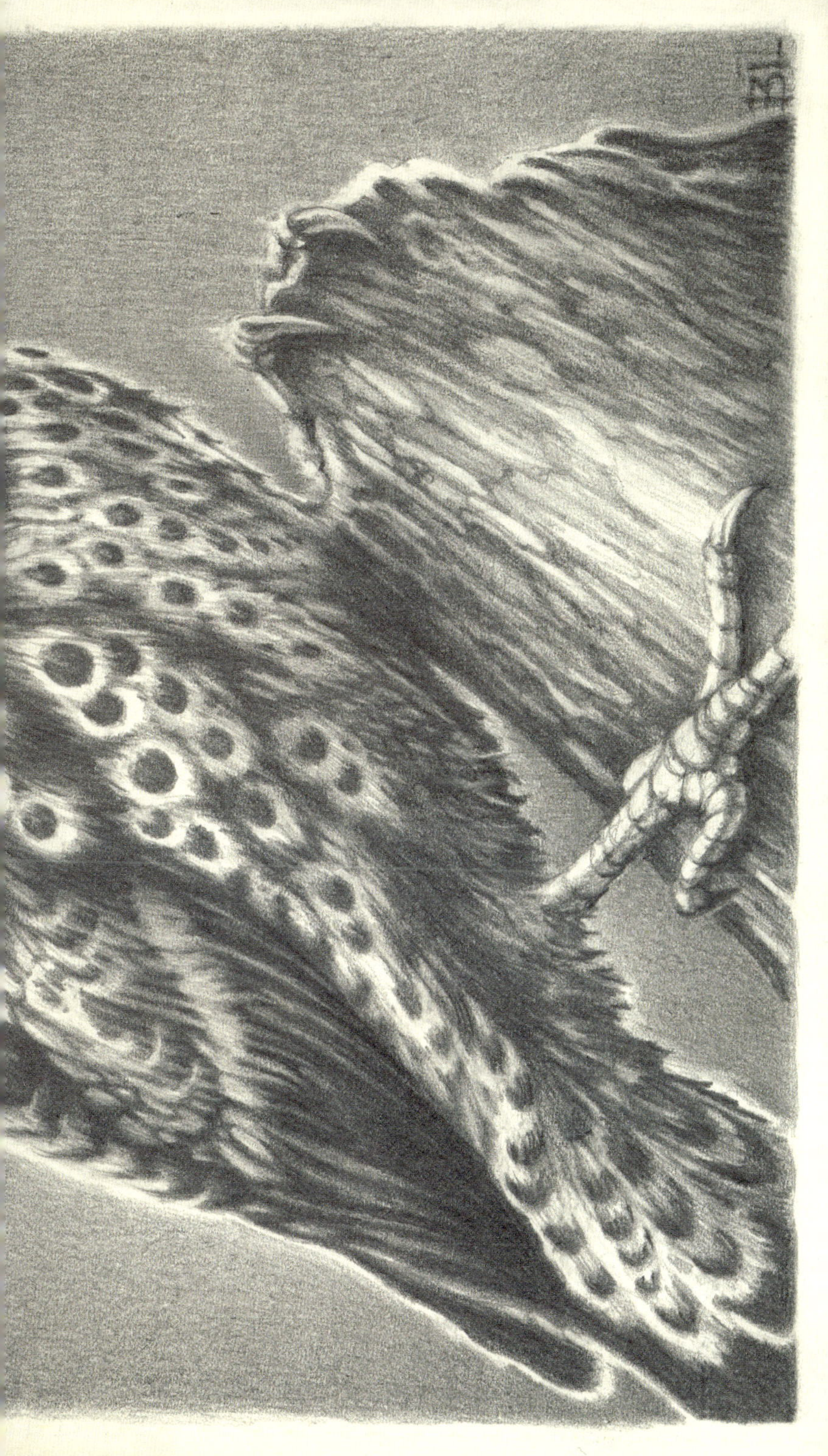

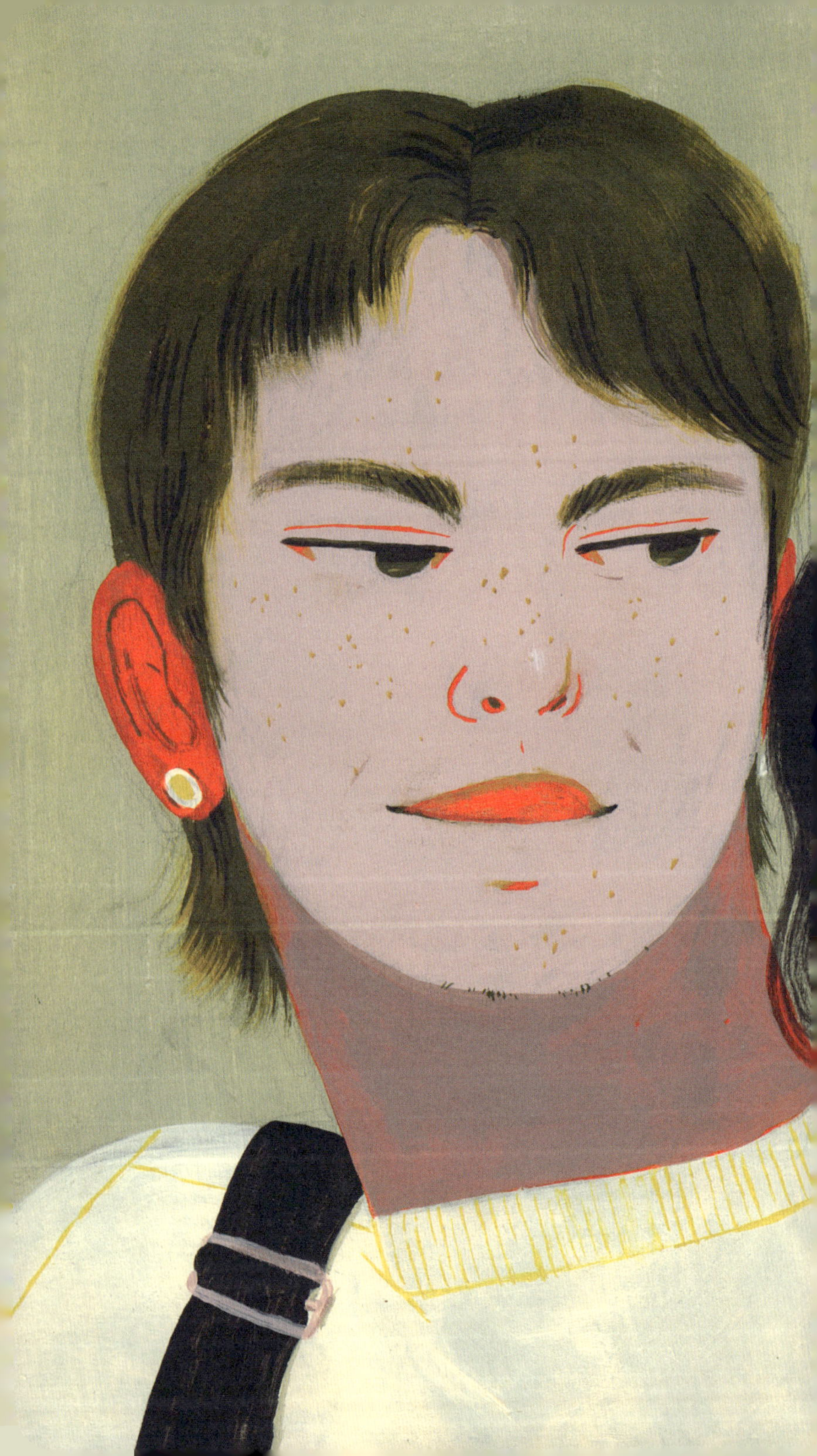

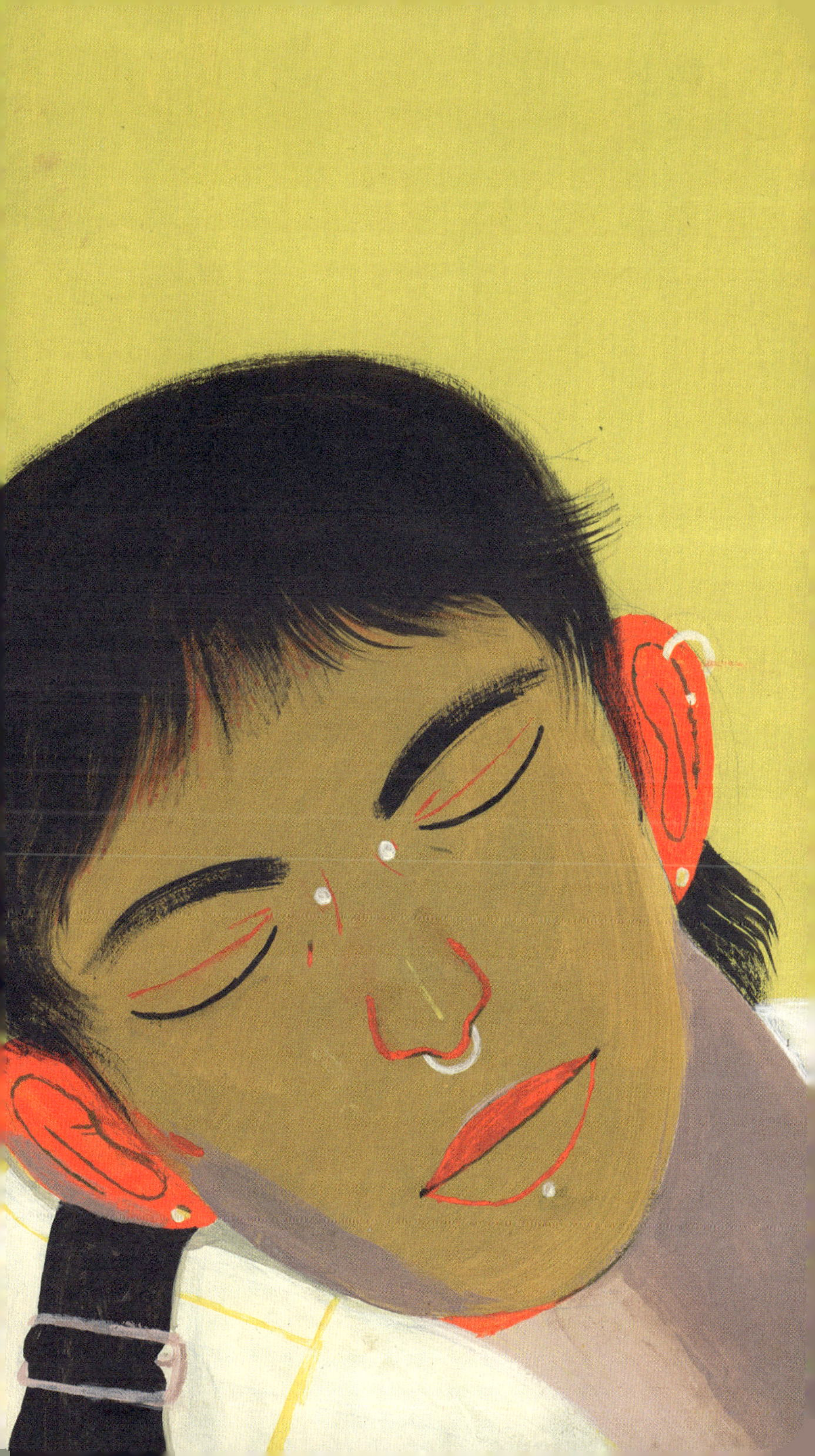

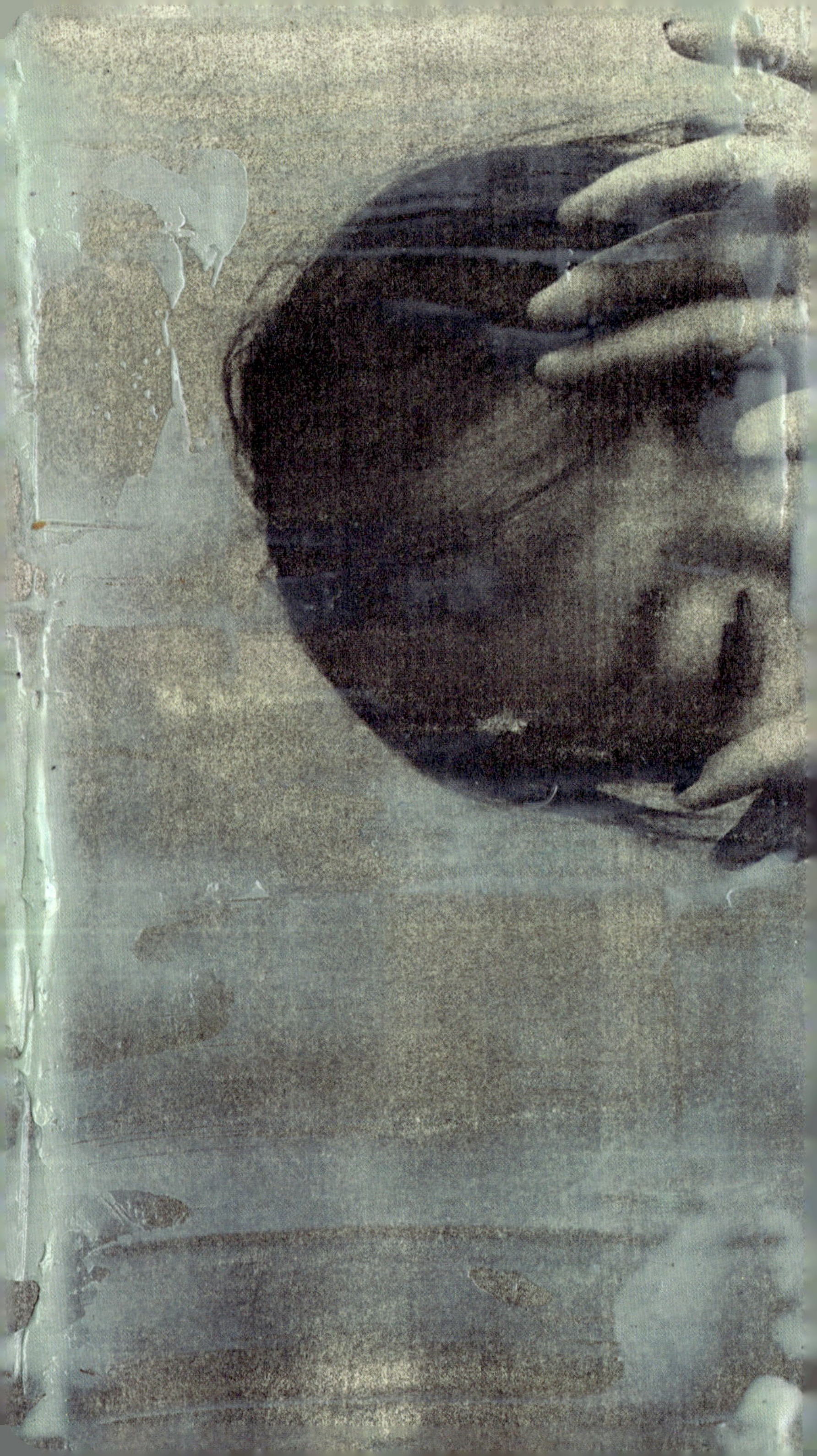

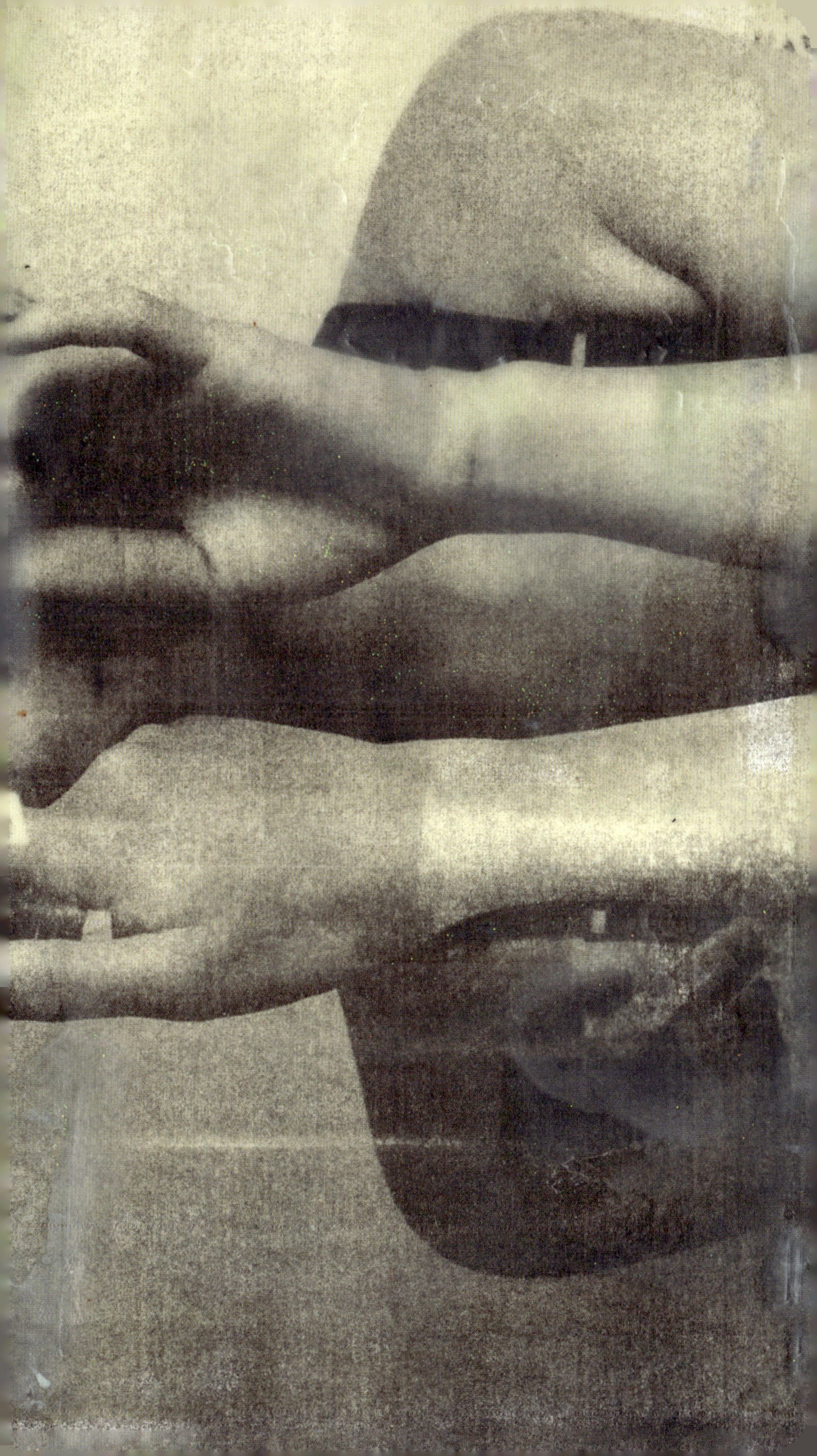

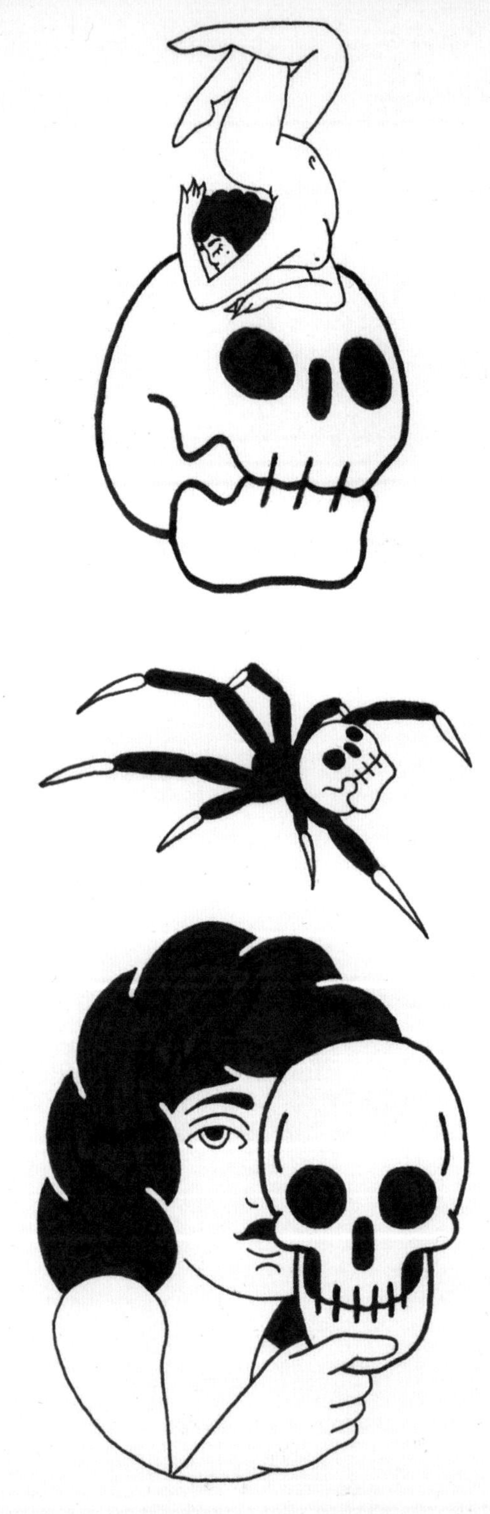

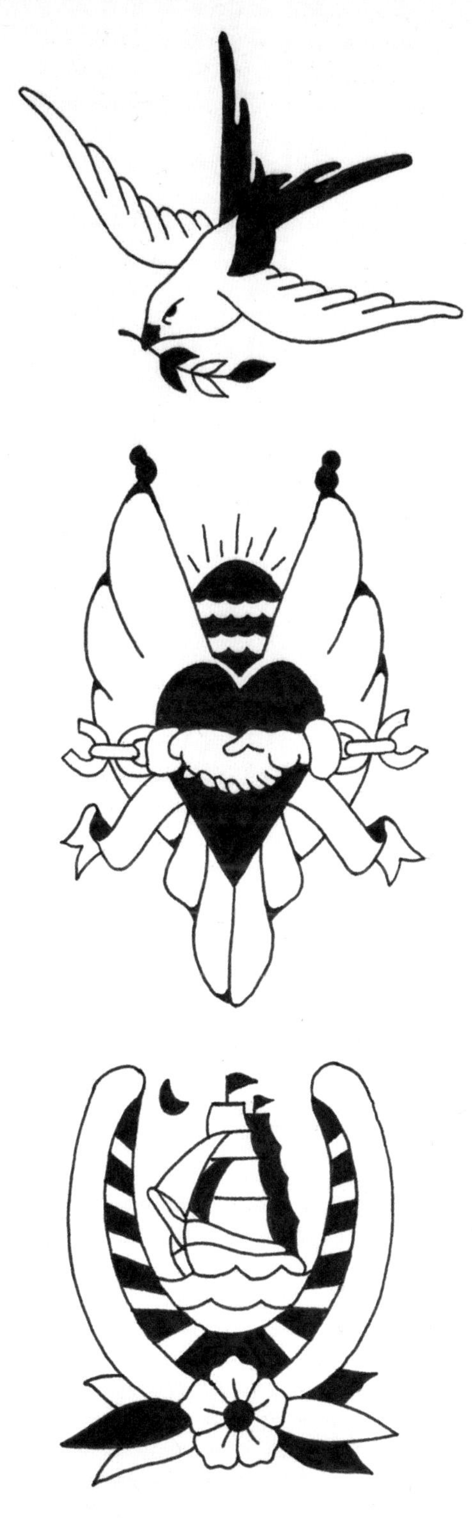

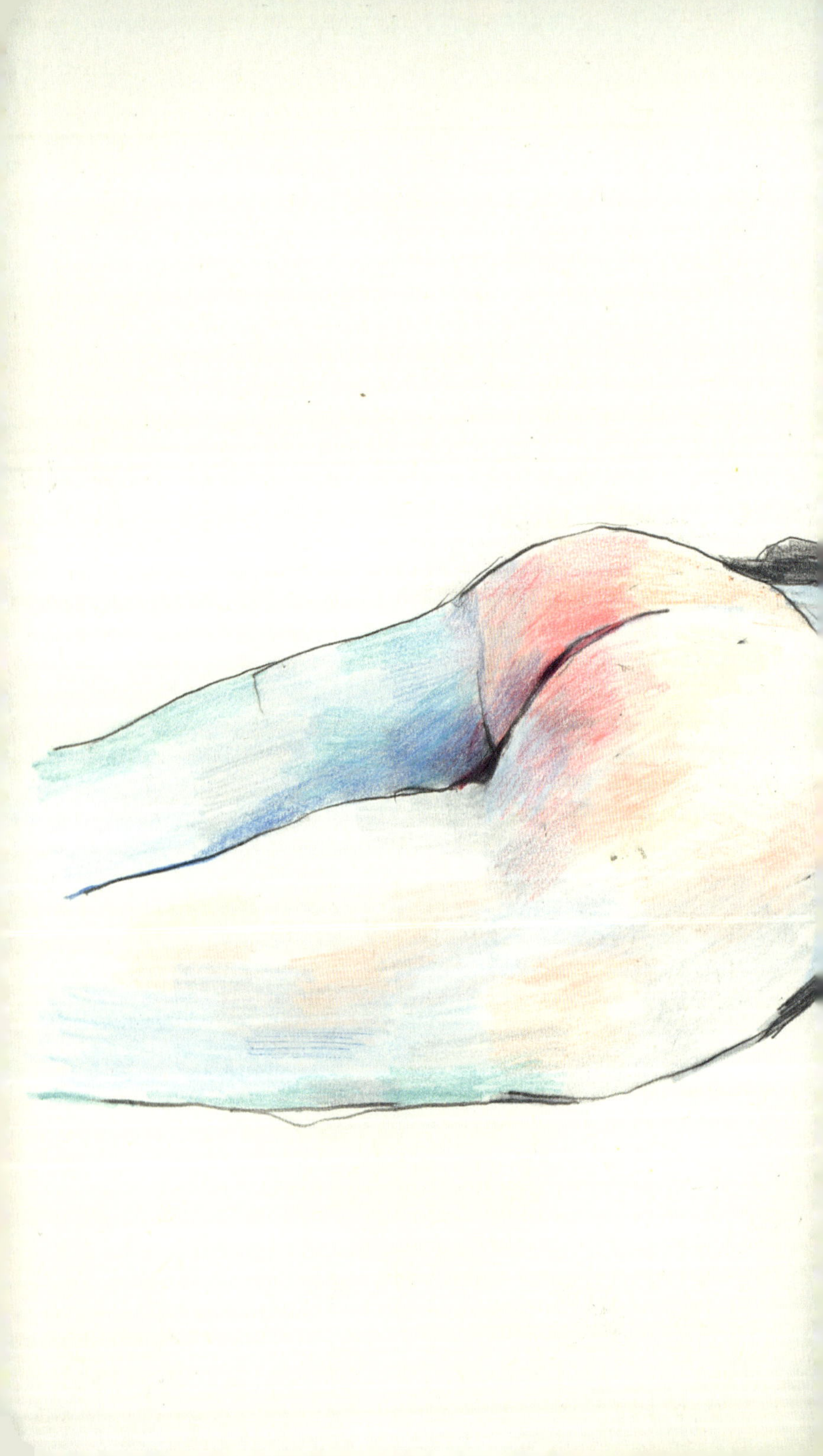

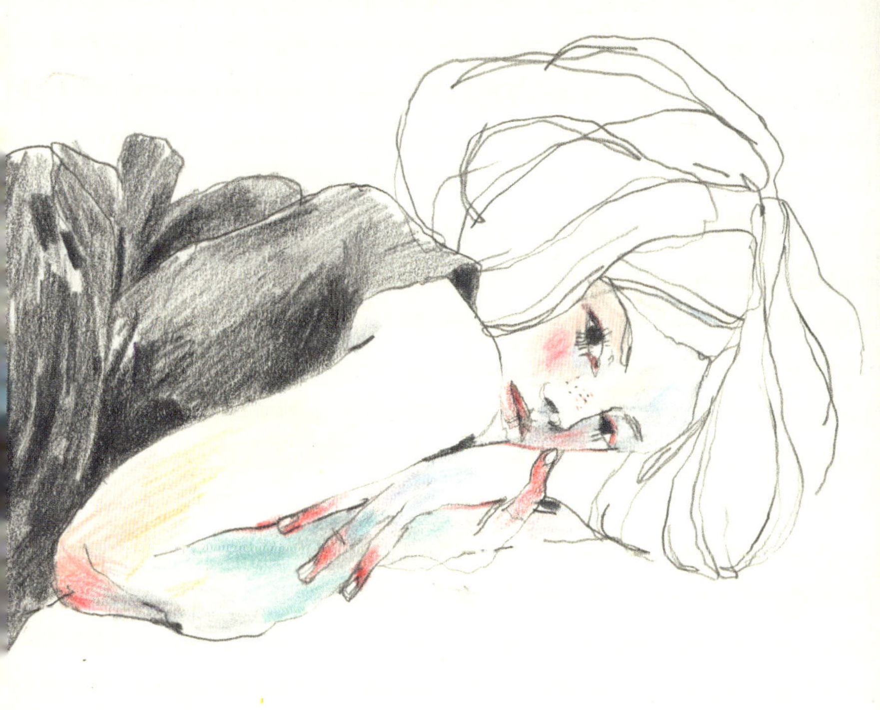

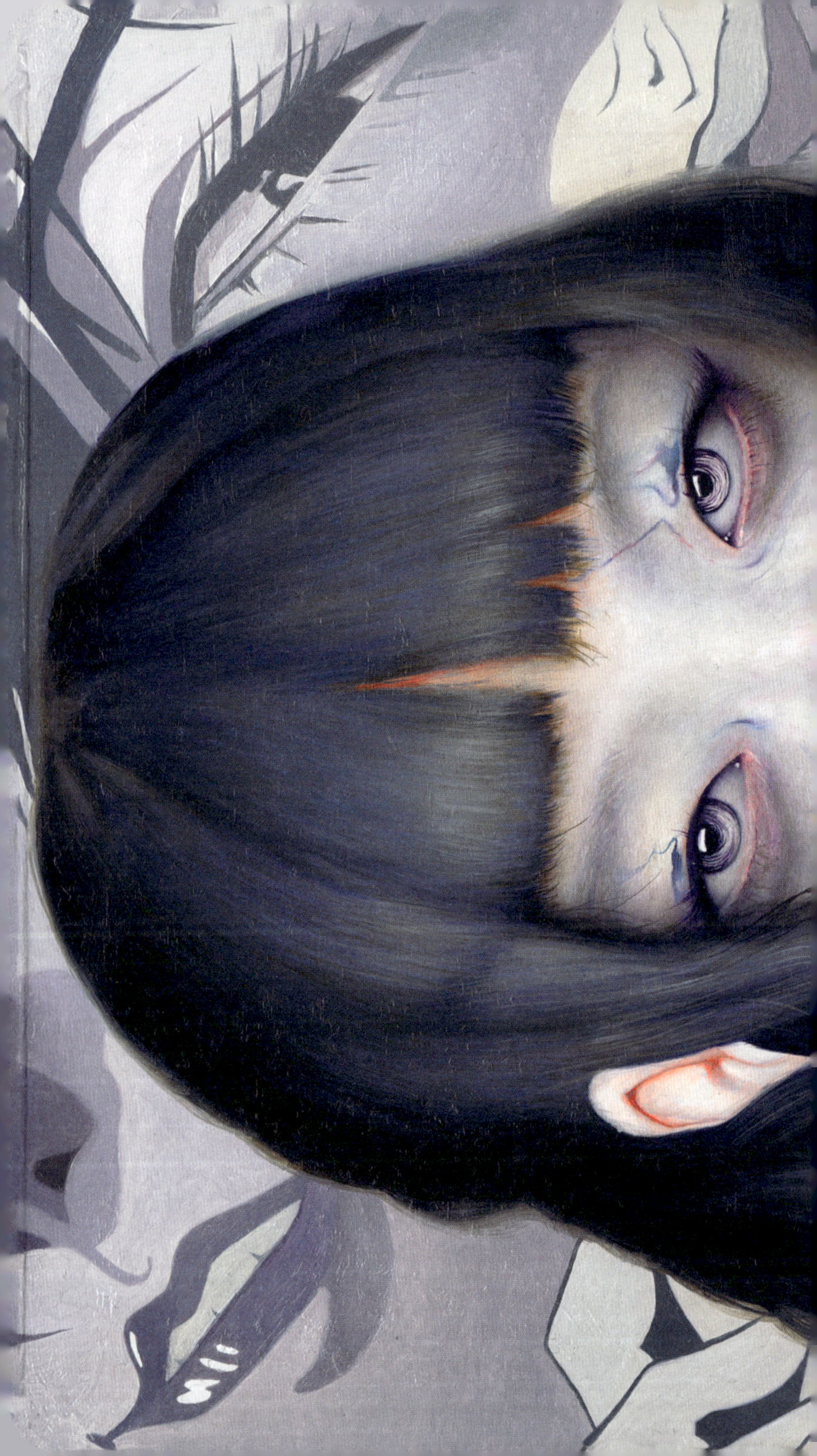

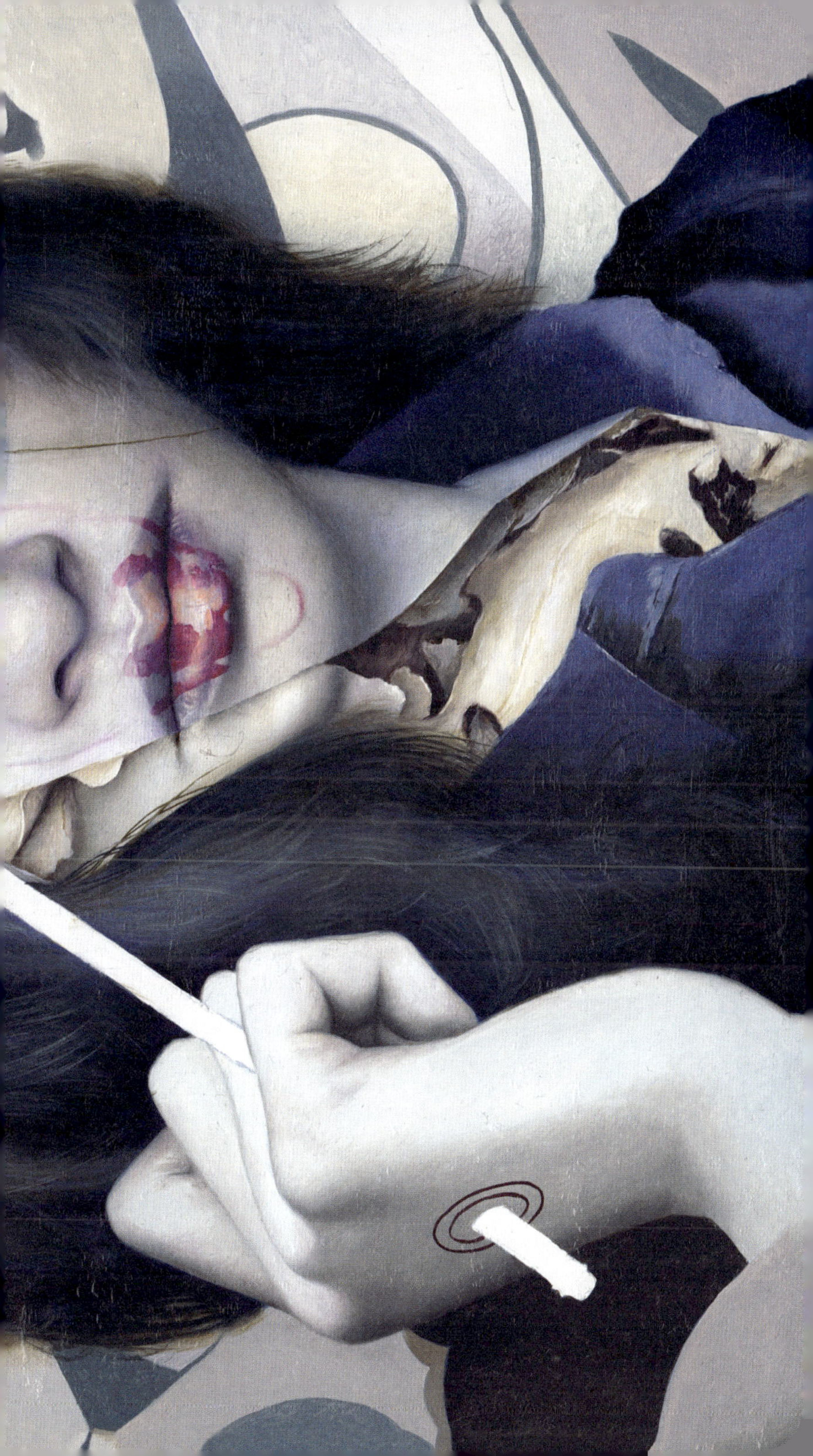

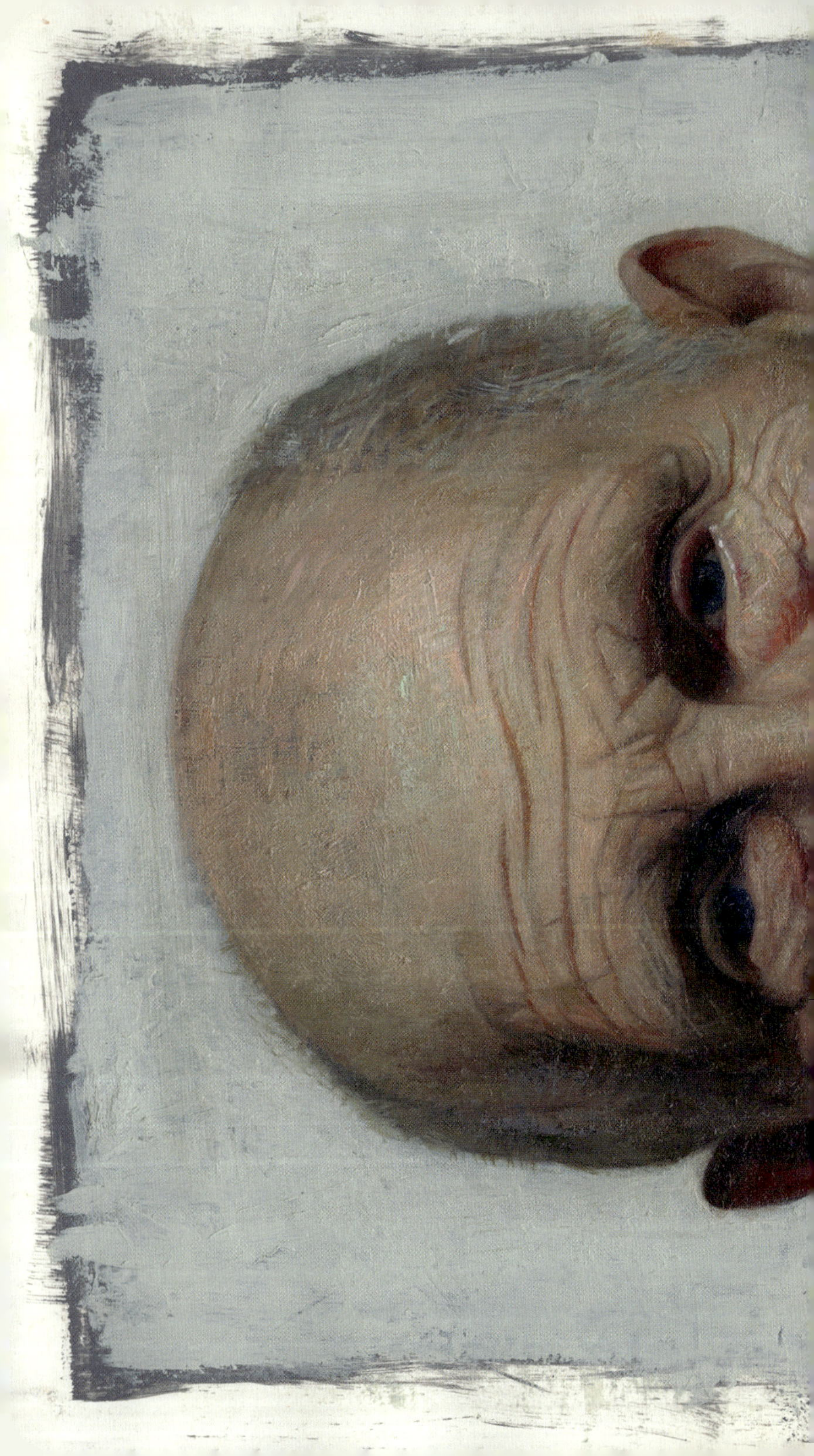

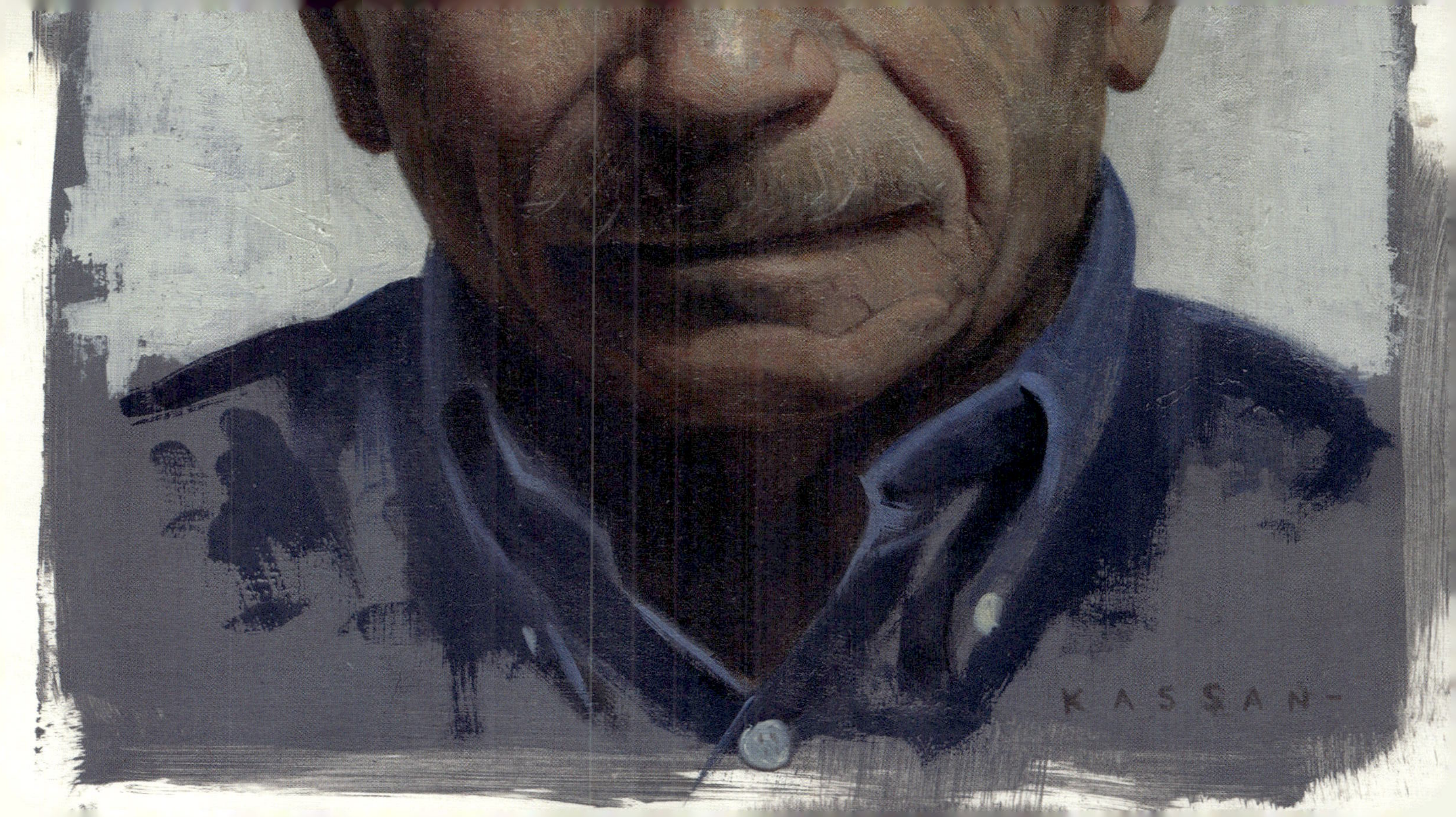

KASSAN

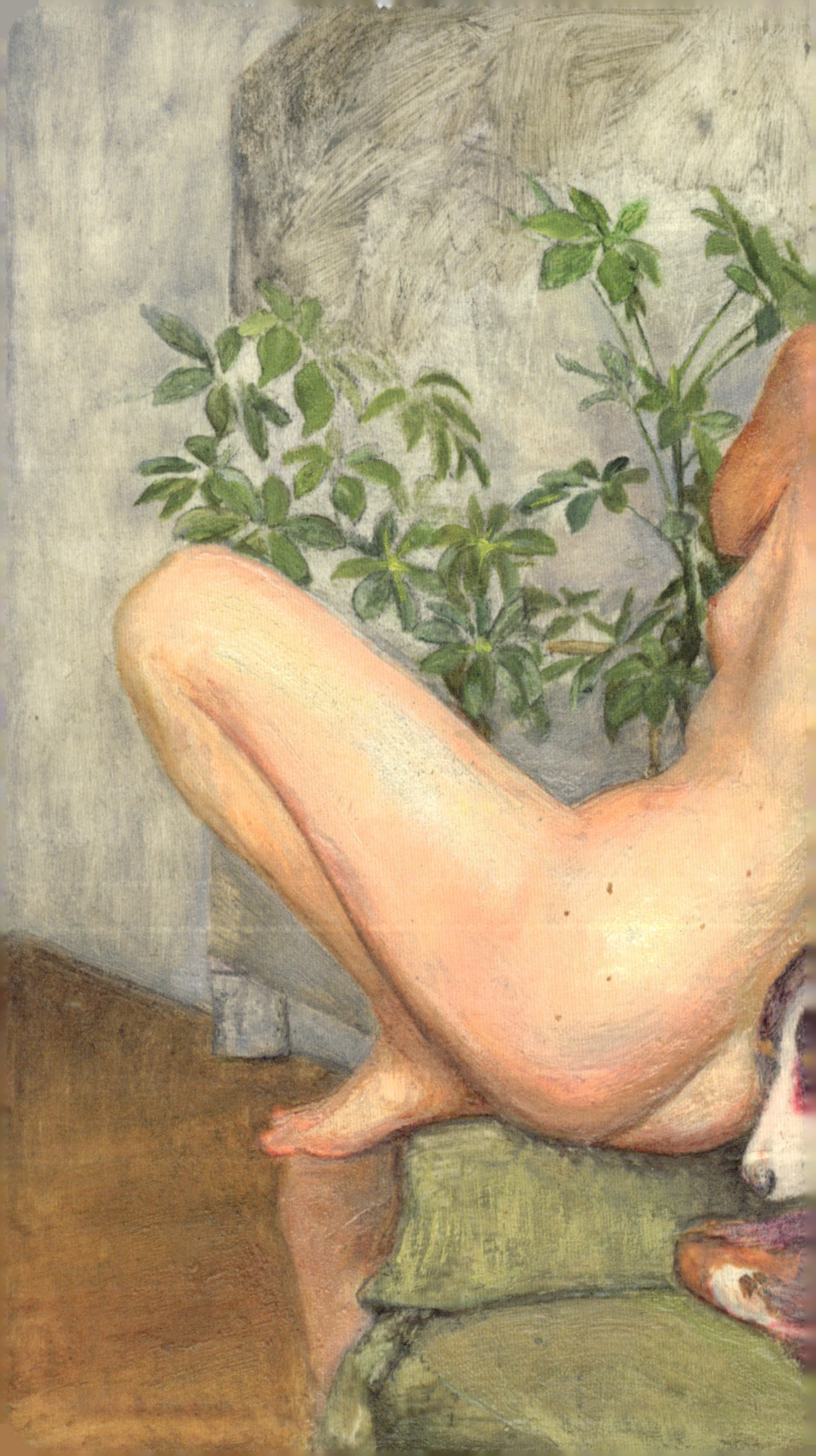

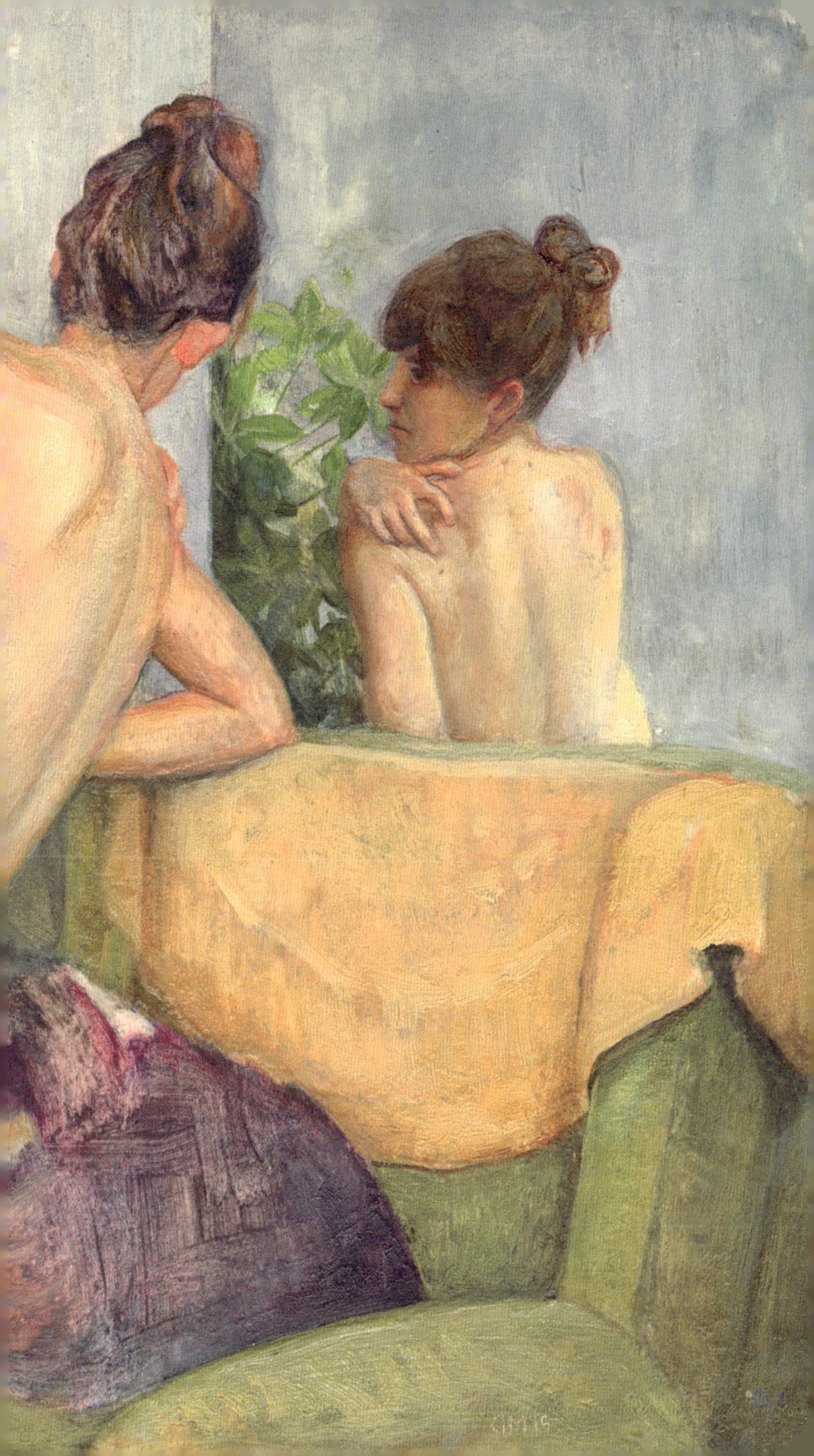

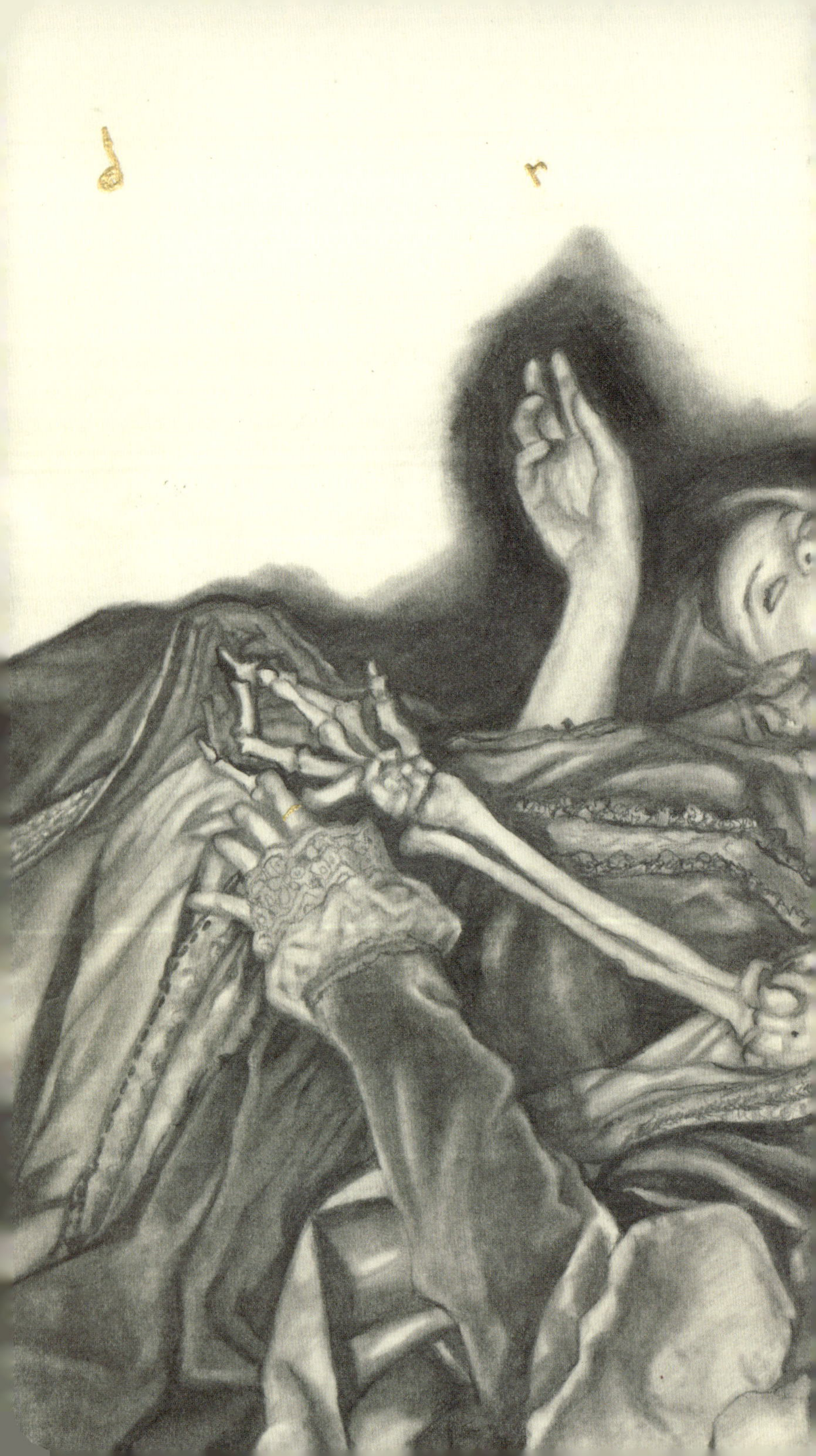

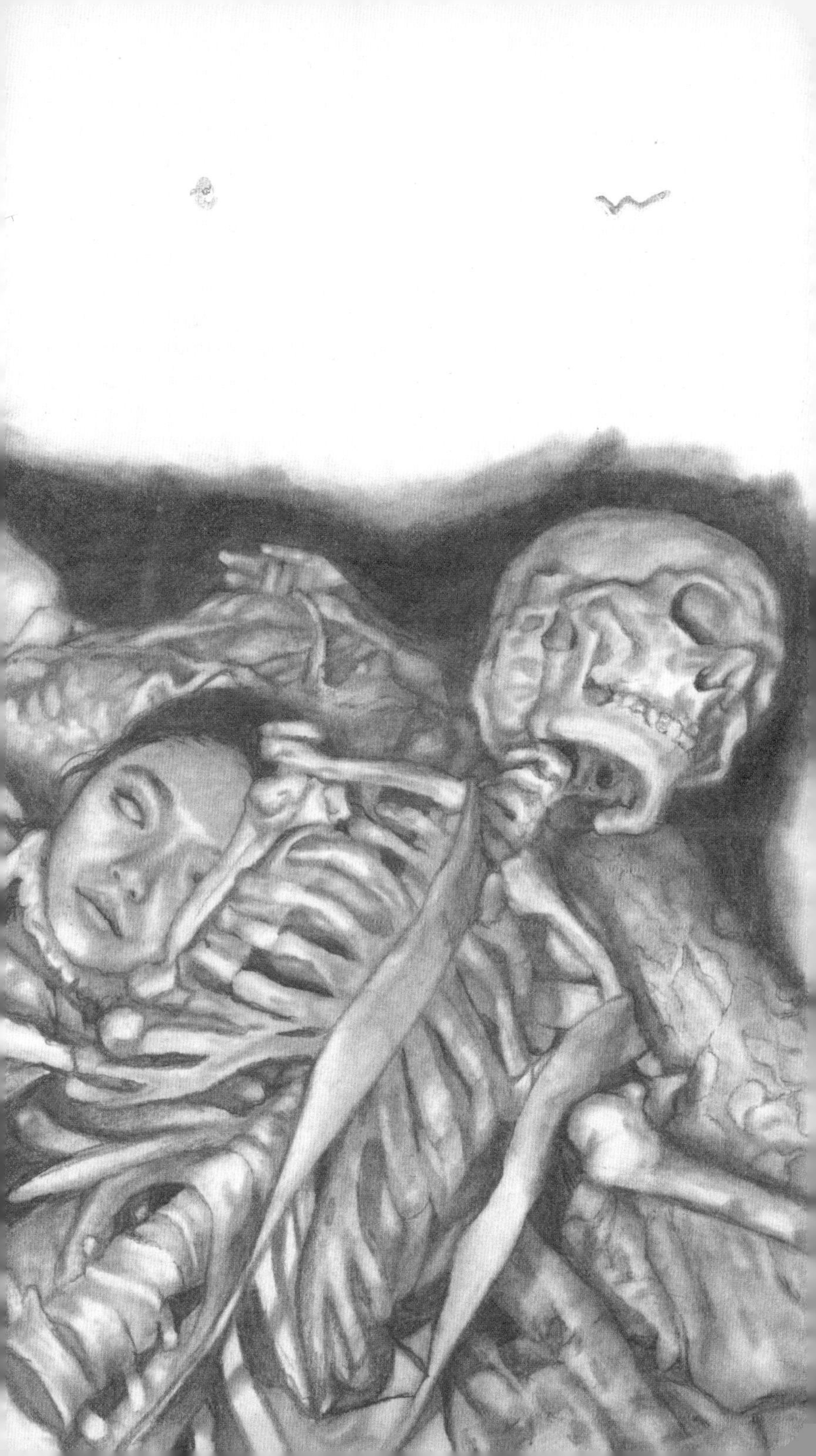

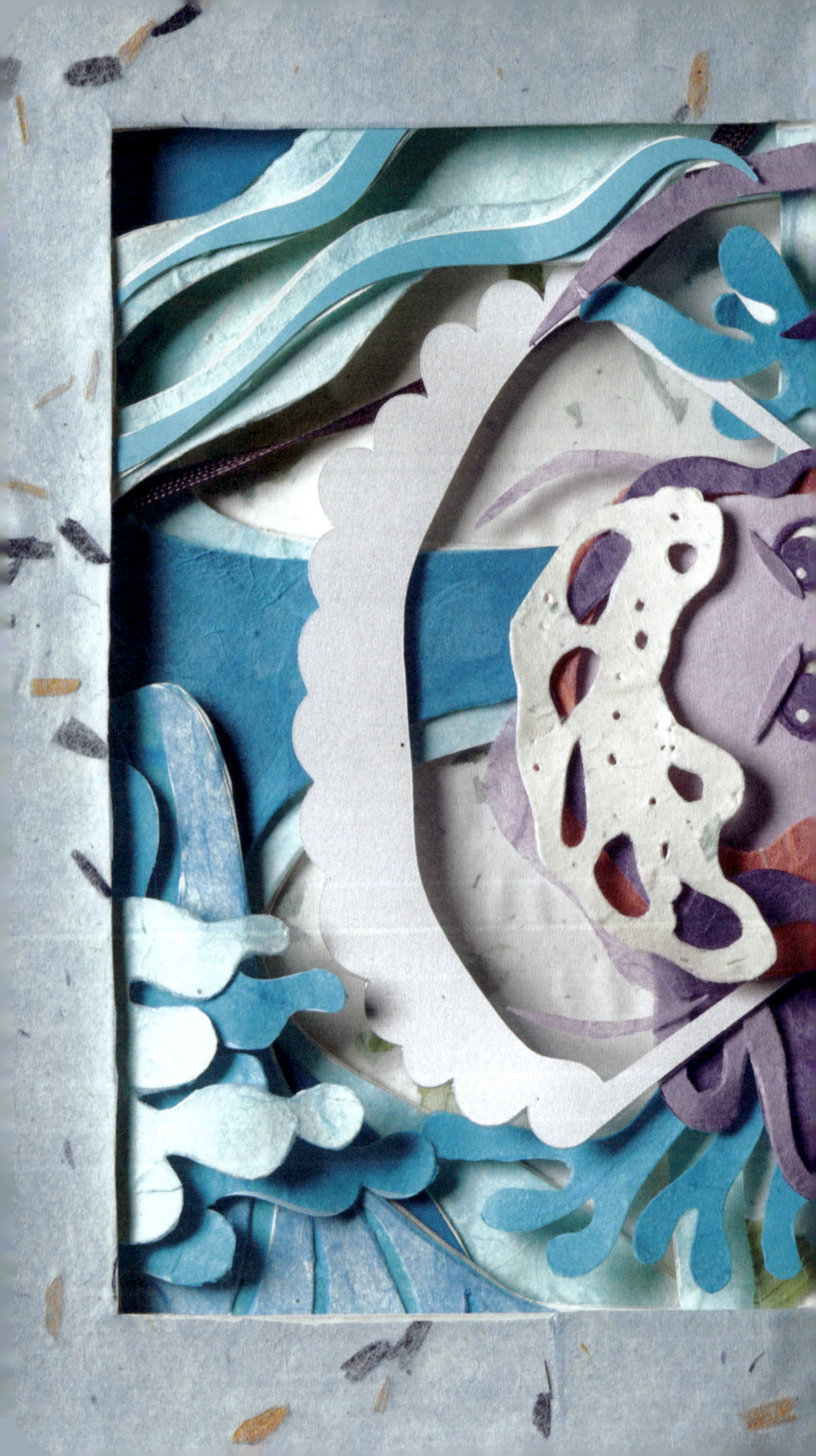

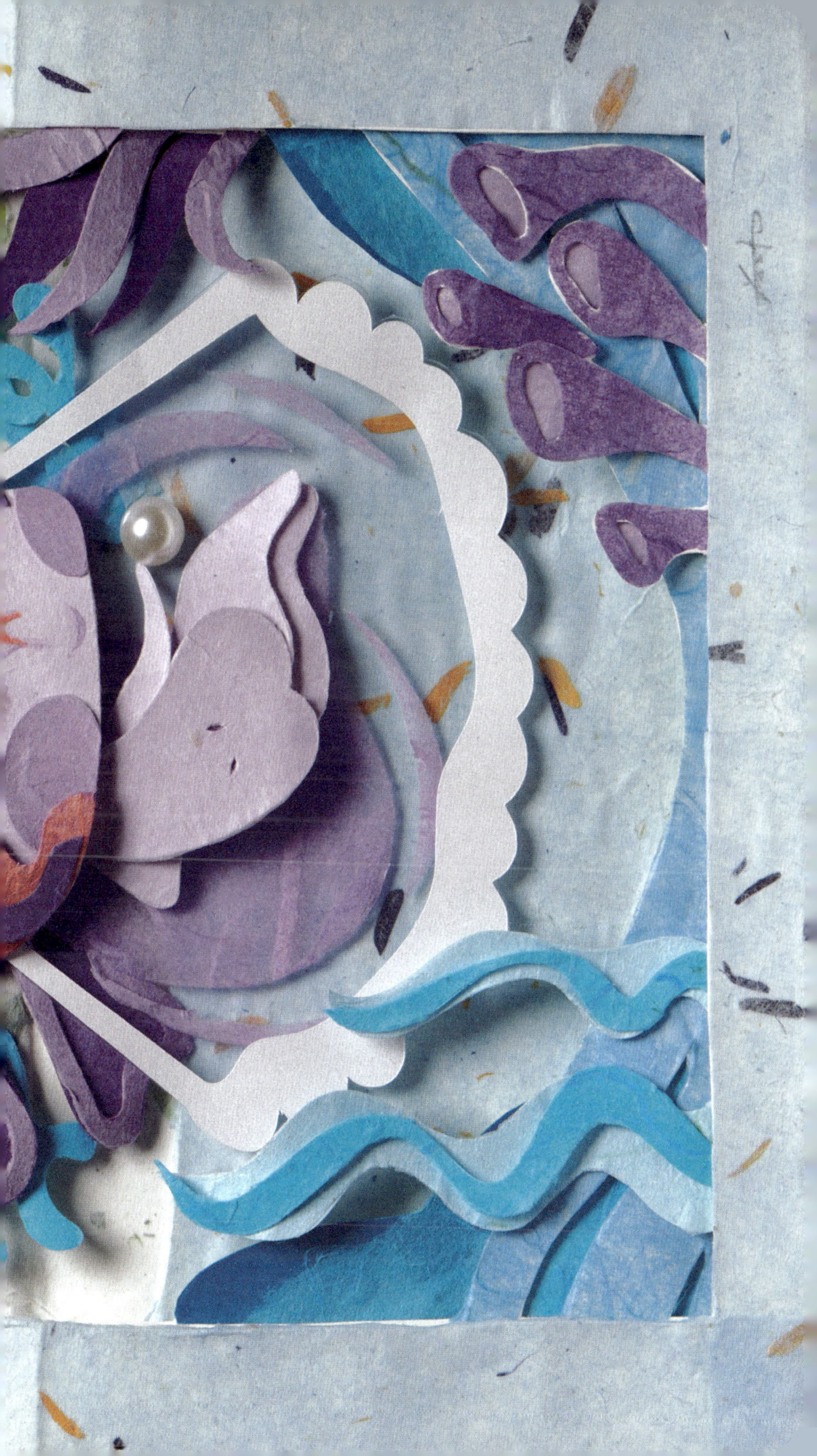

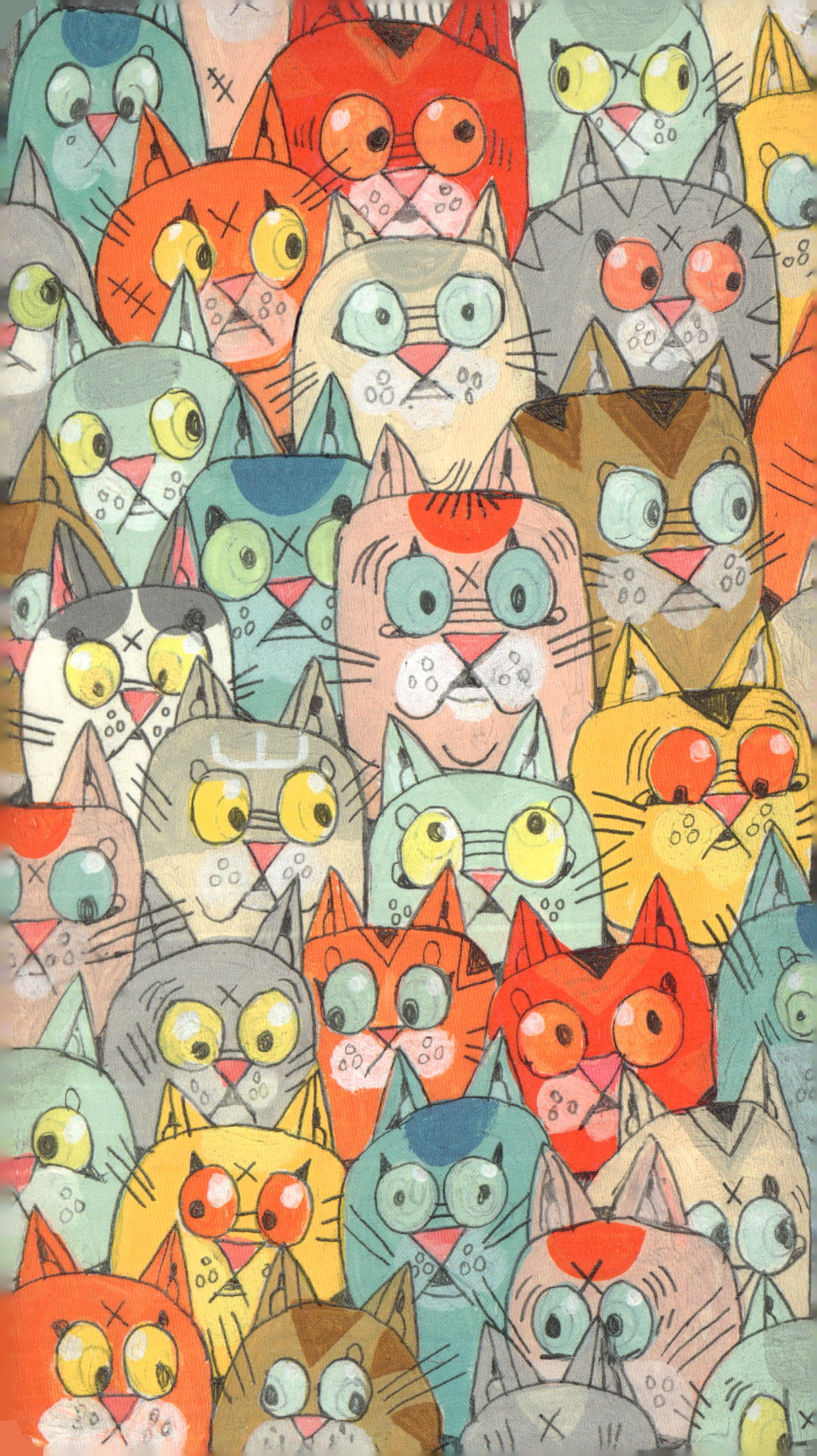

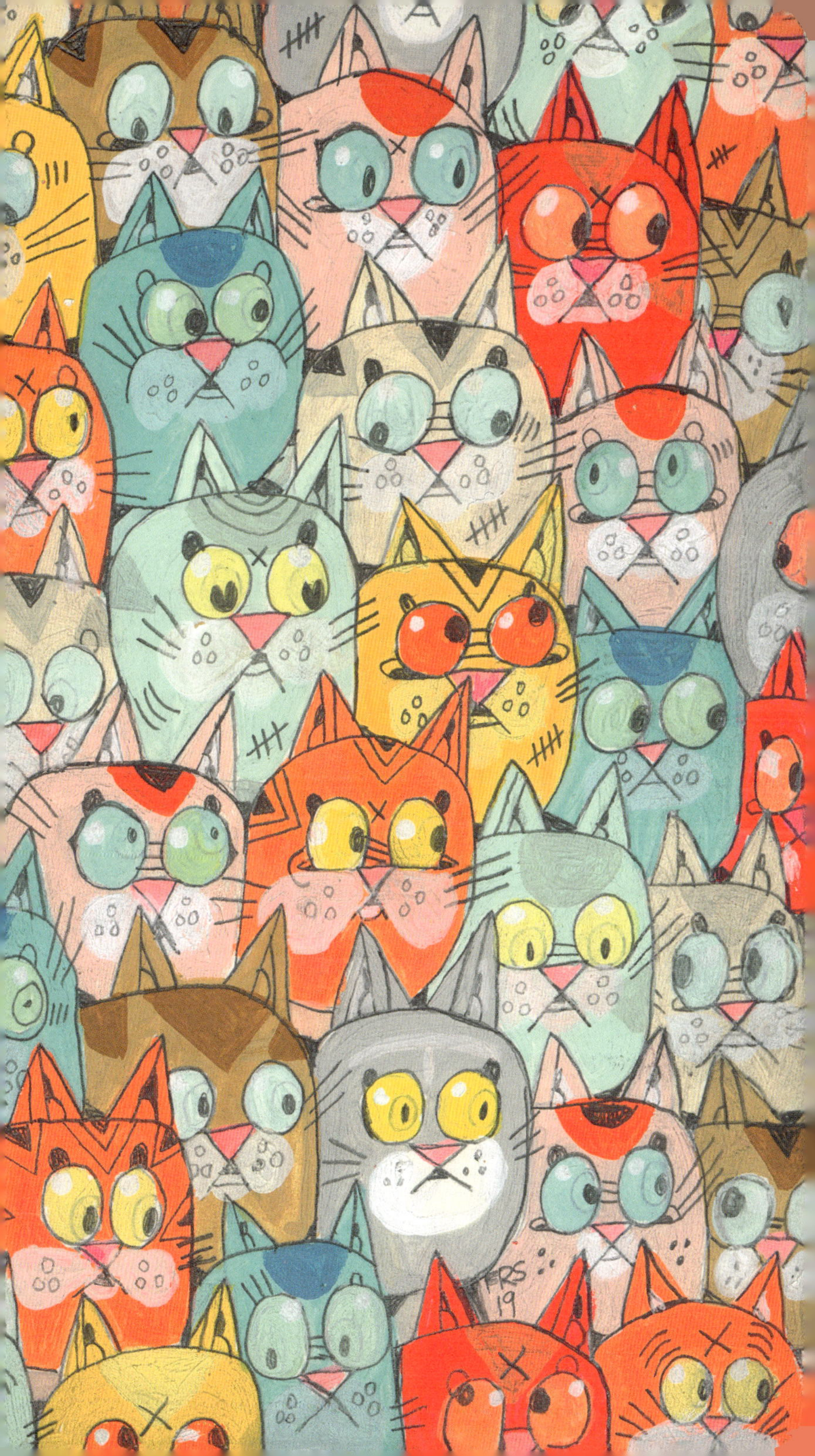

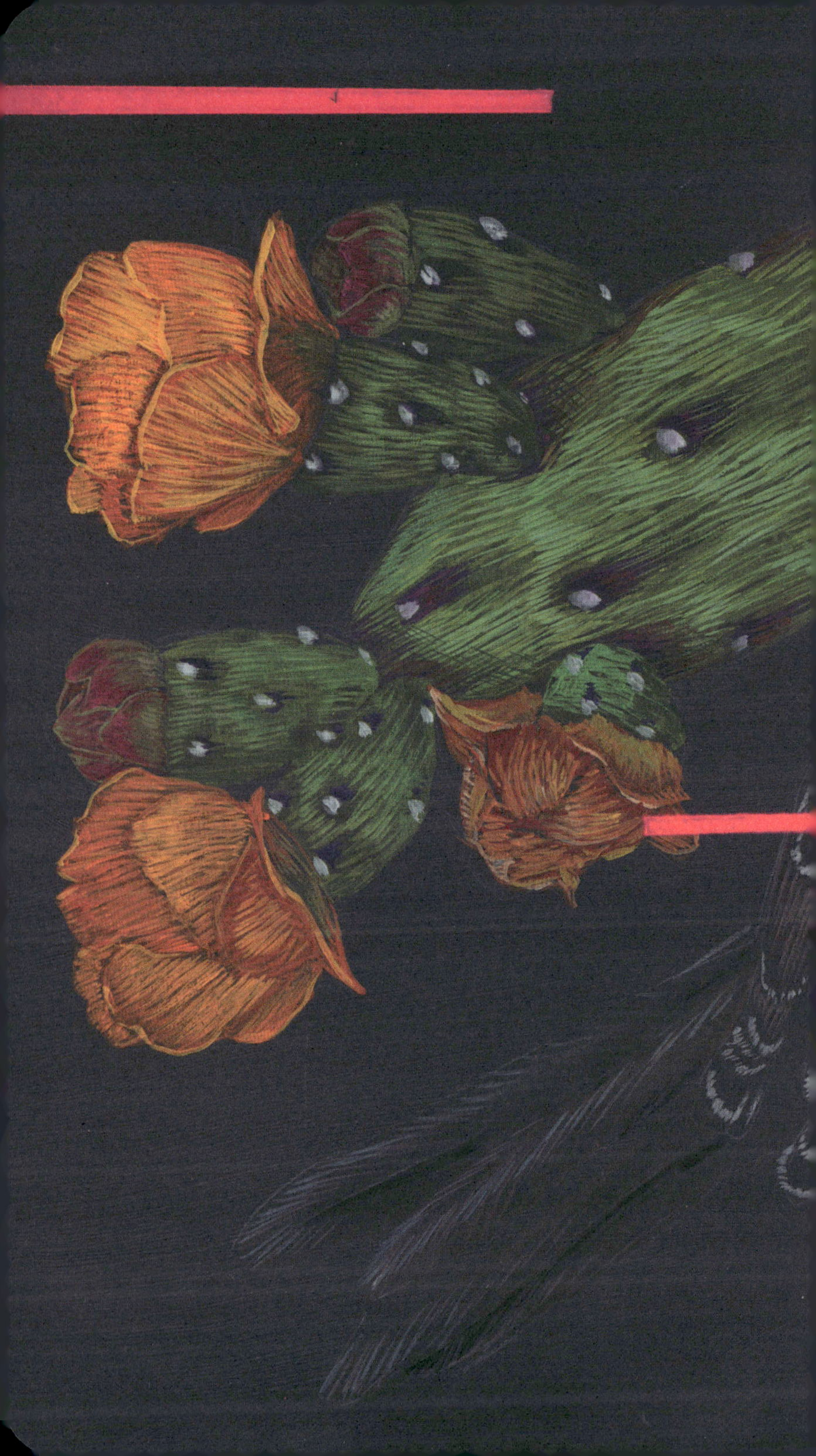

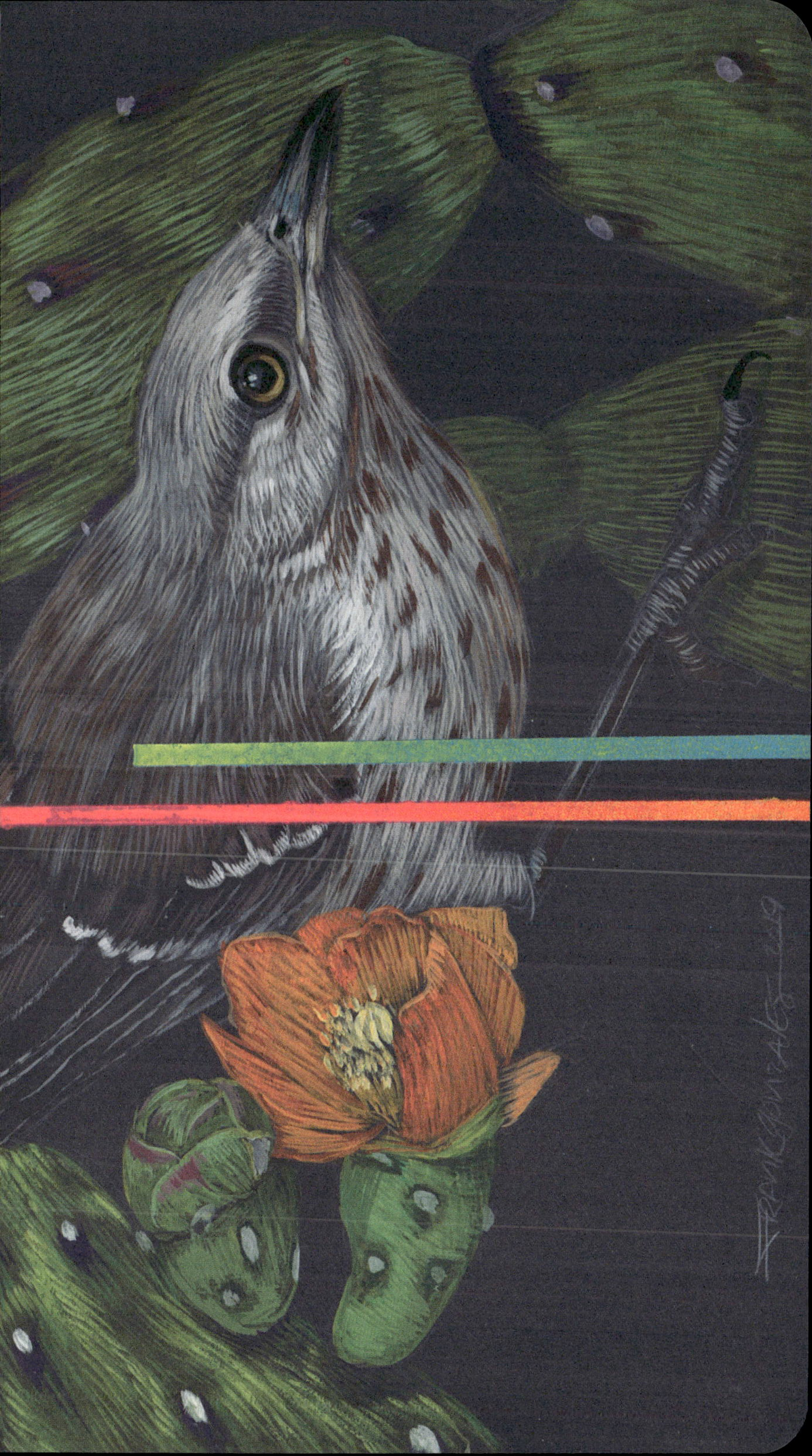

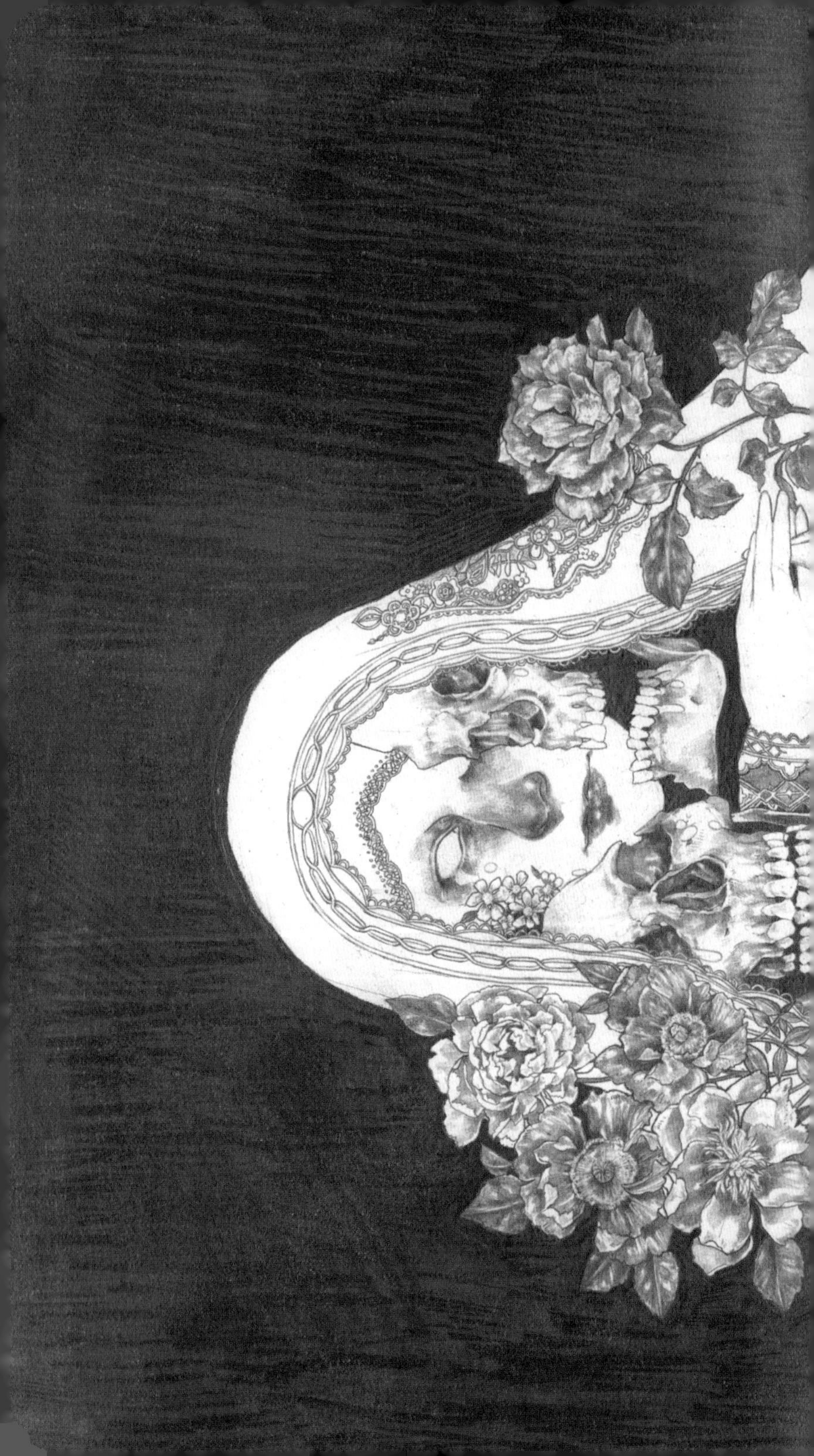

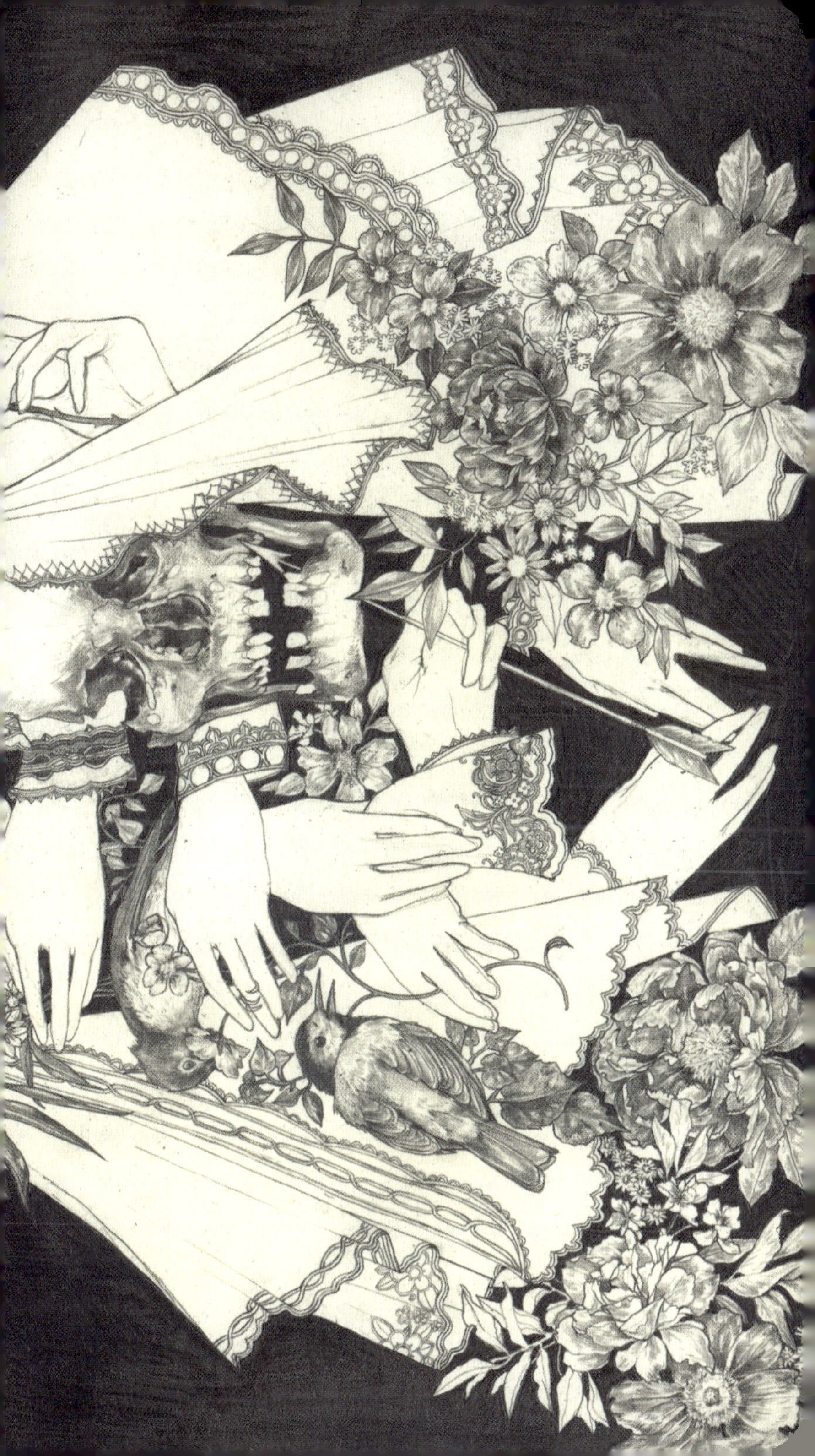

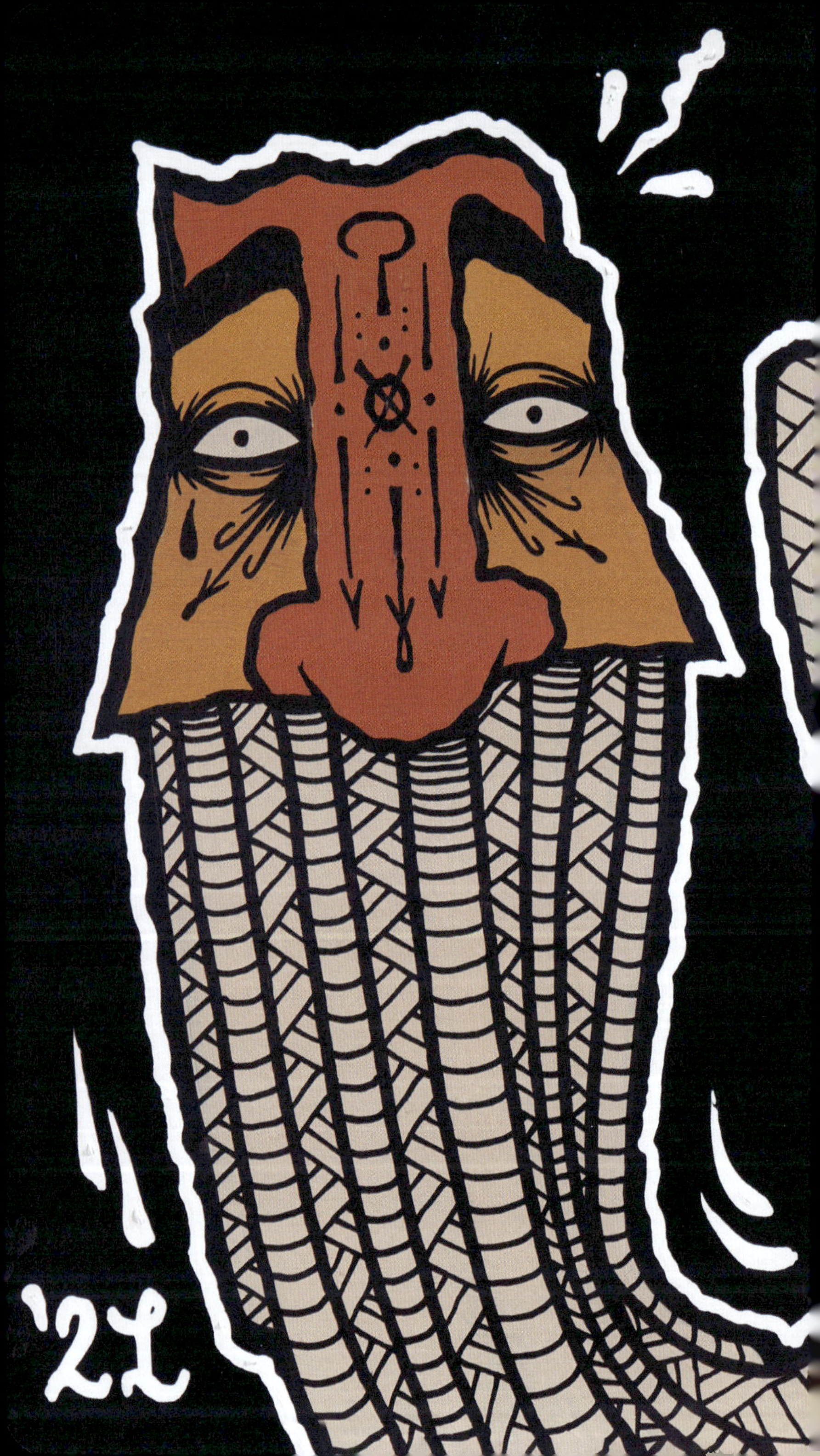
'22

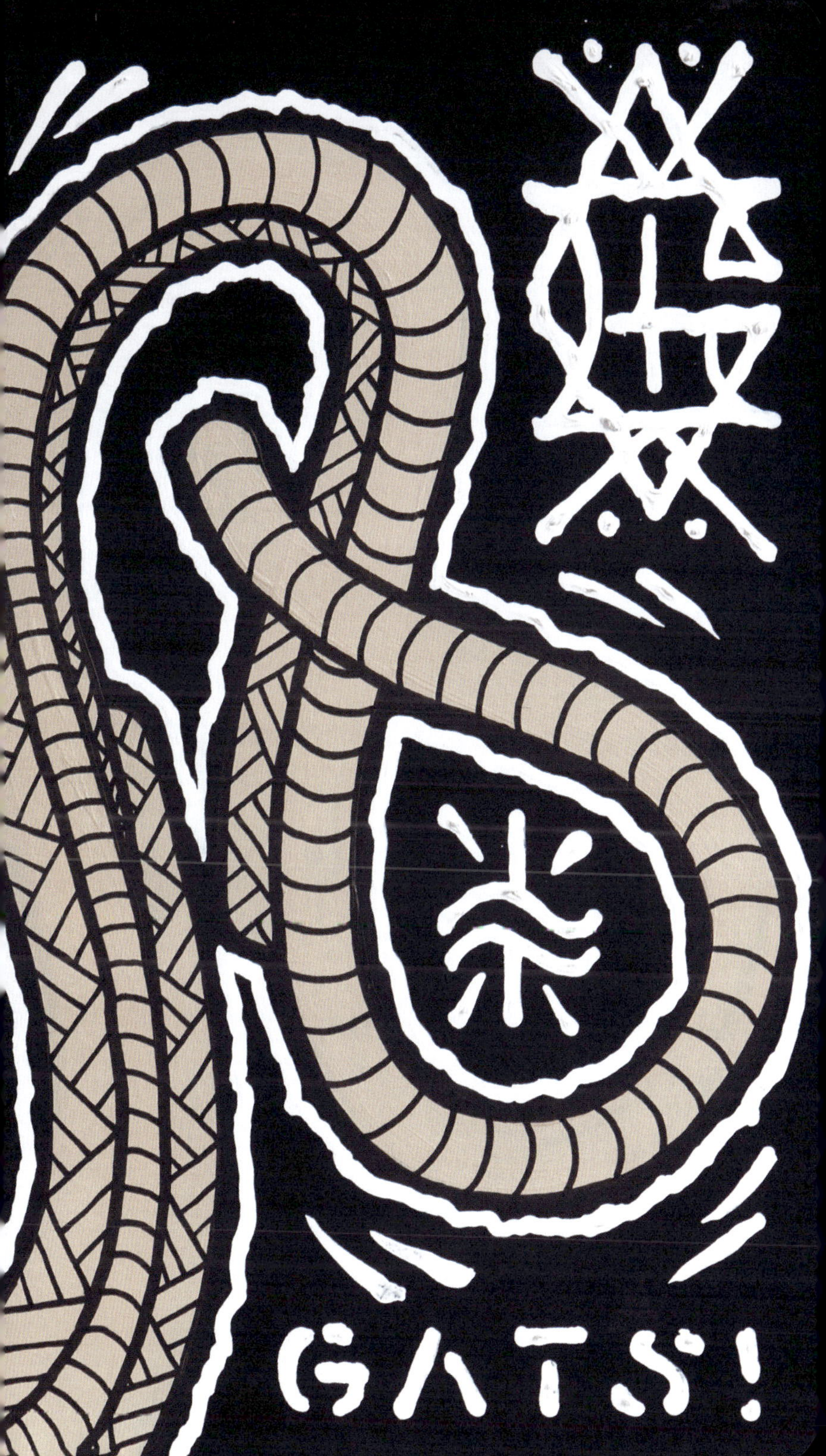
GATS!

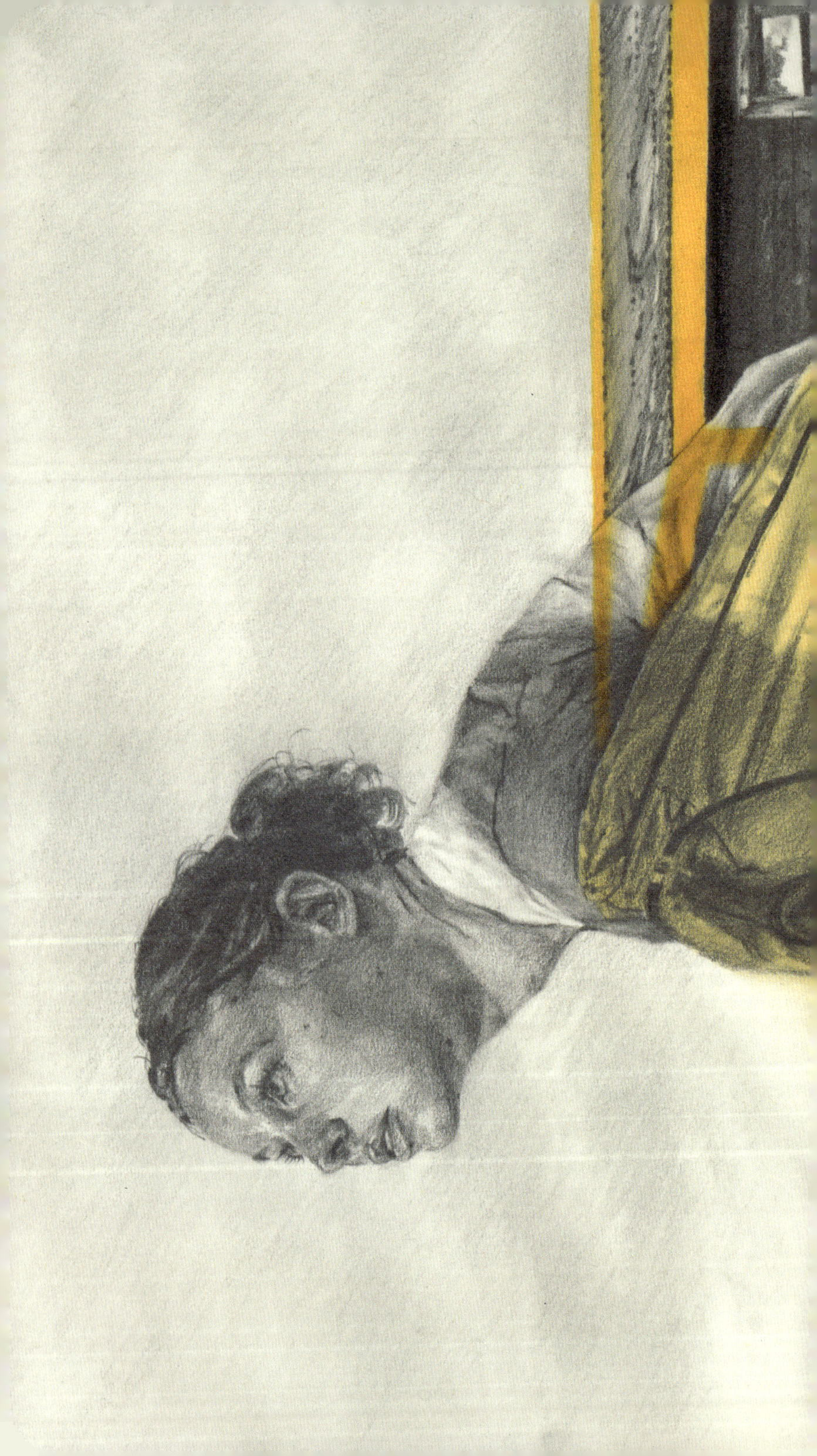

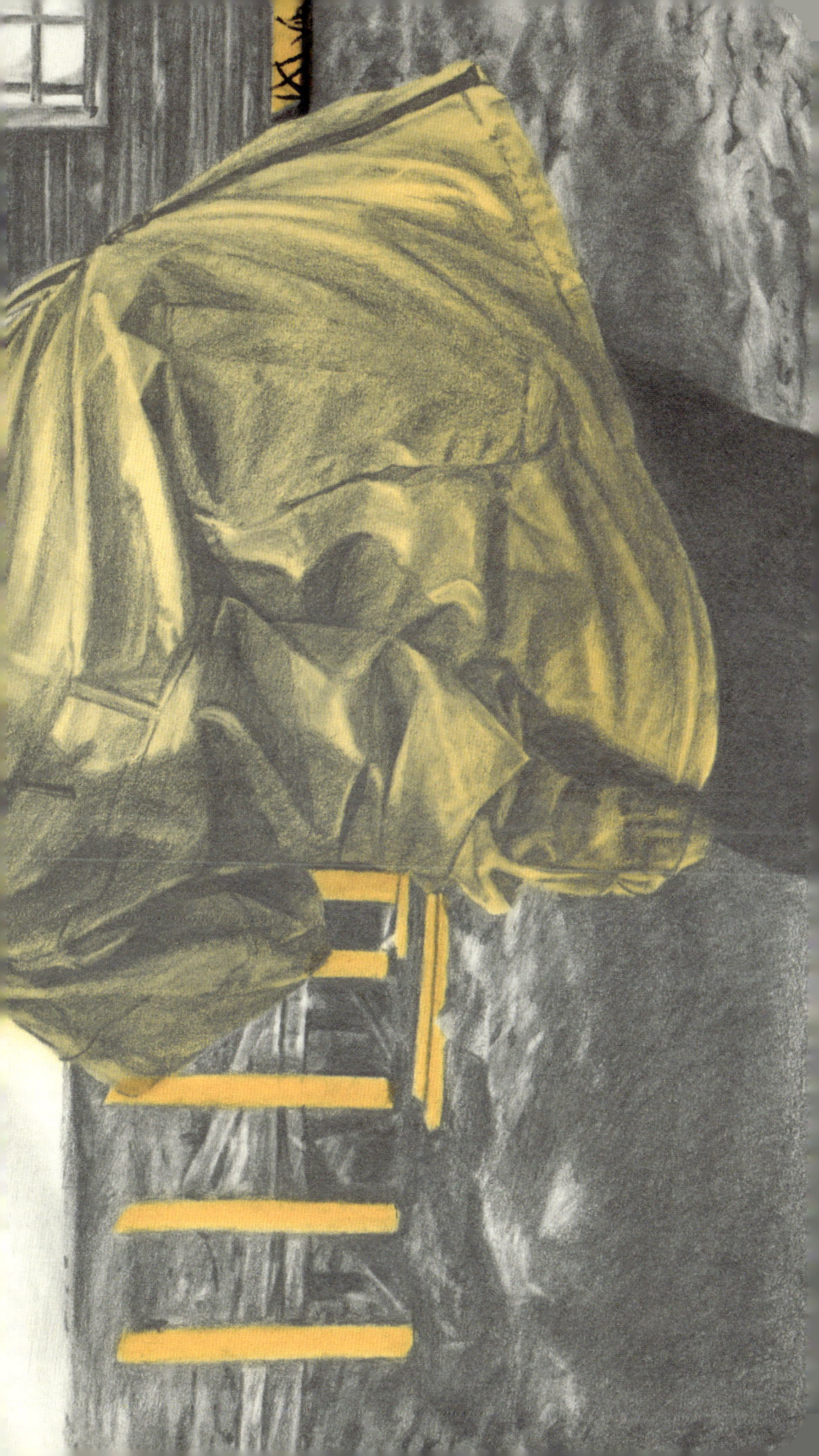

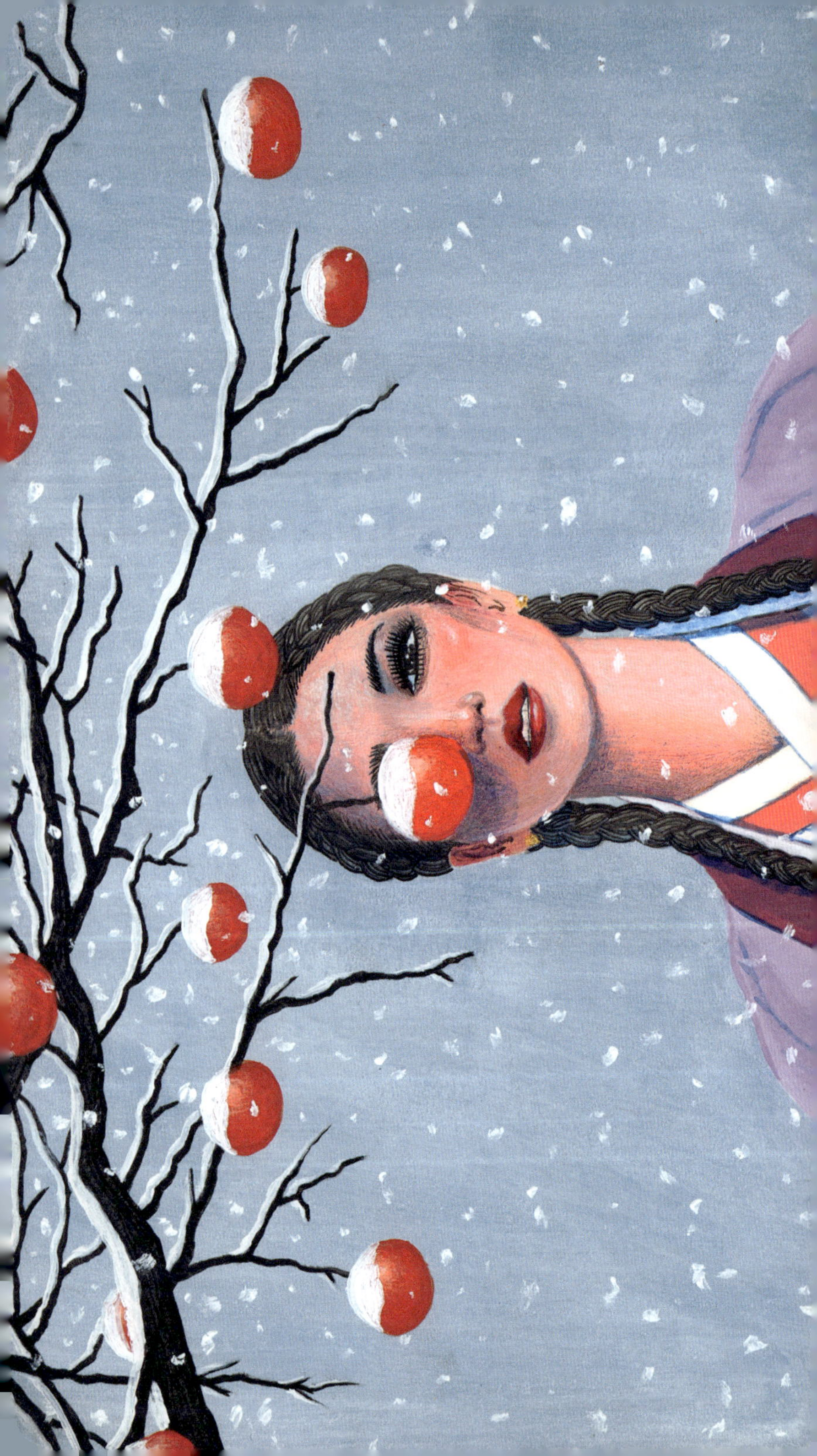

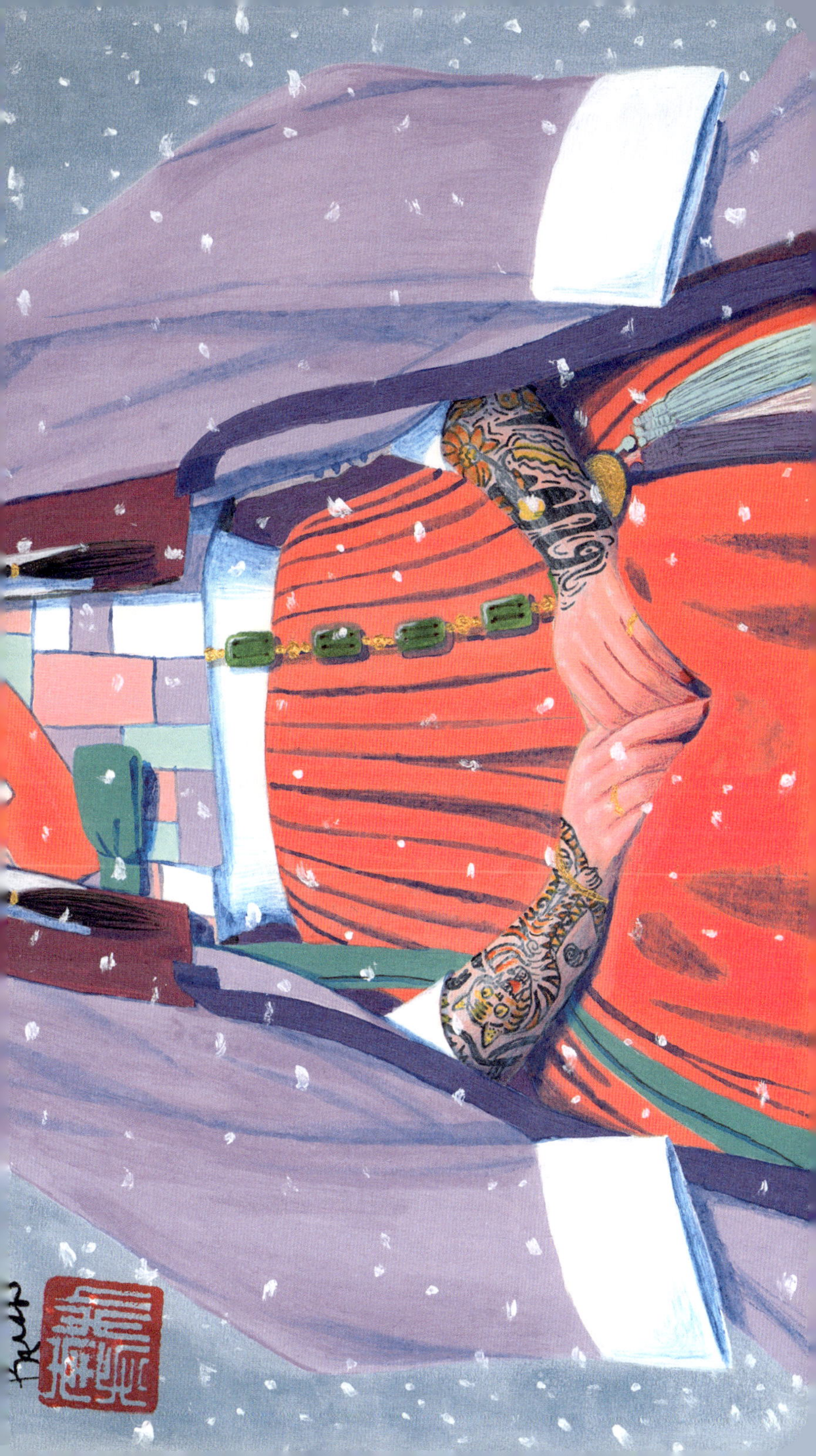

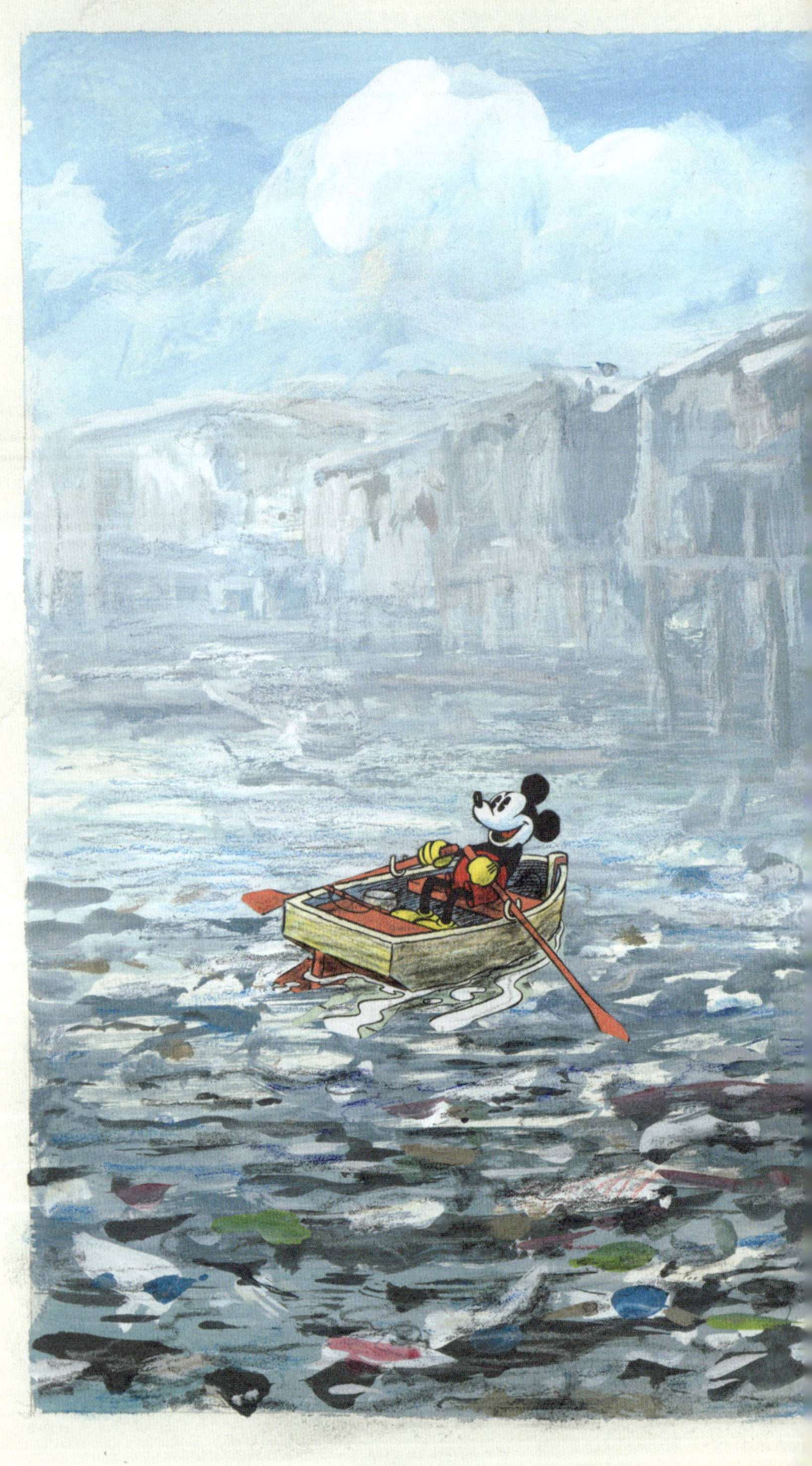

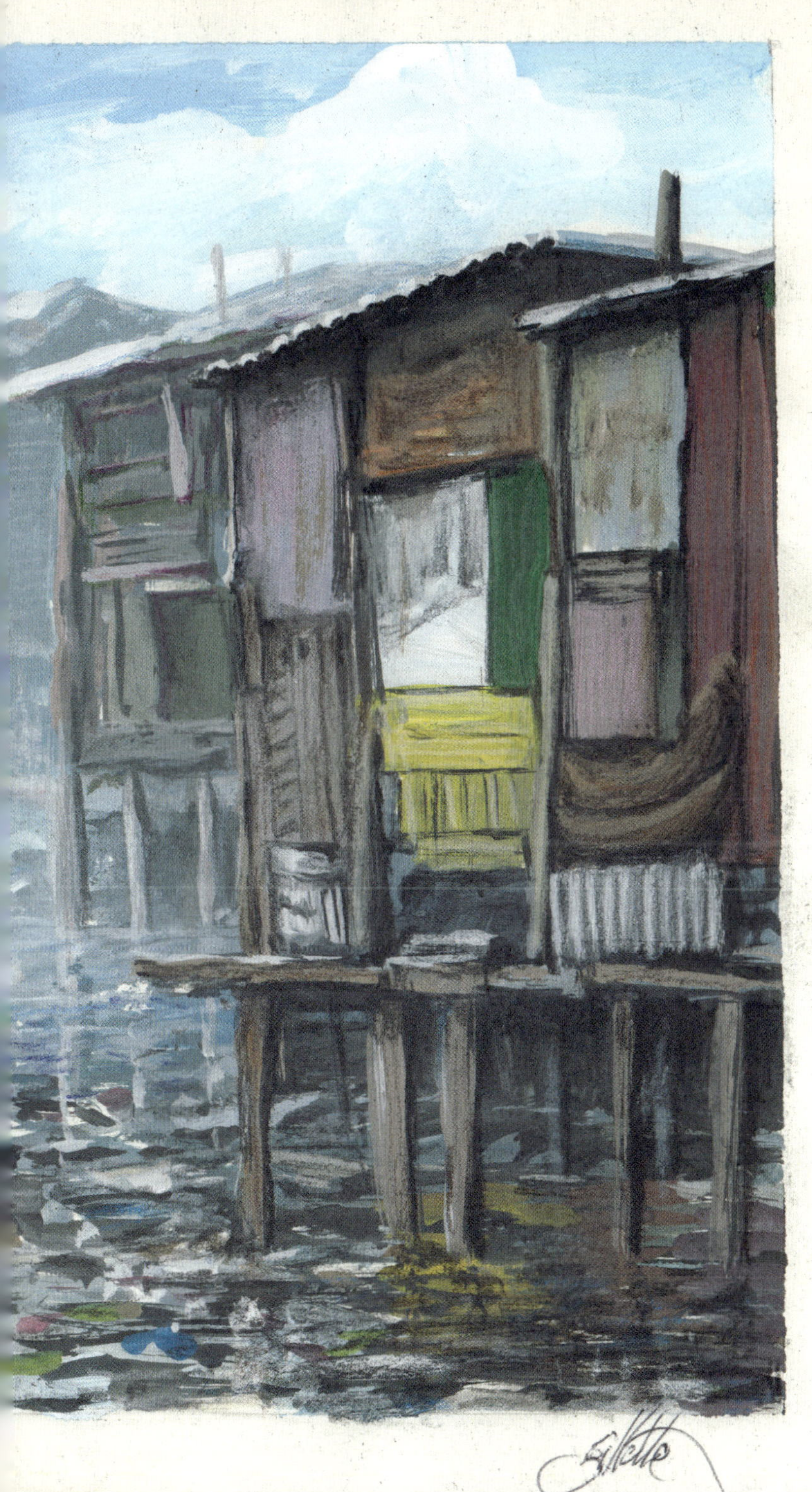

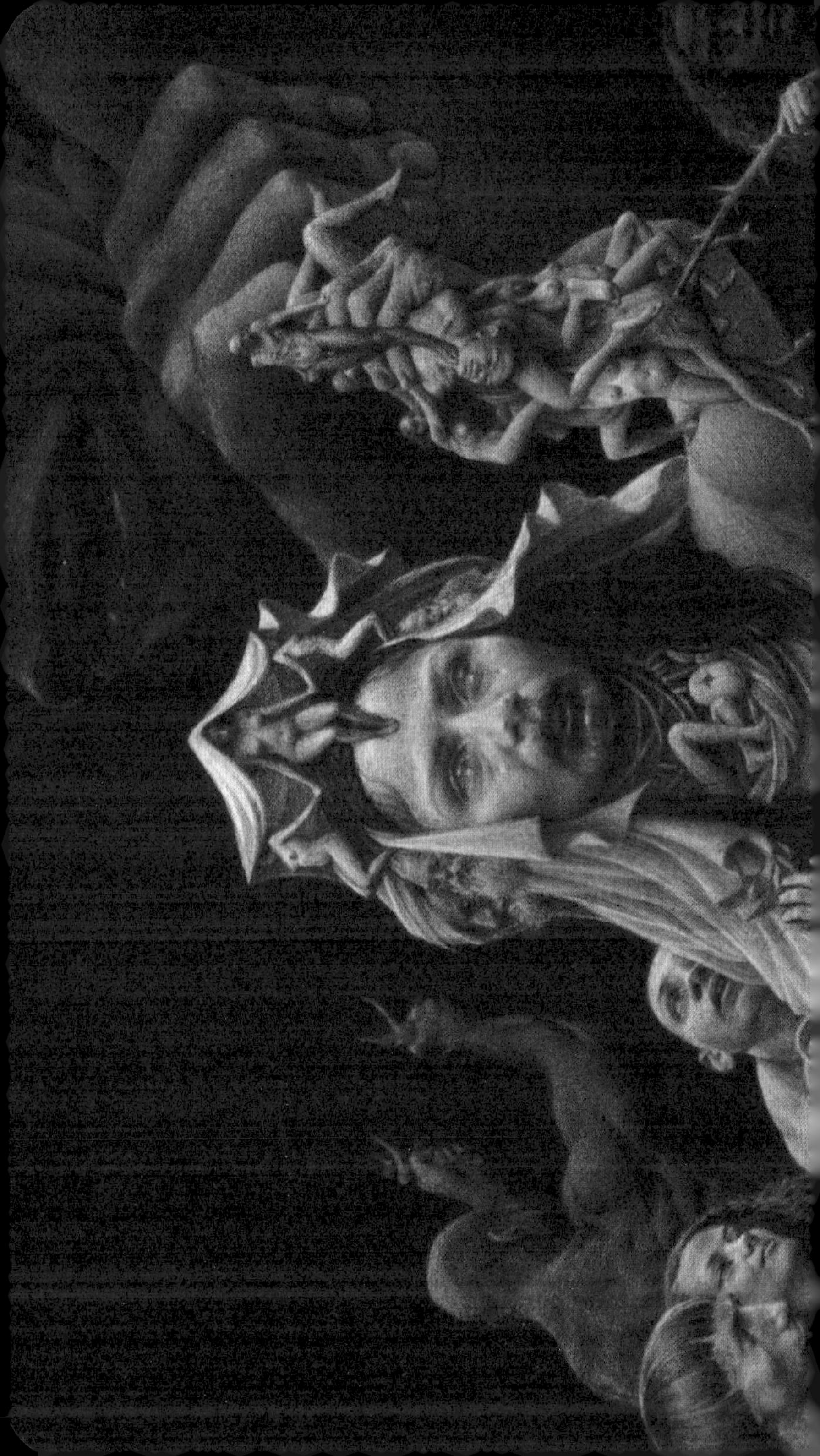

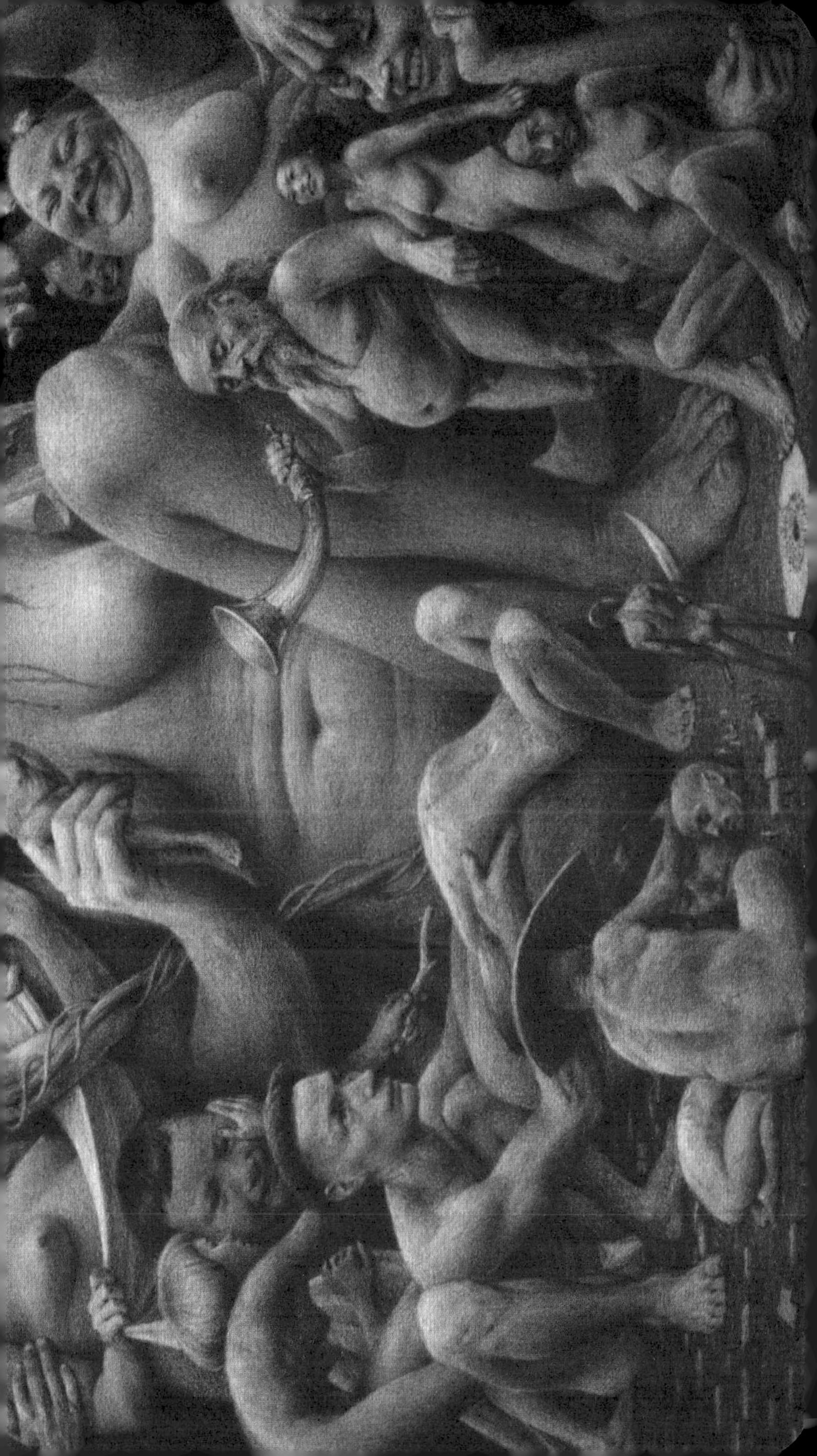

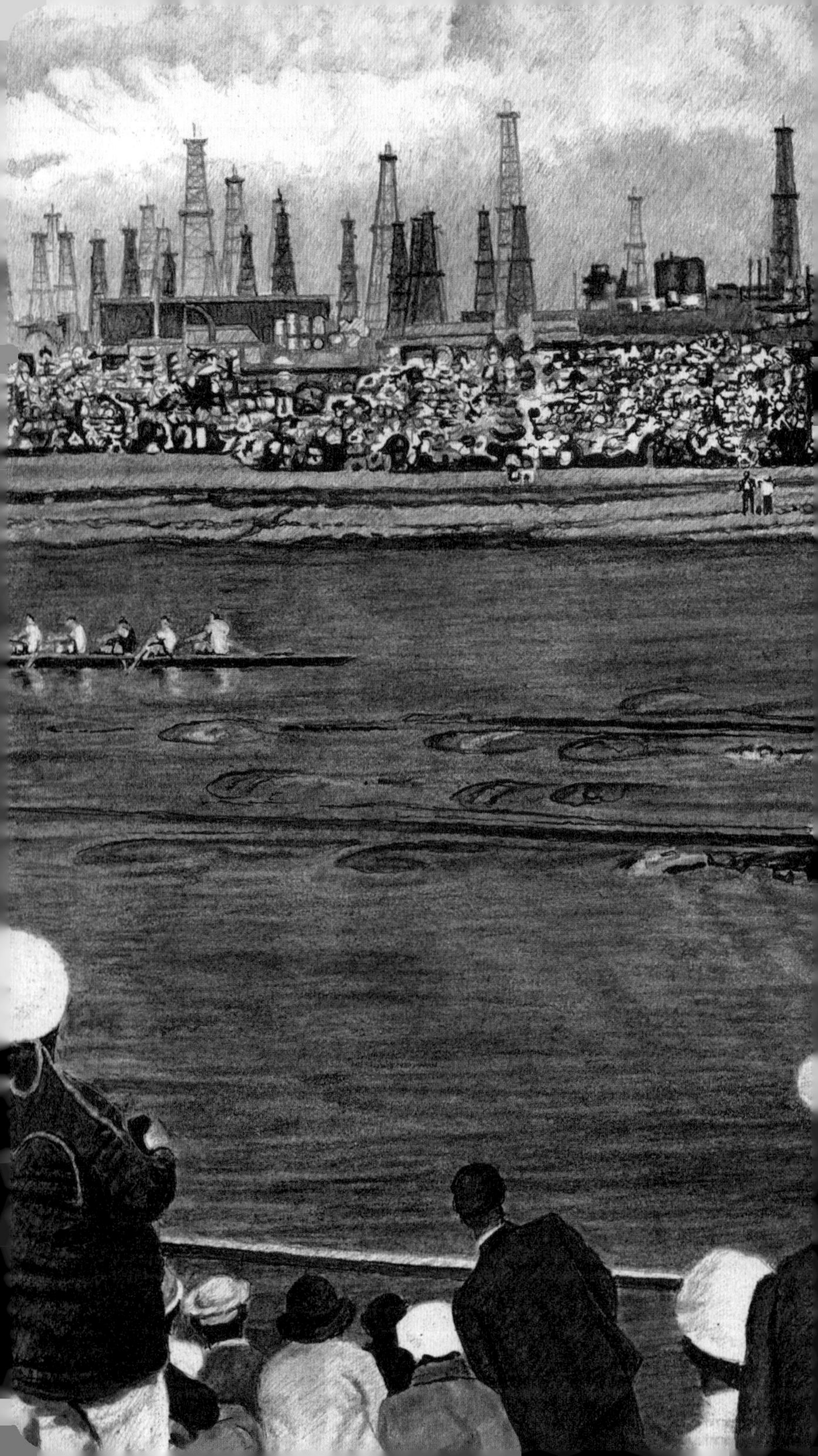

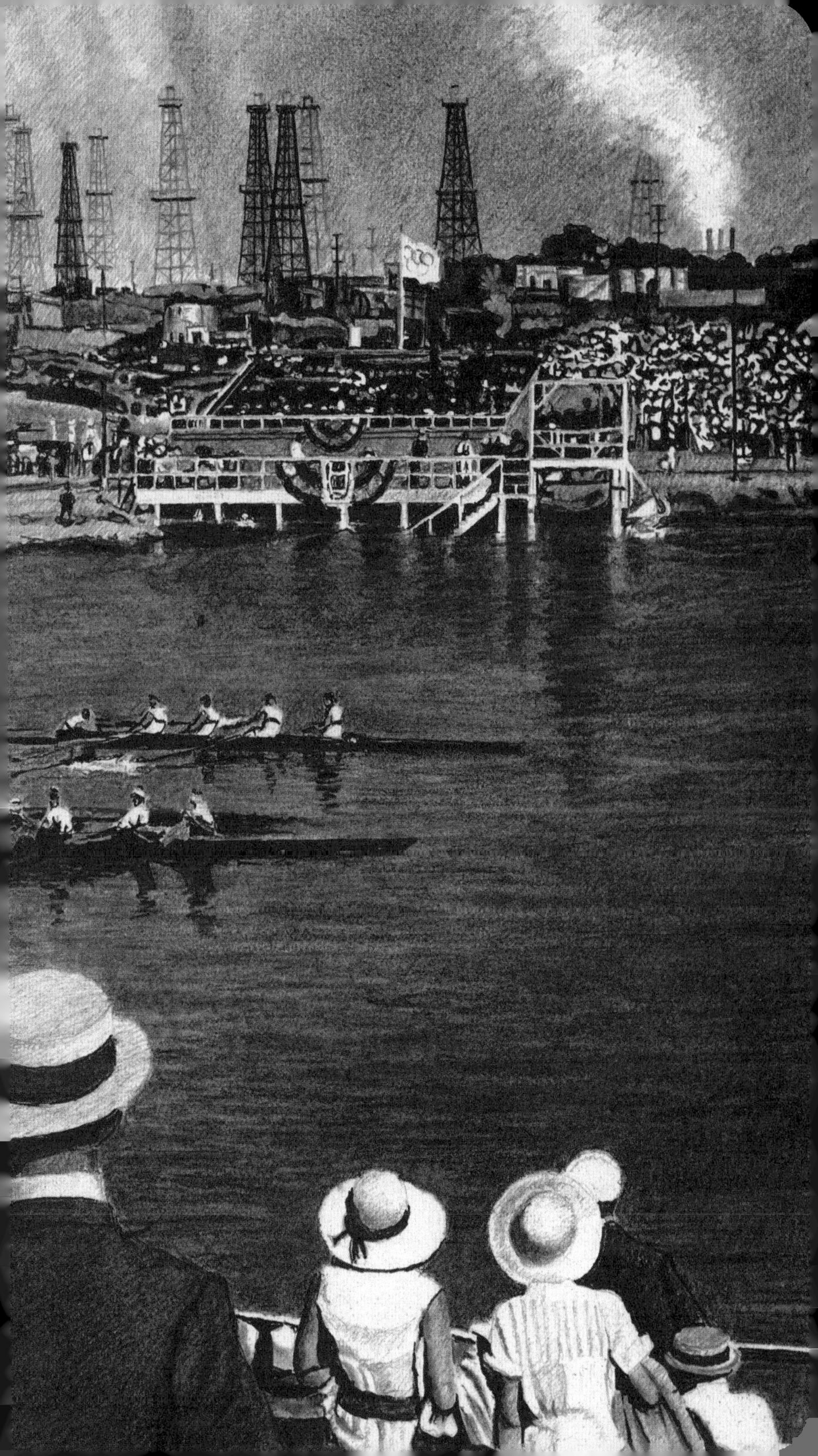

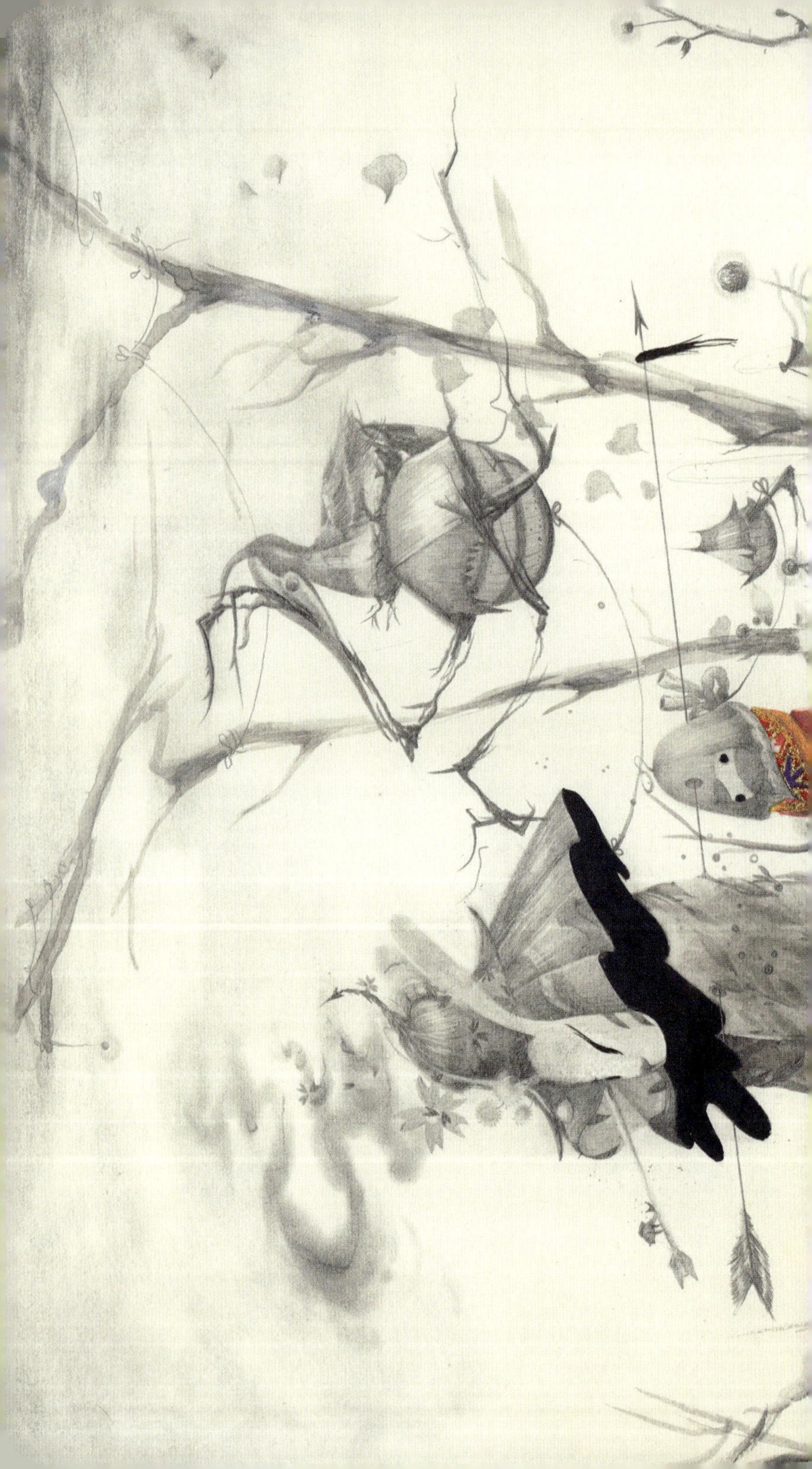

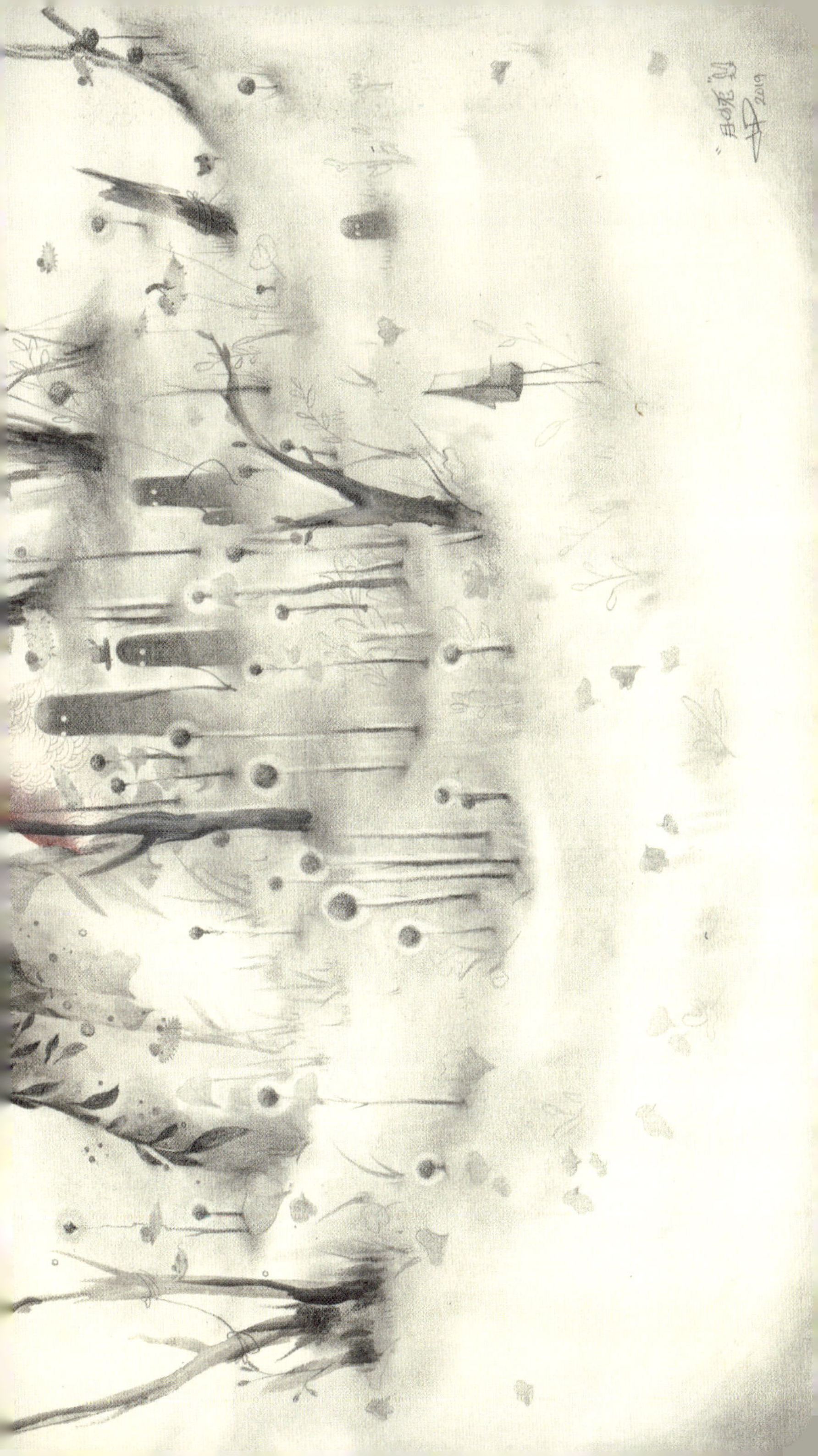

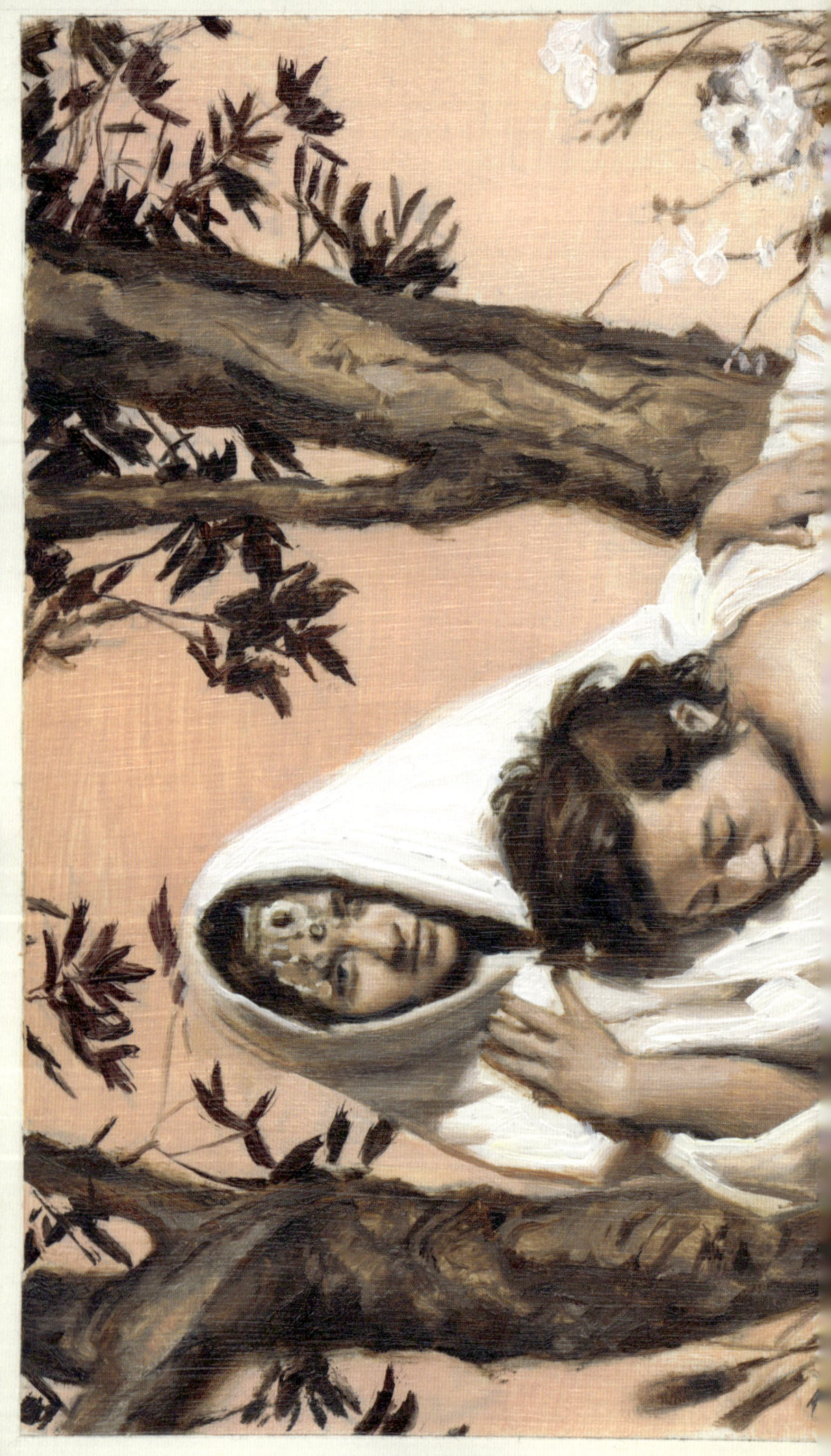

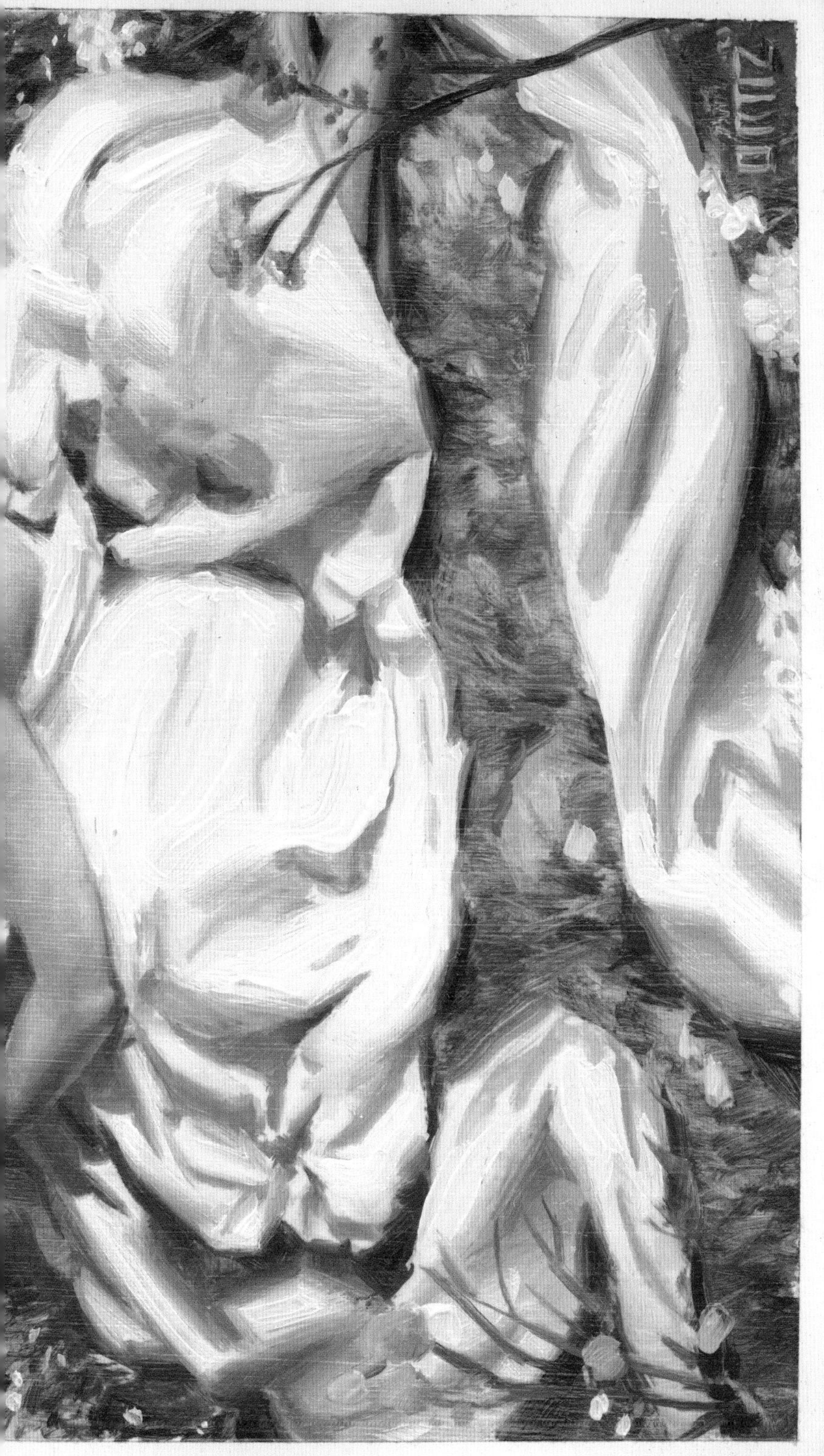

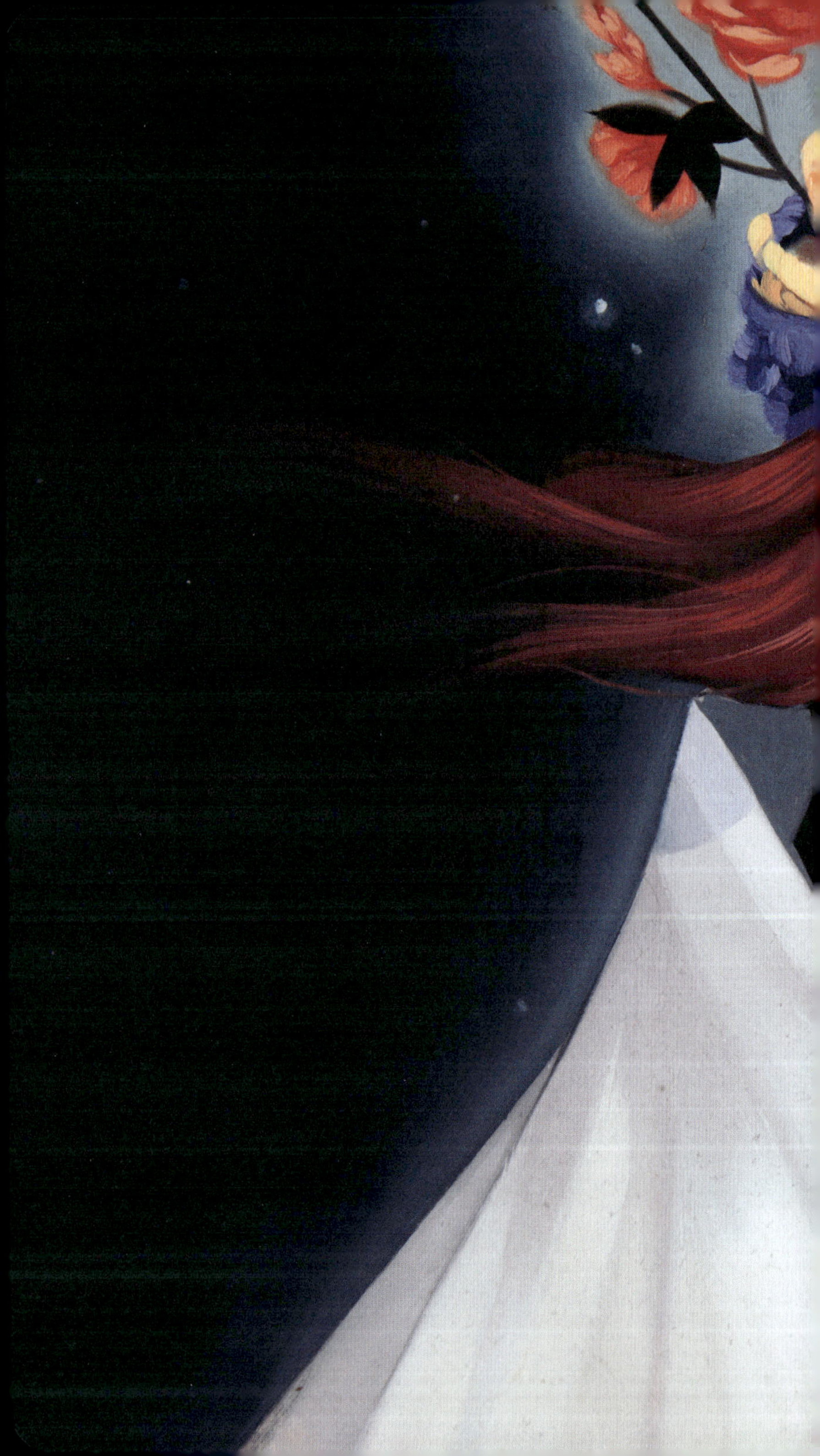

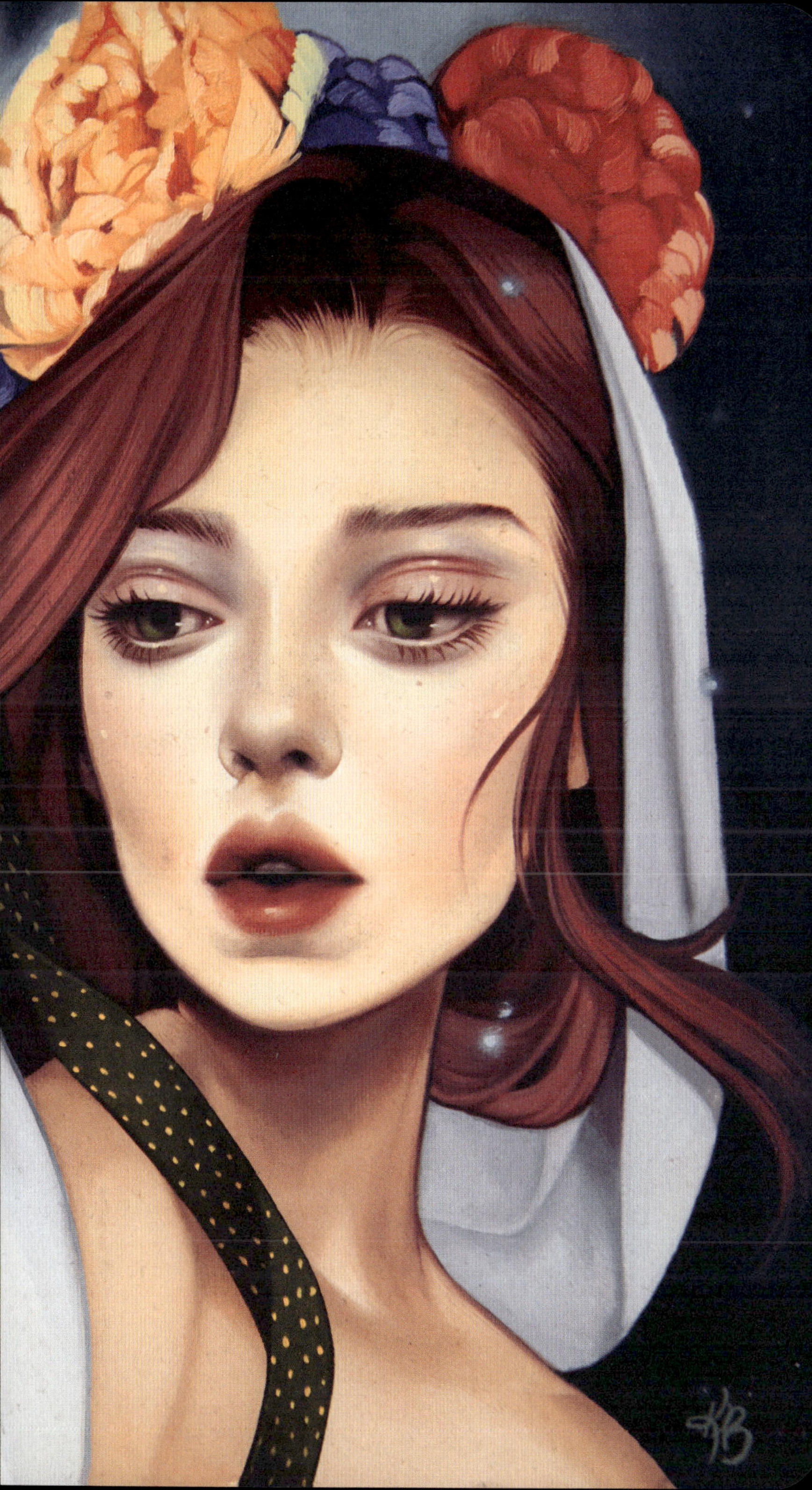

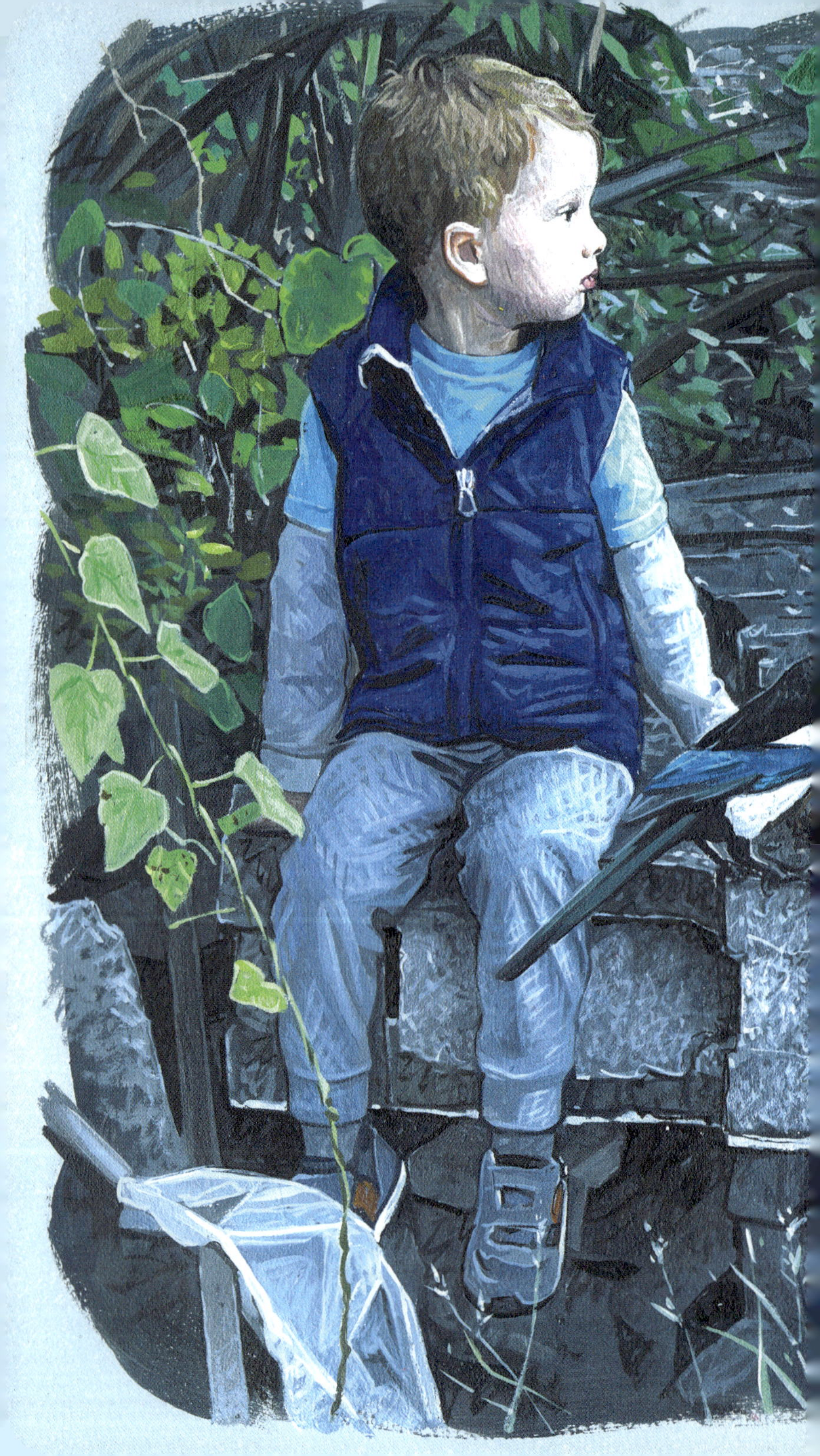

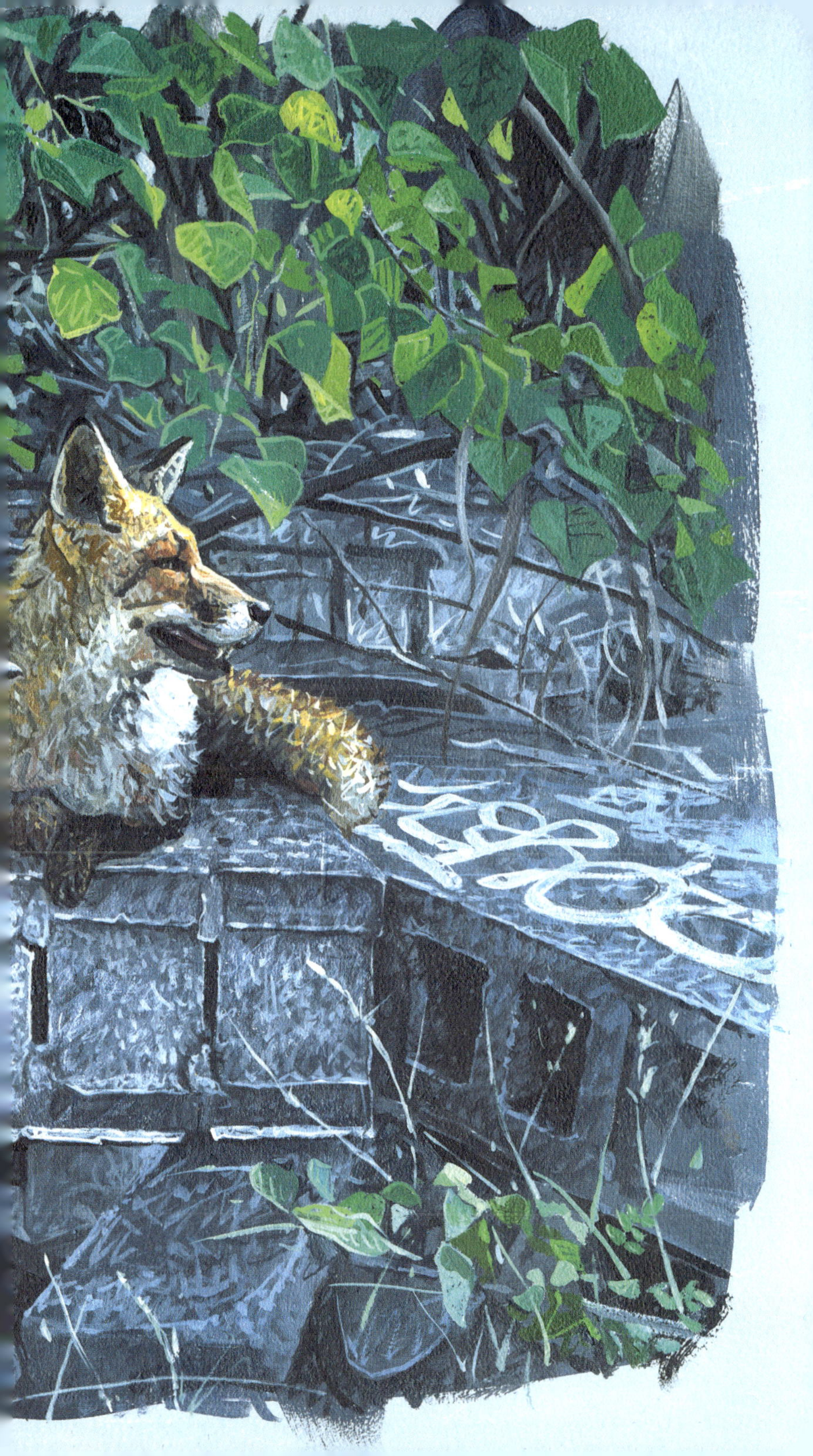

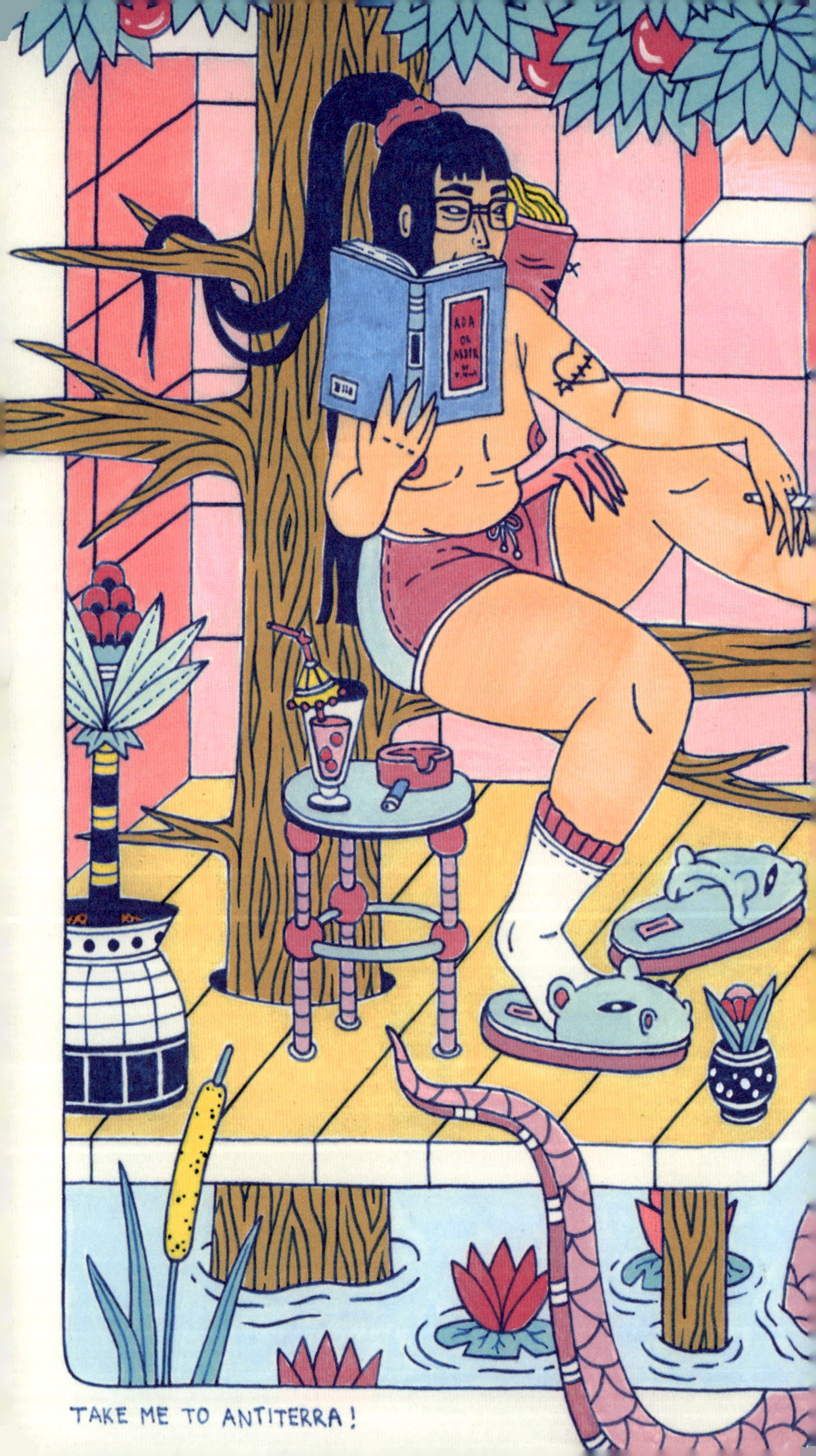

TAKE ME TO ANTITERRA!

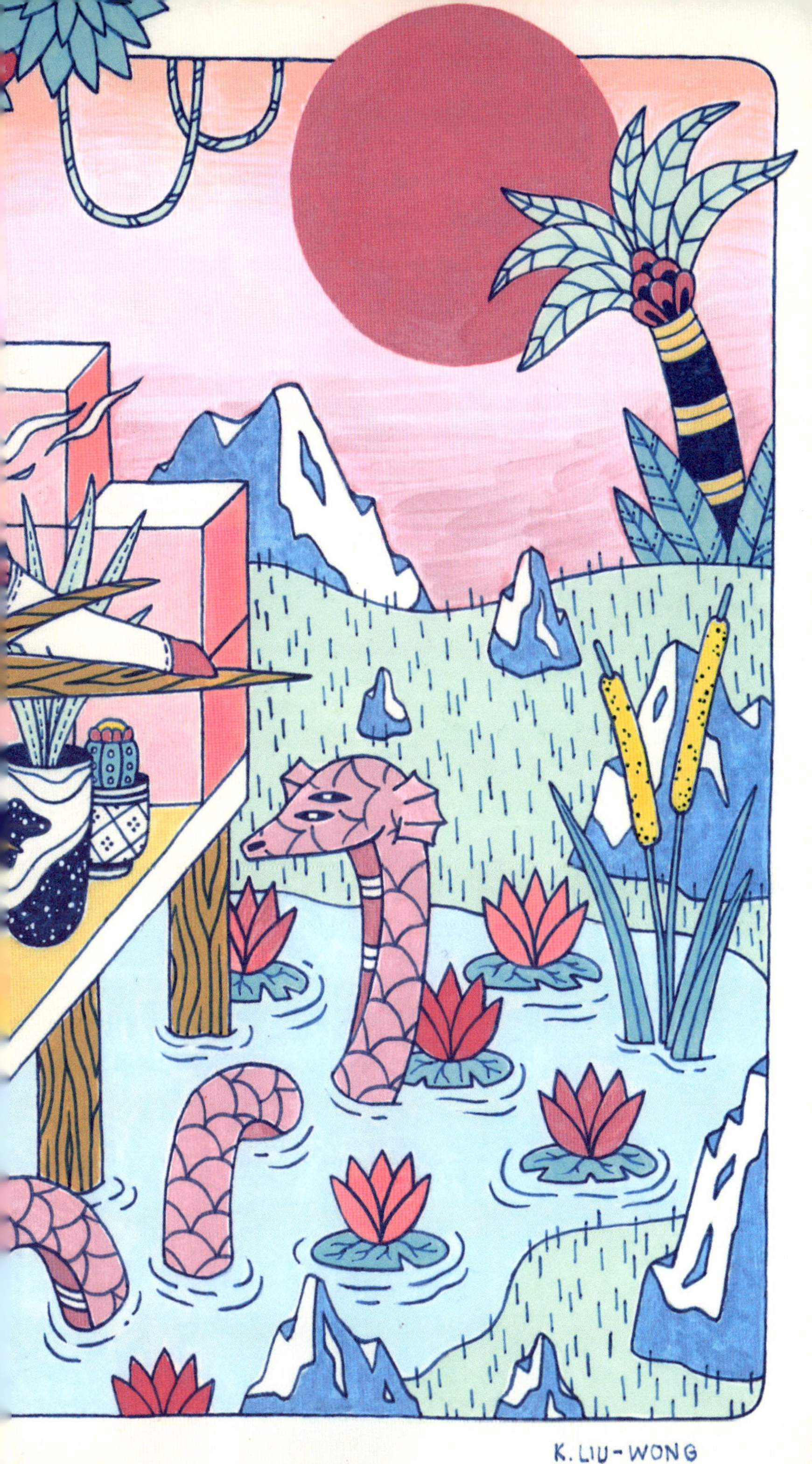
K. LIU-WONG

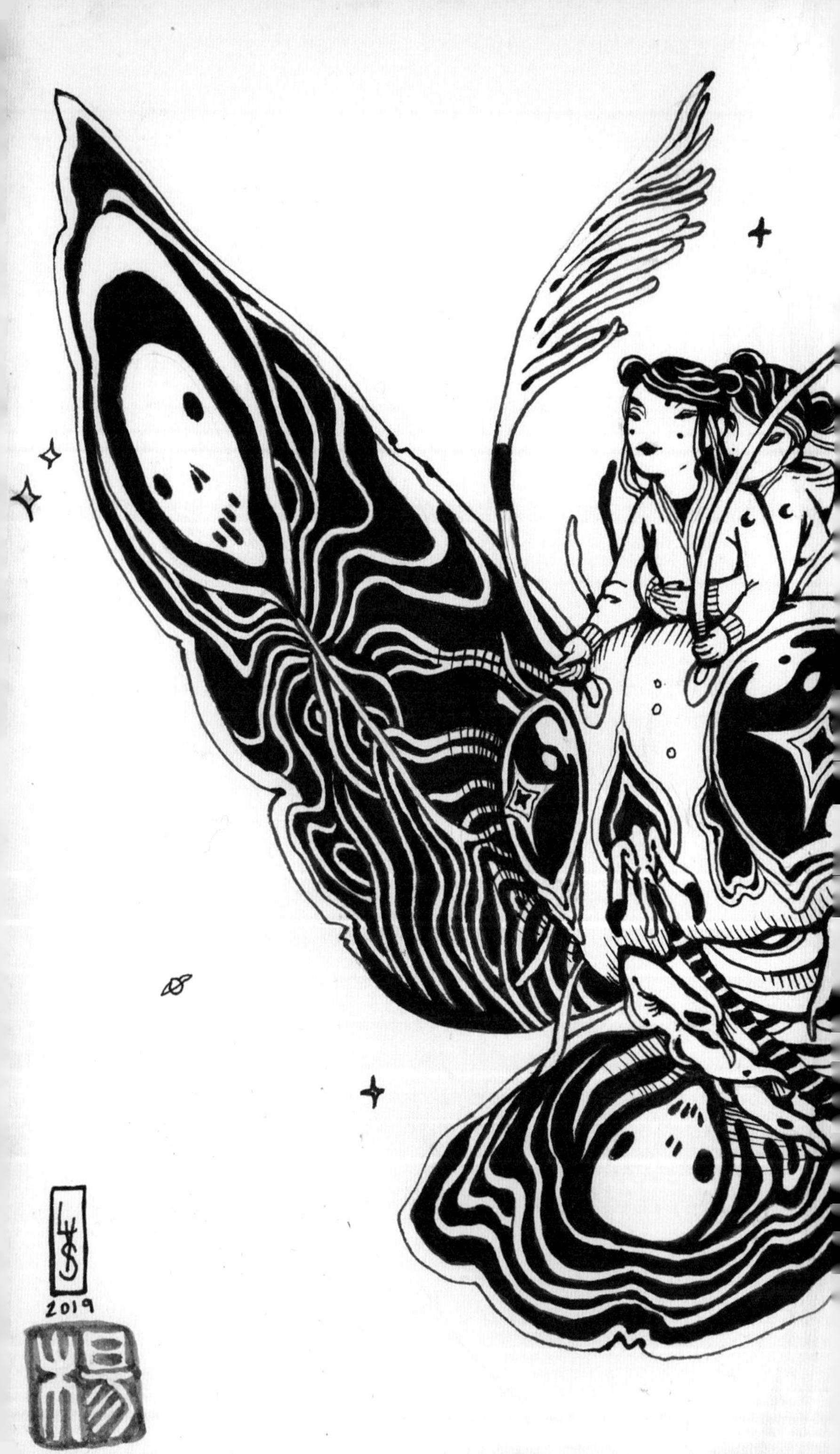

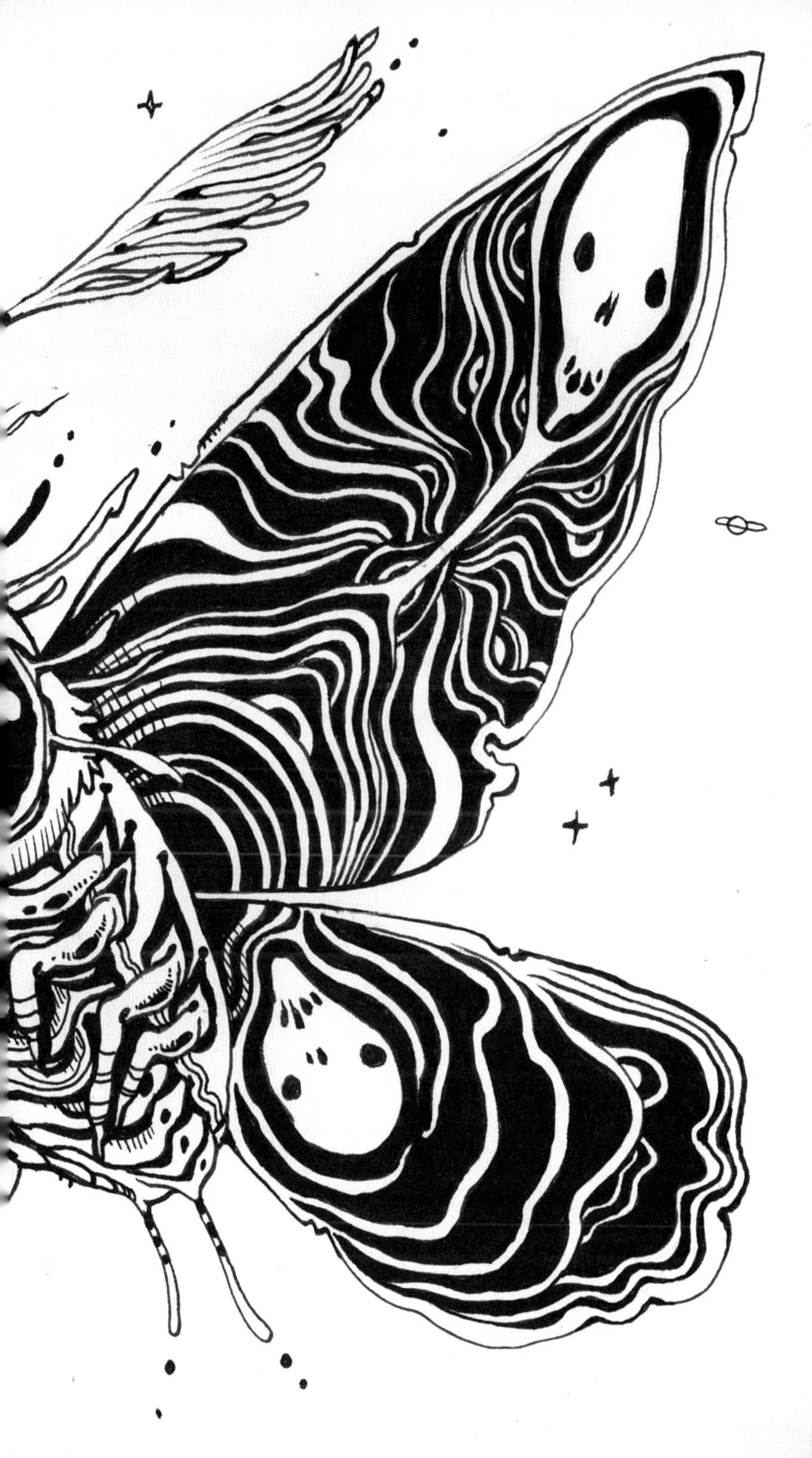

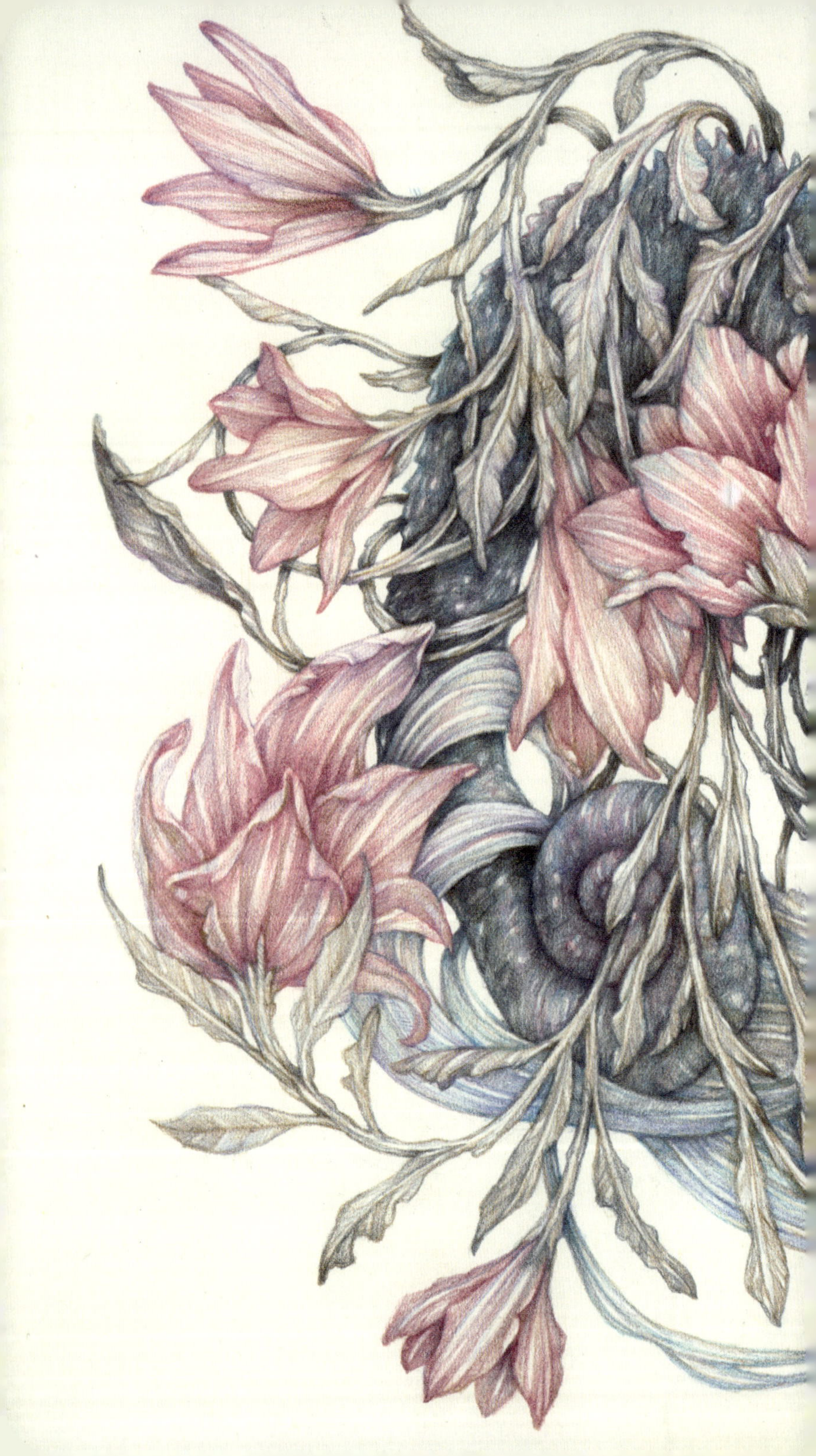

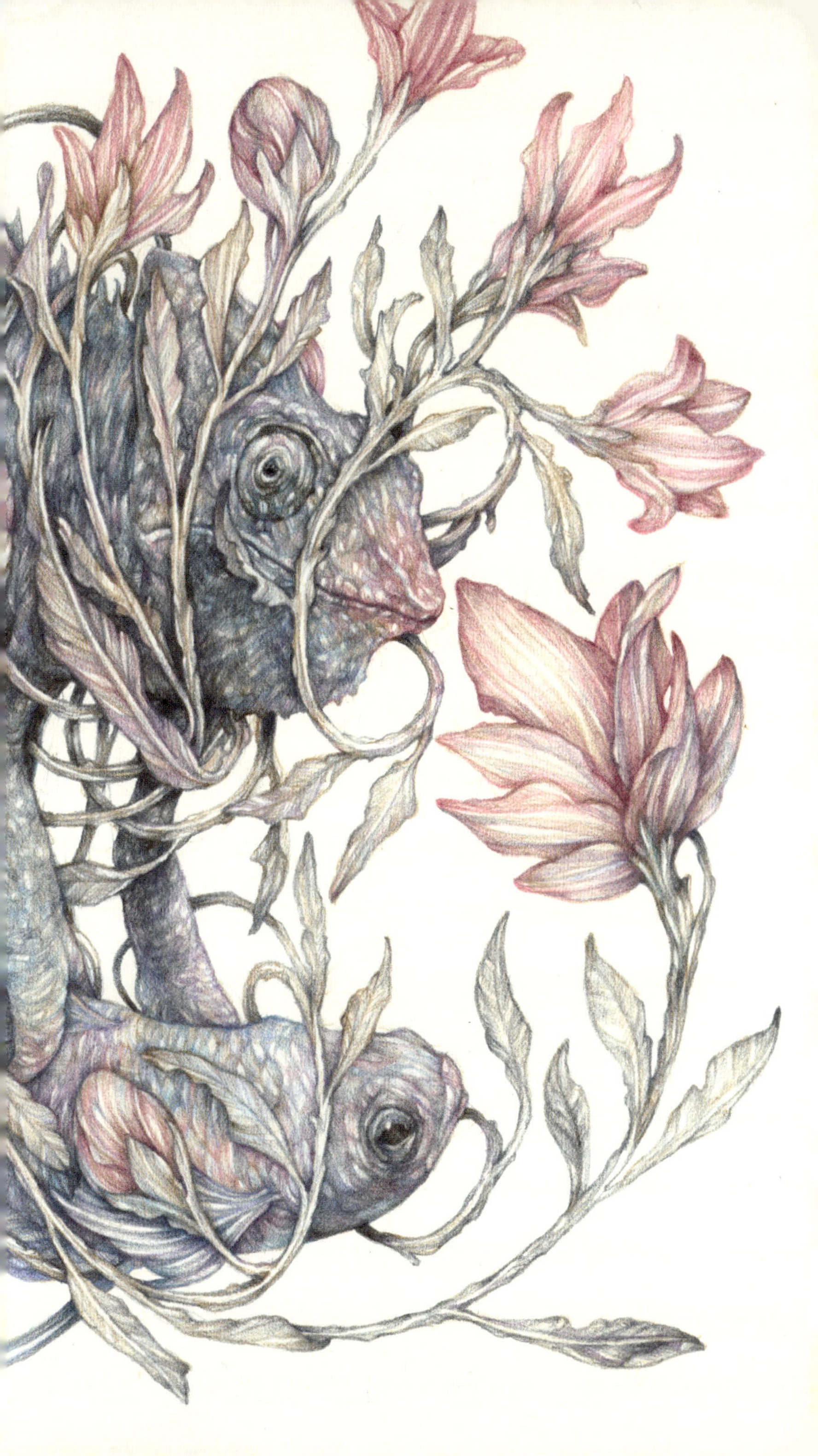

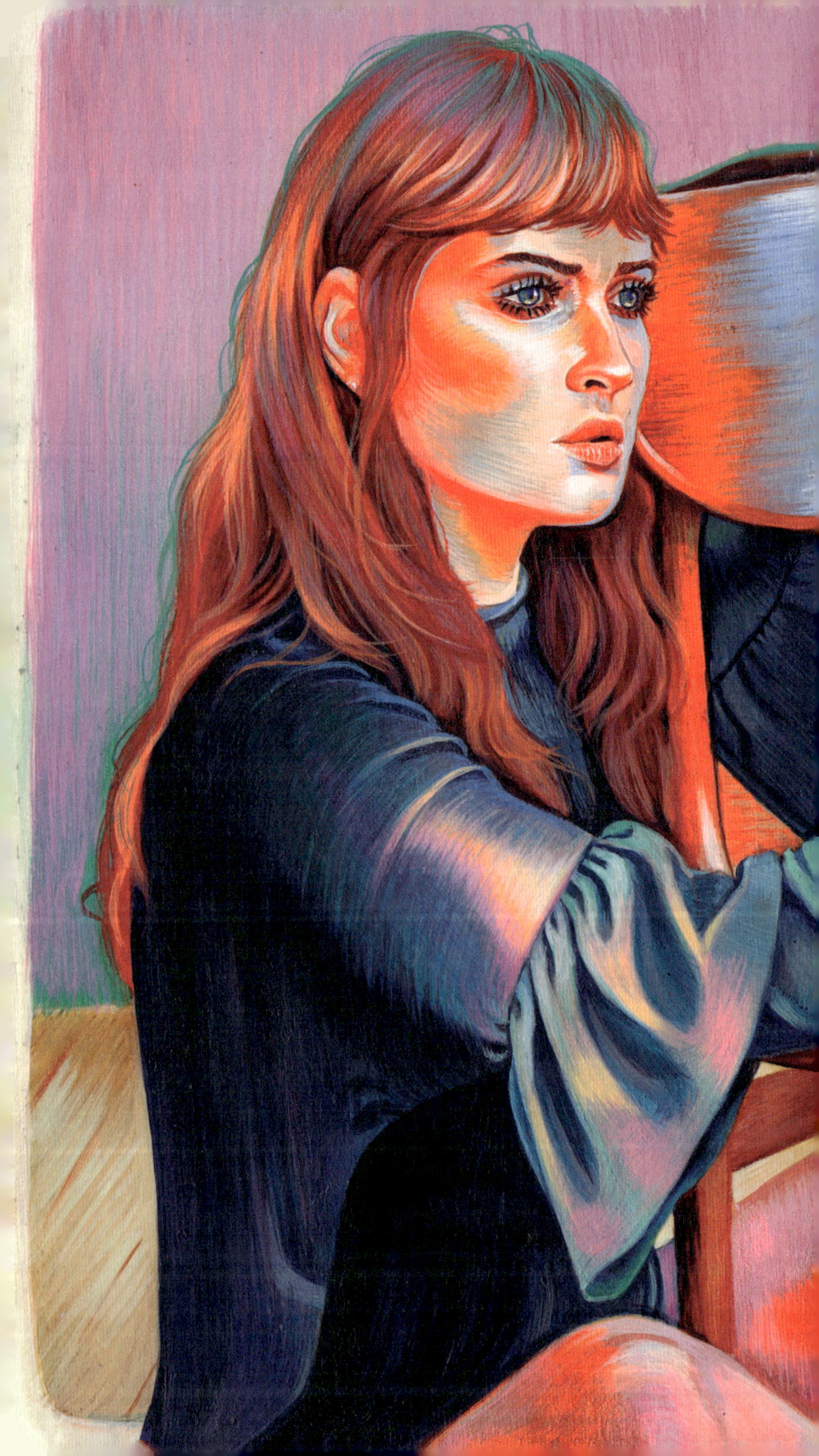

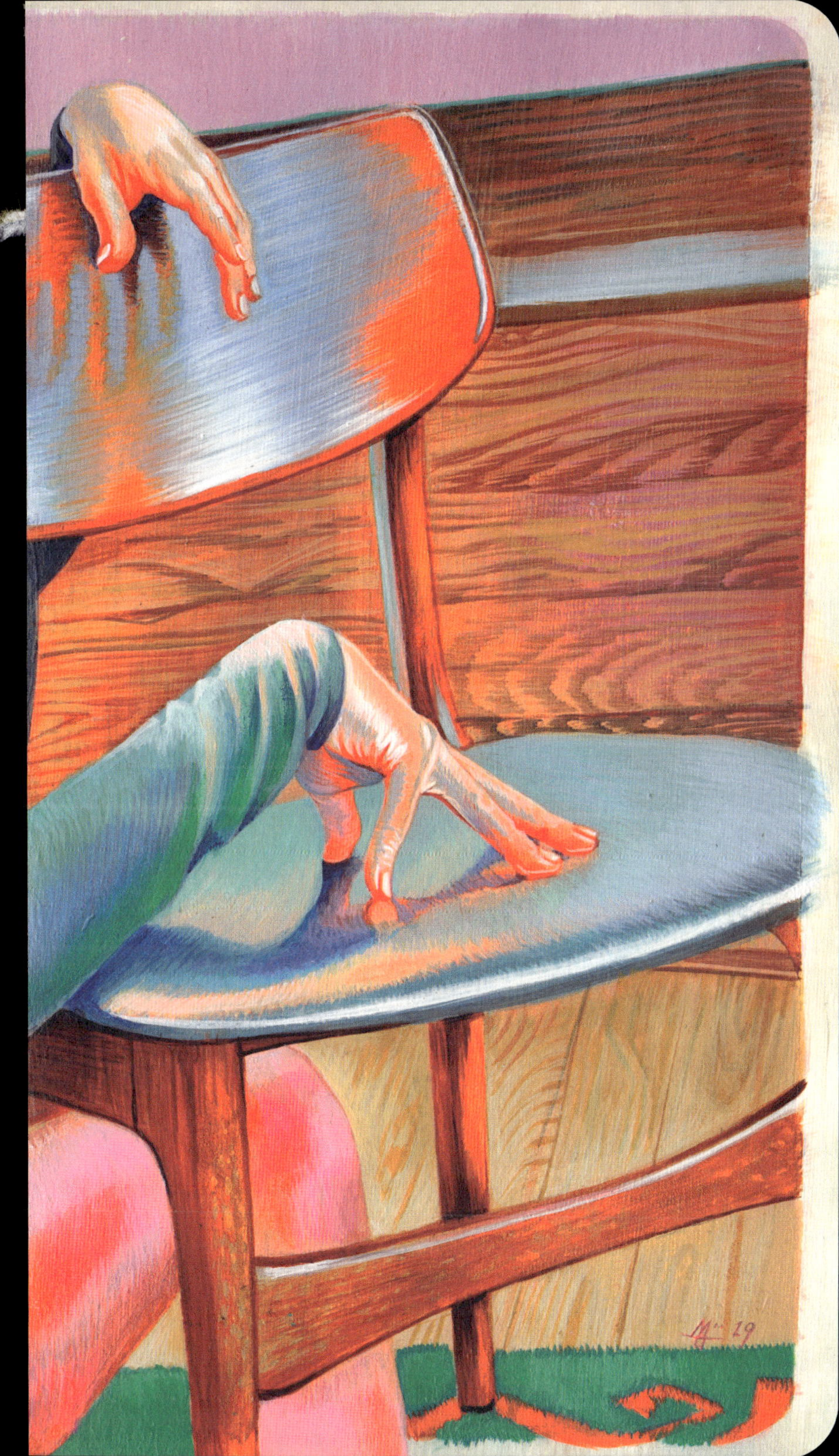

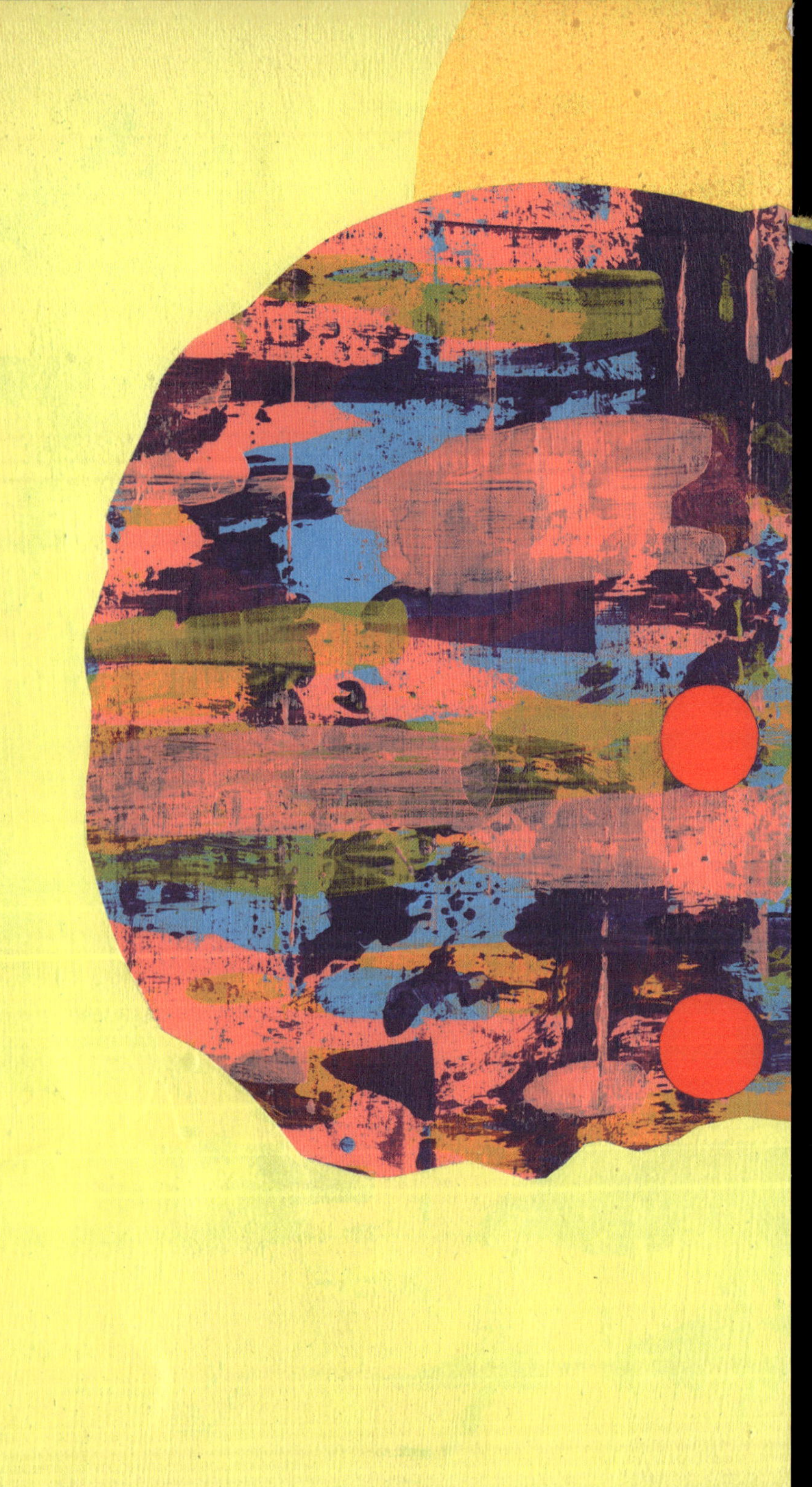

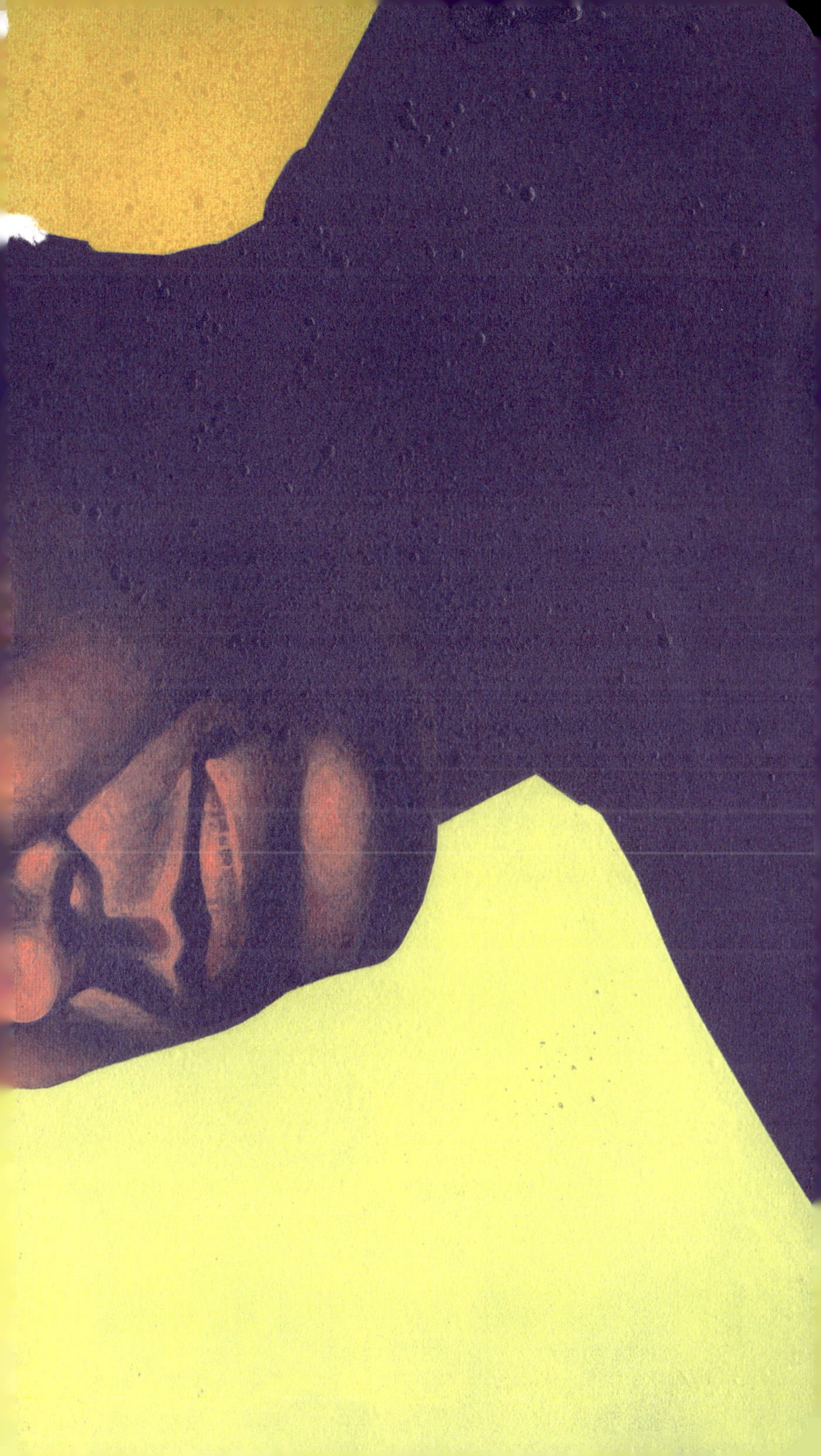

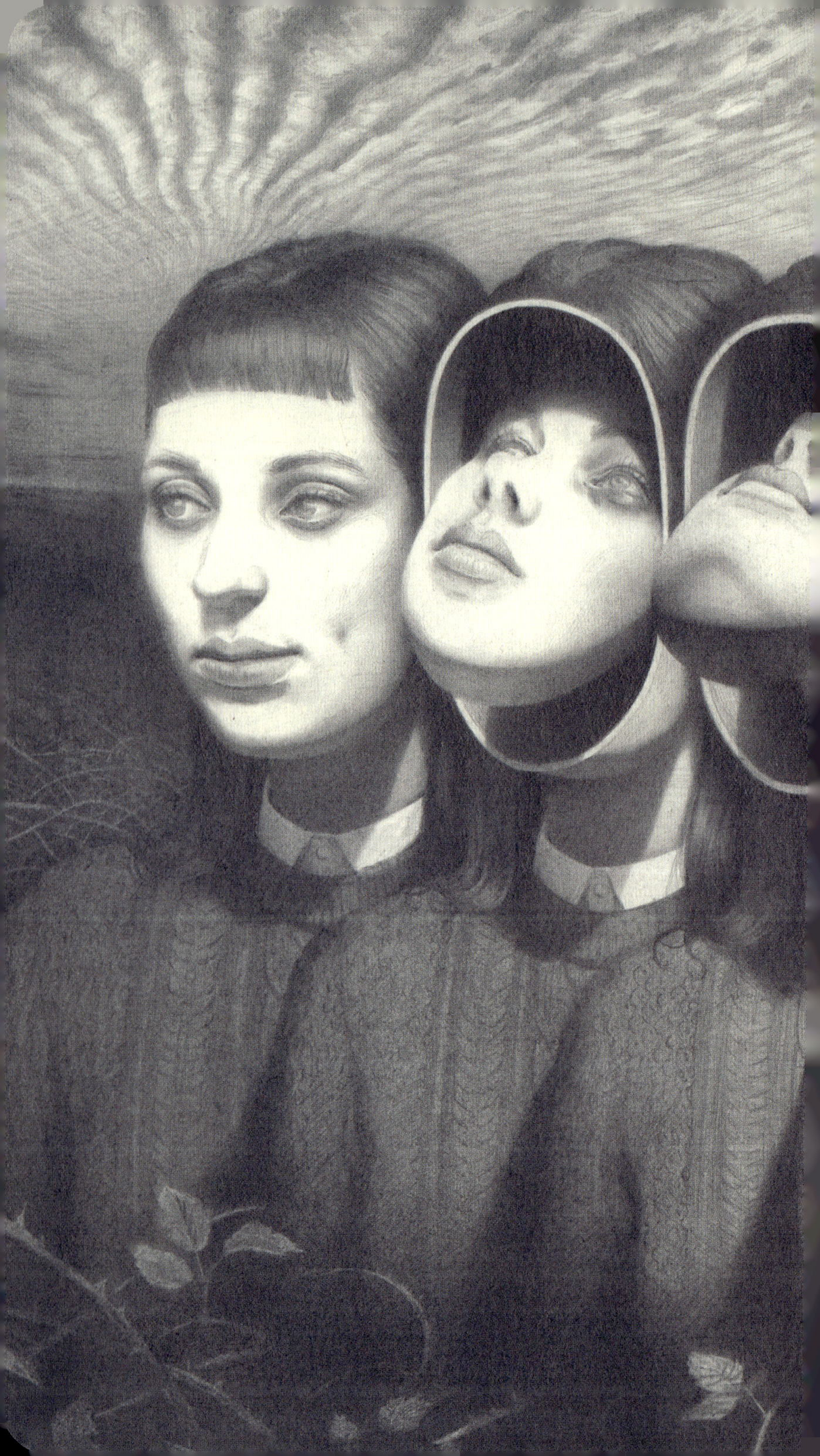

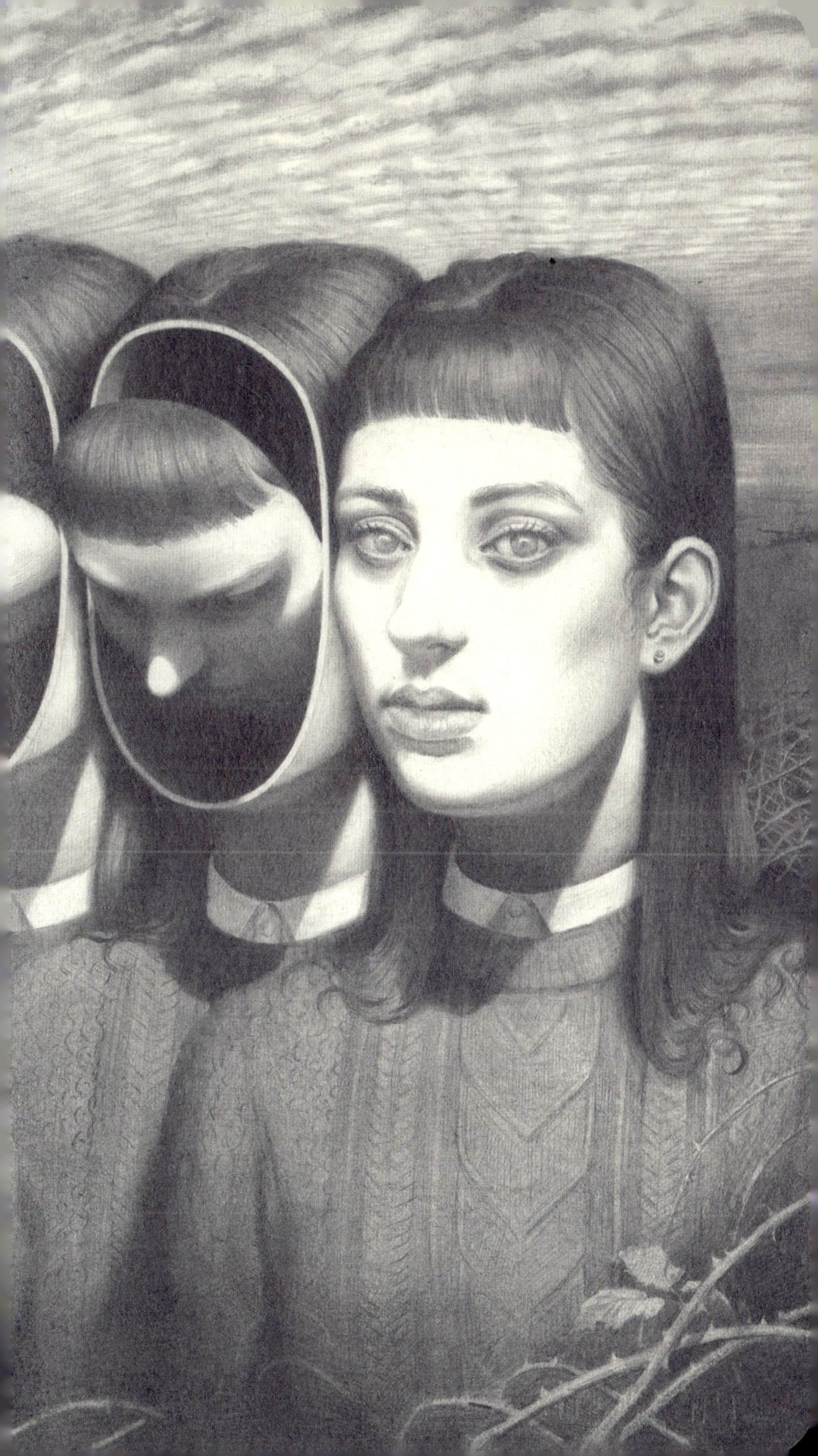

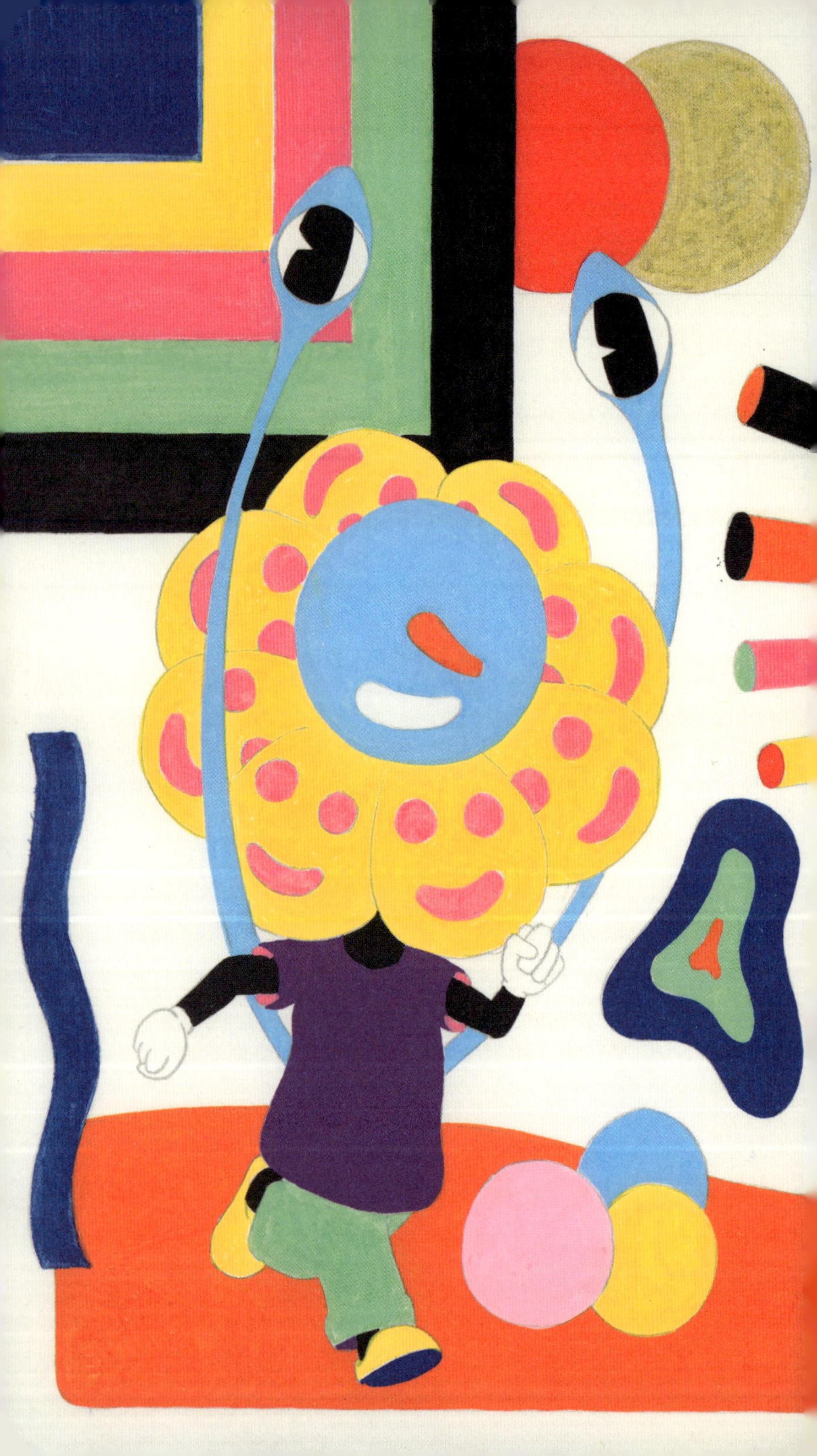

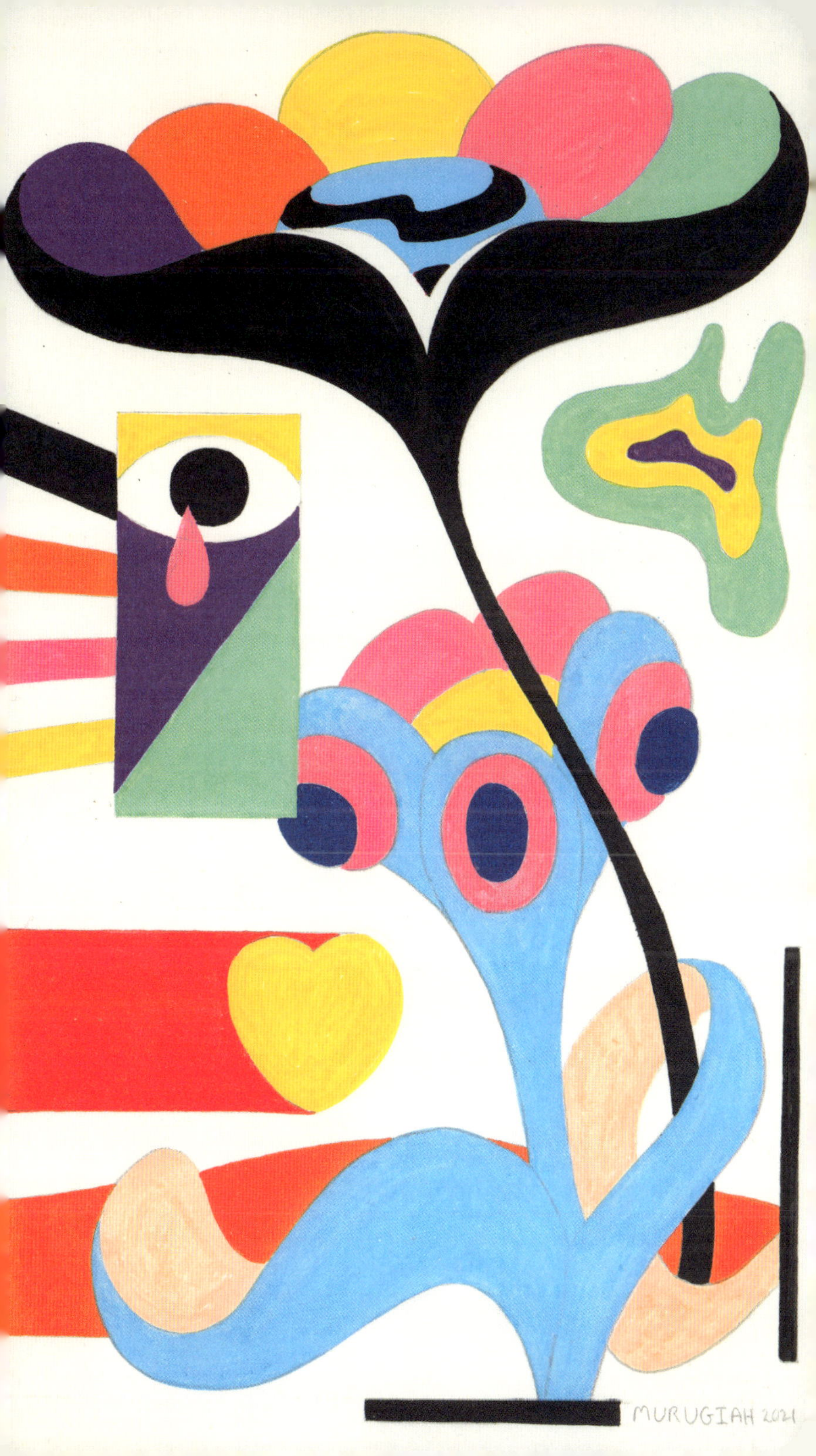

MURUGIAH 2021

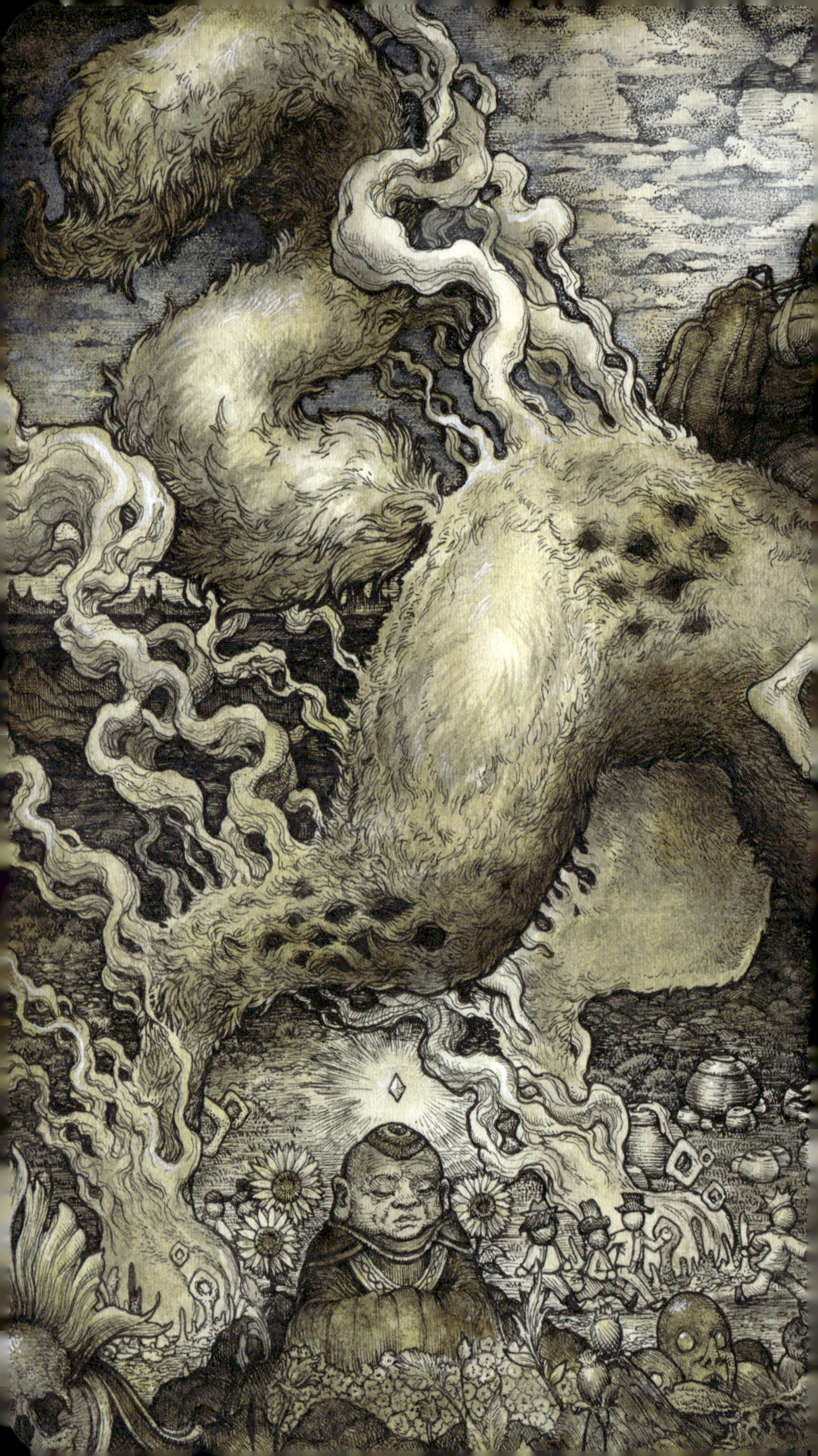

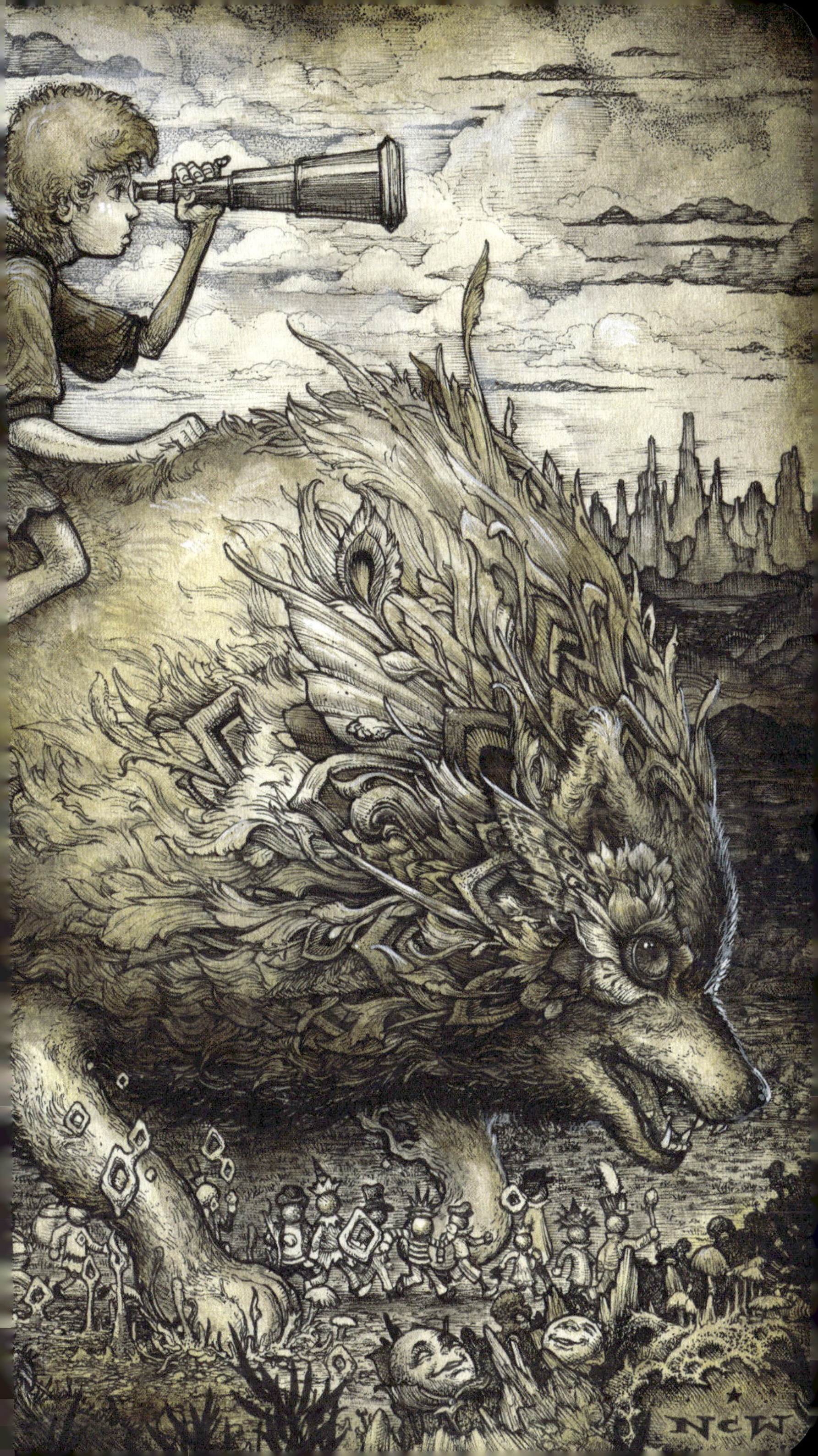

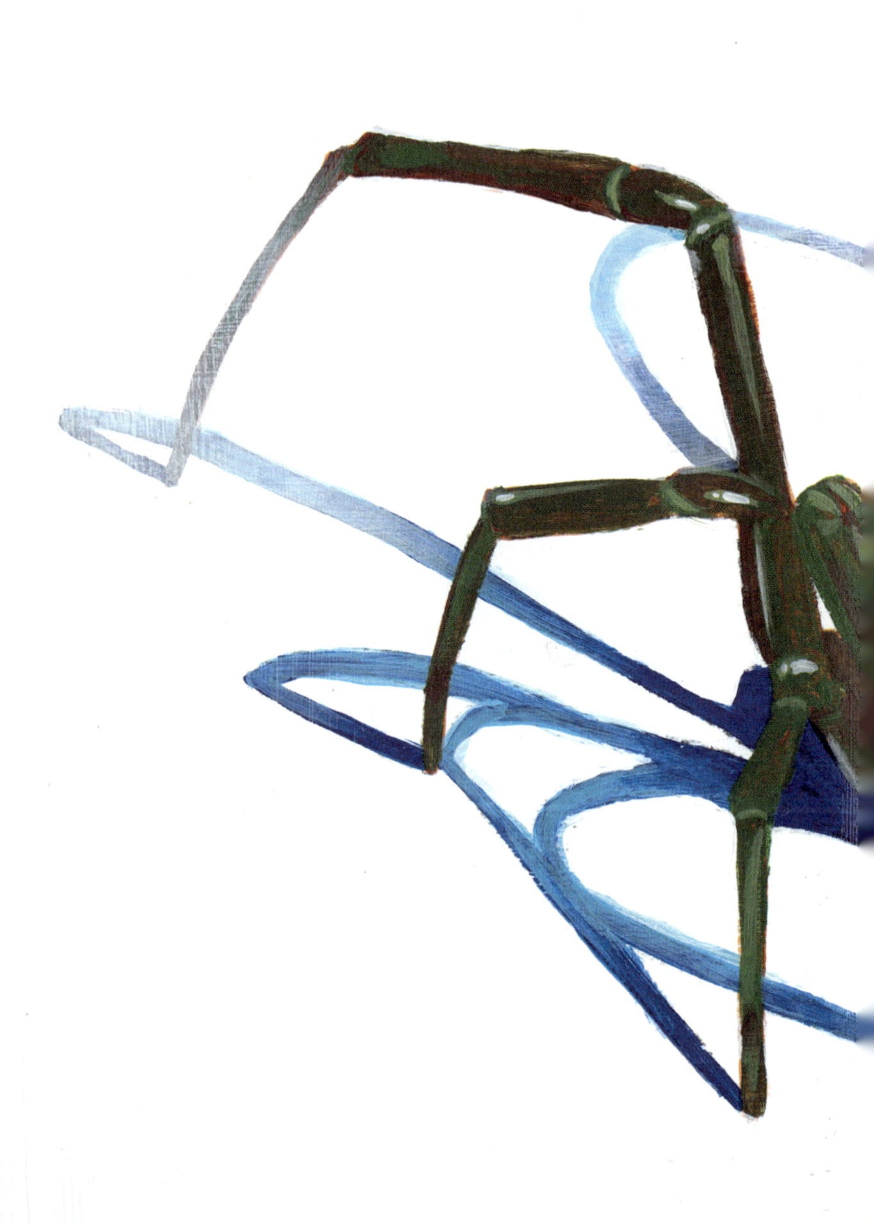

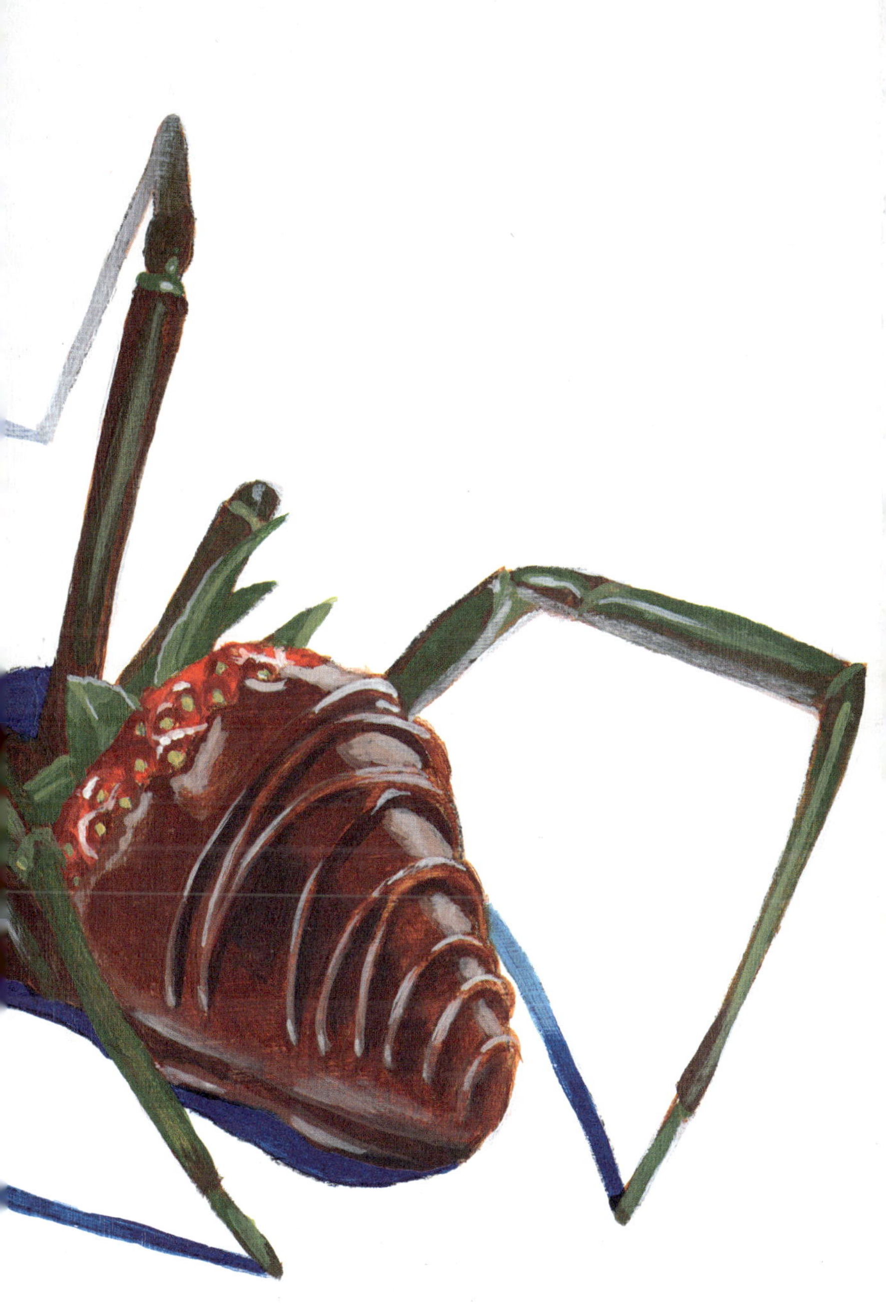

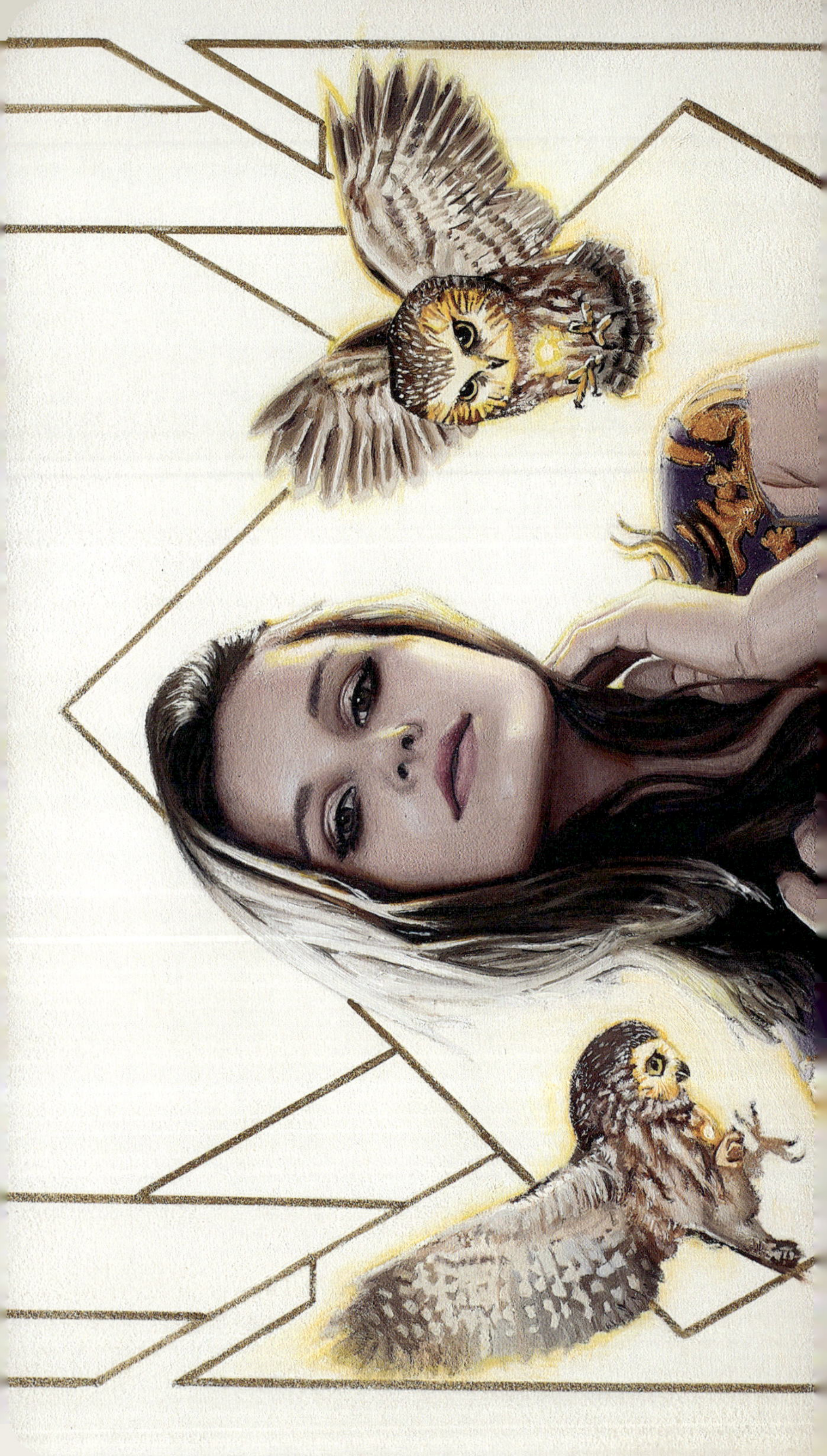

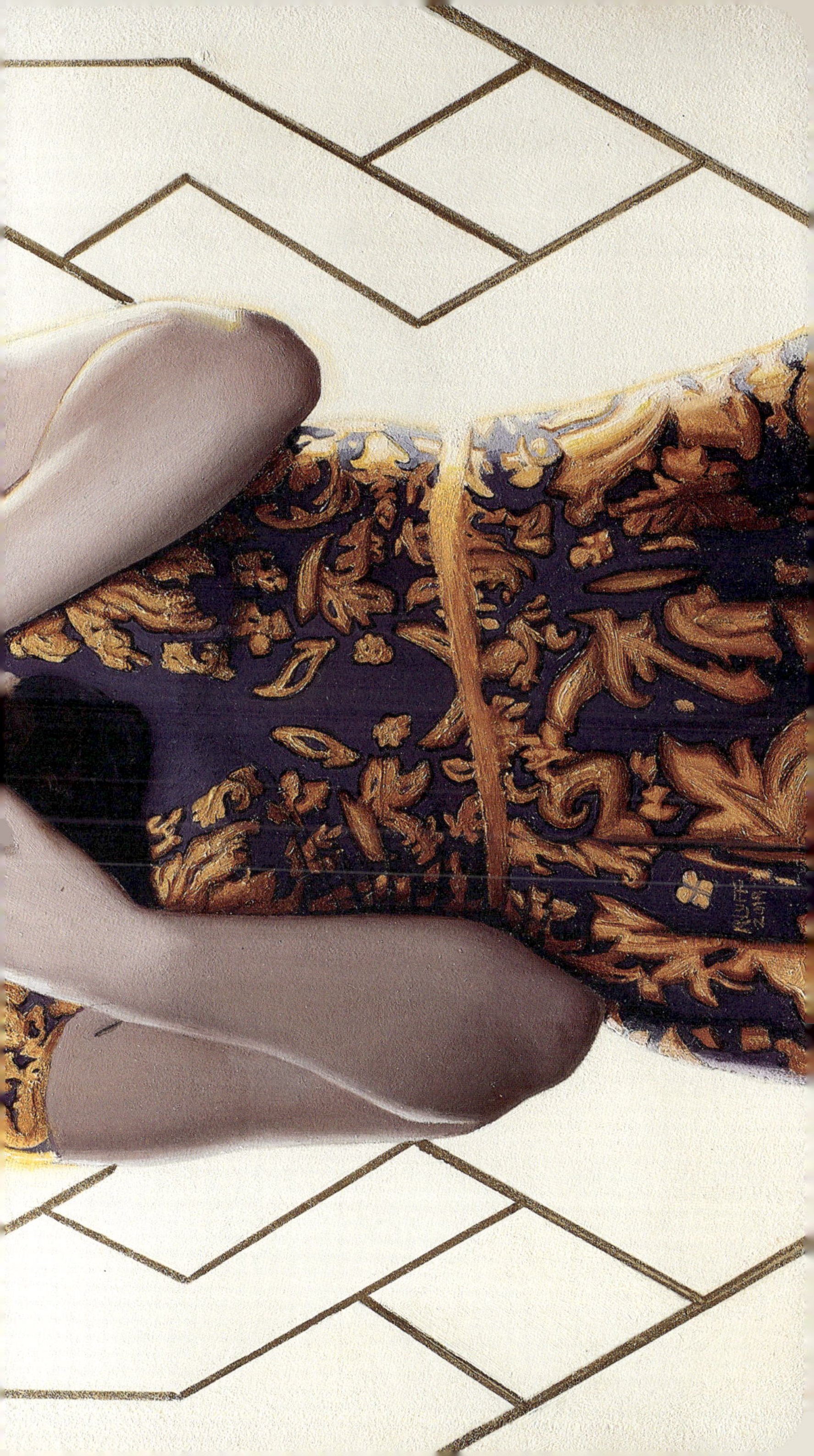

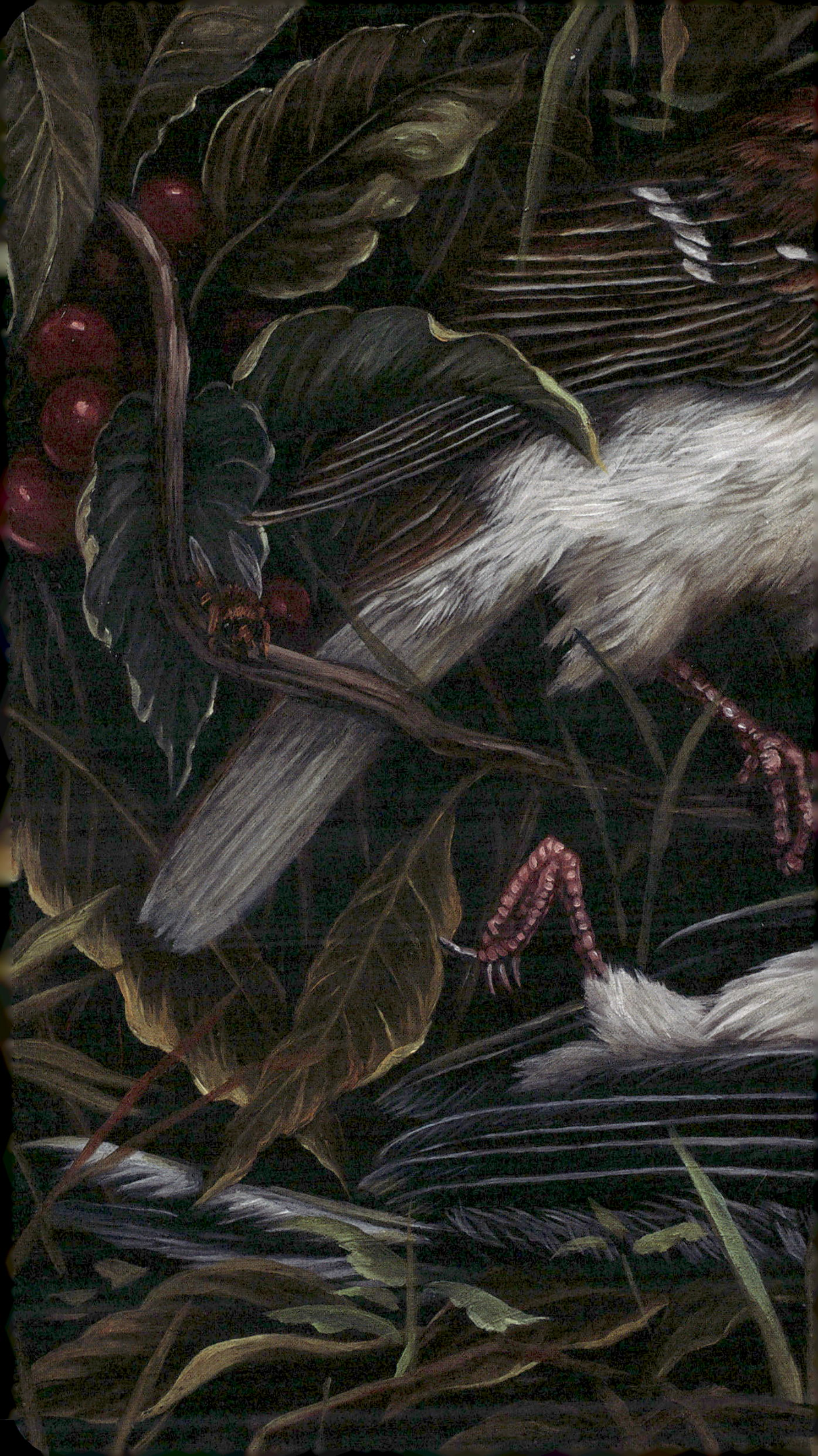

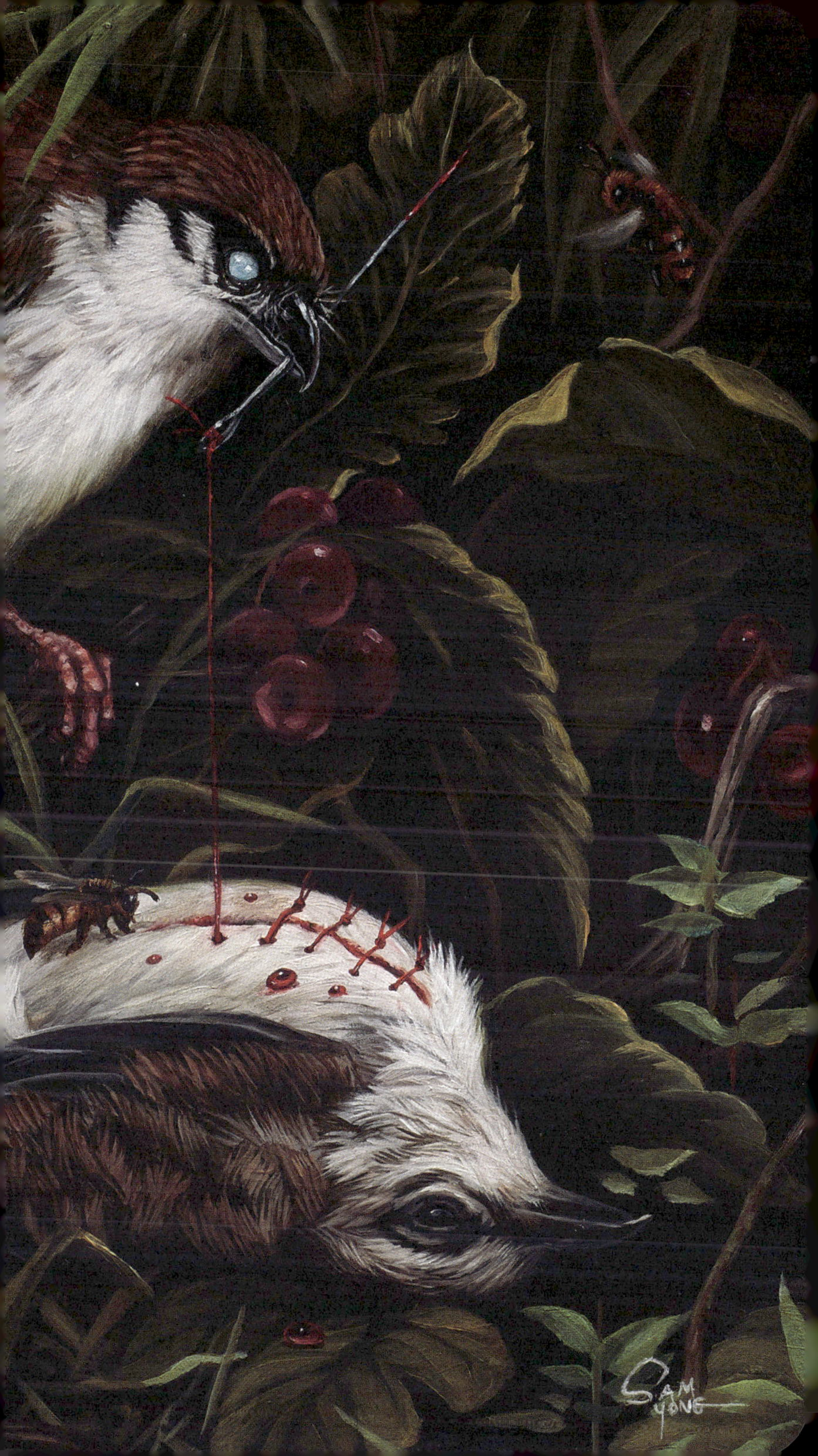
Sam
Yong

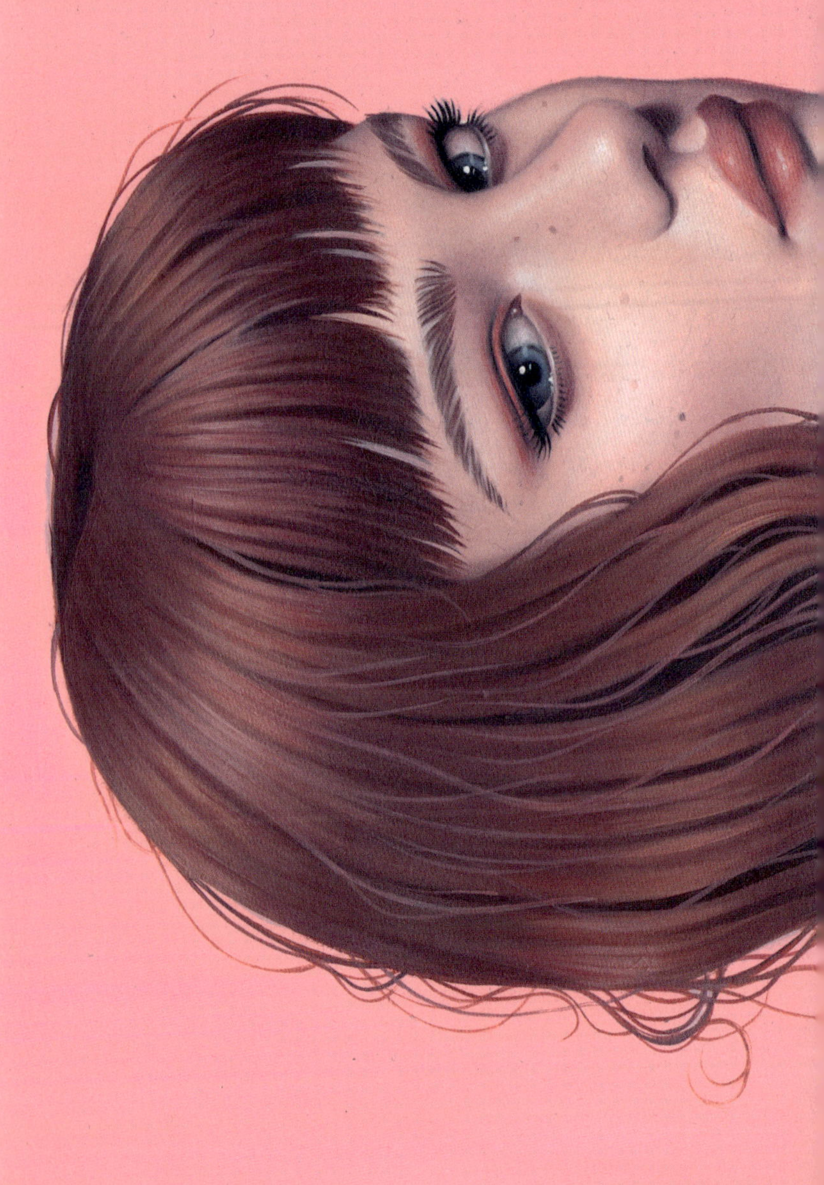

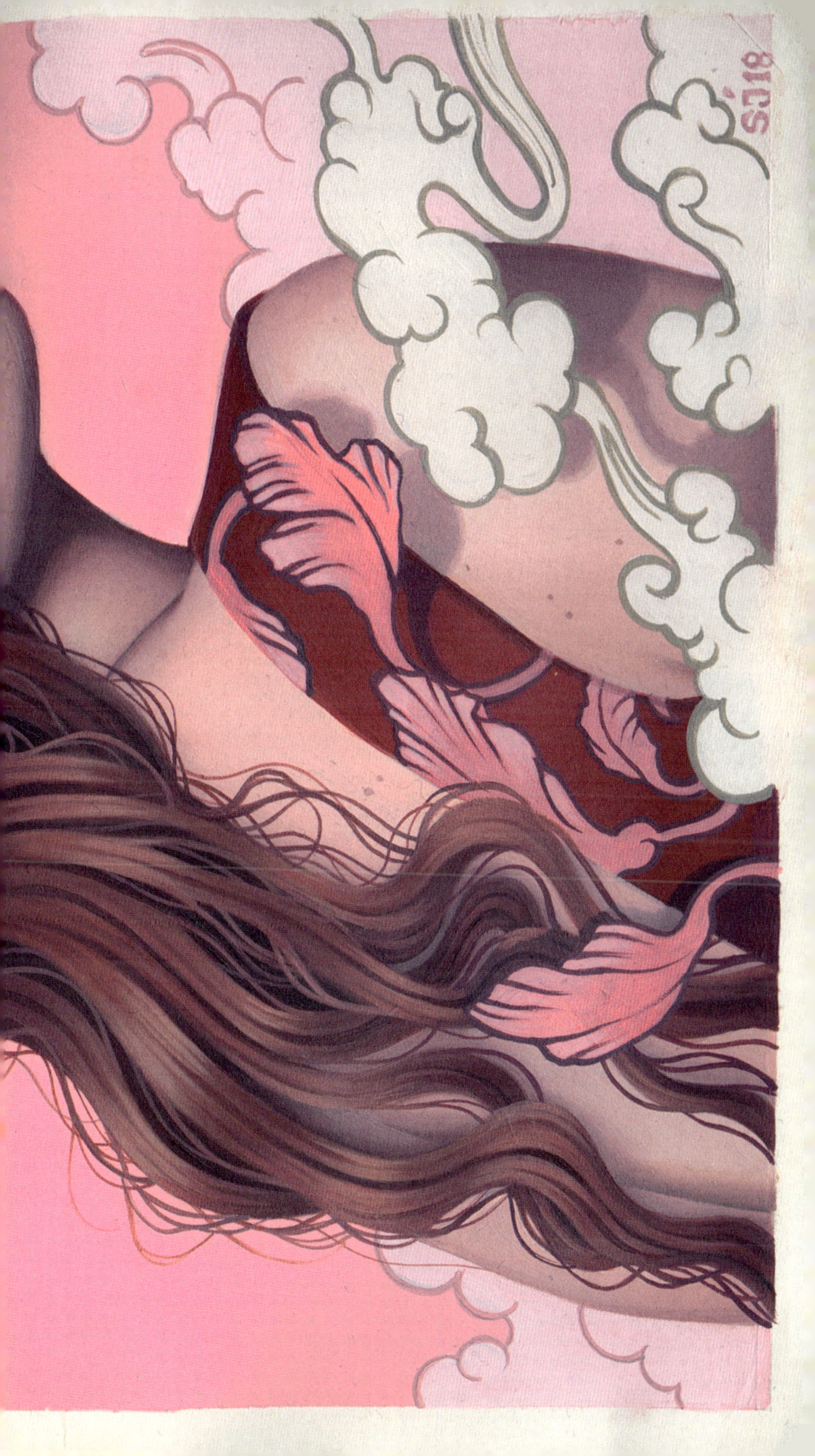

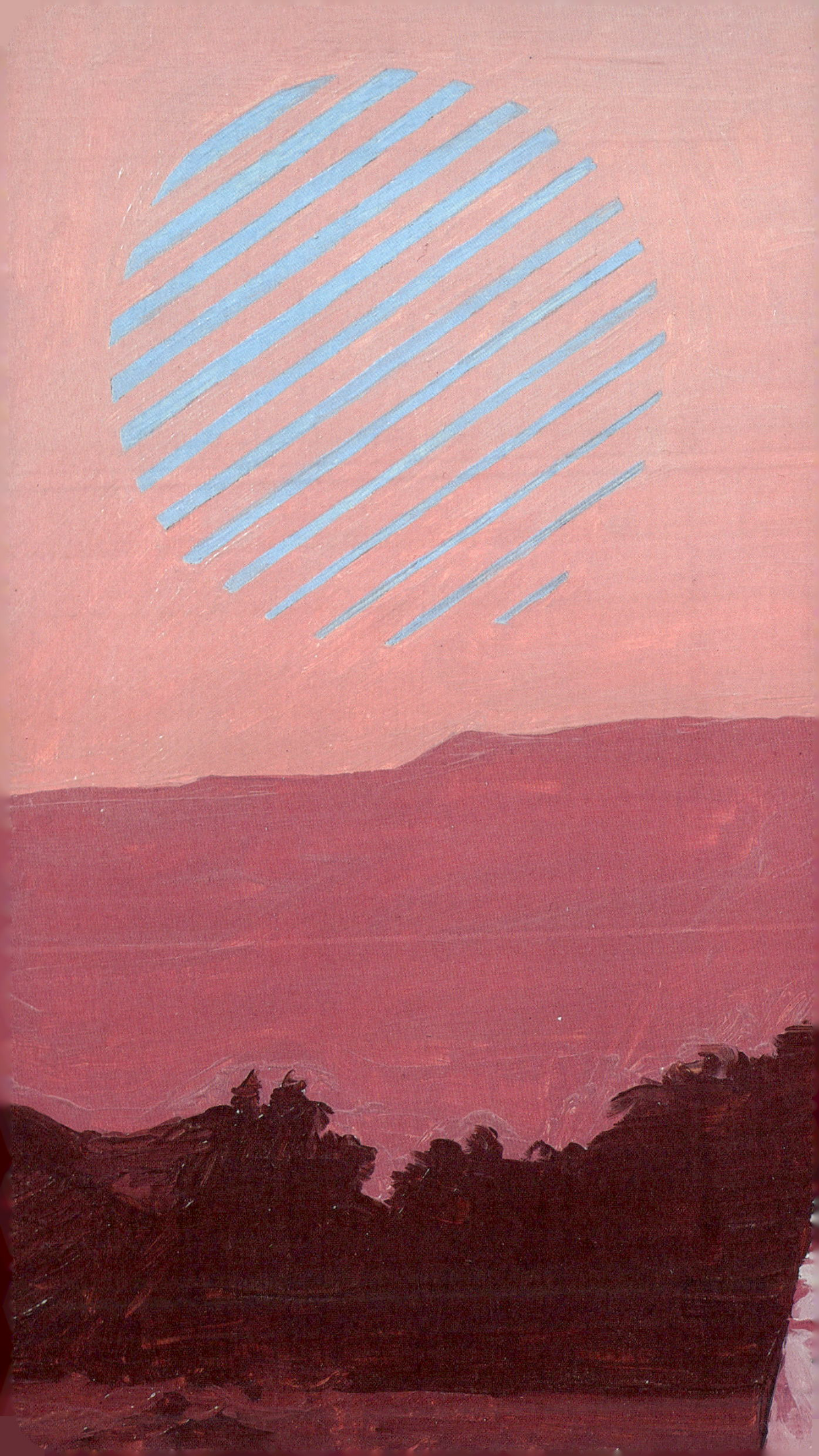

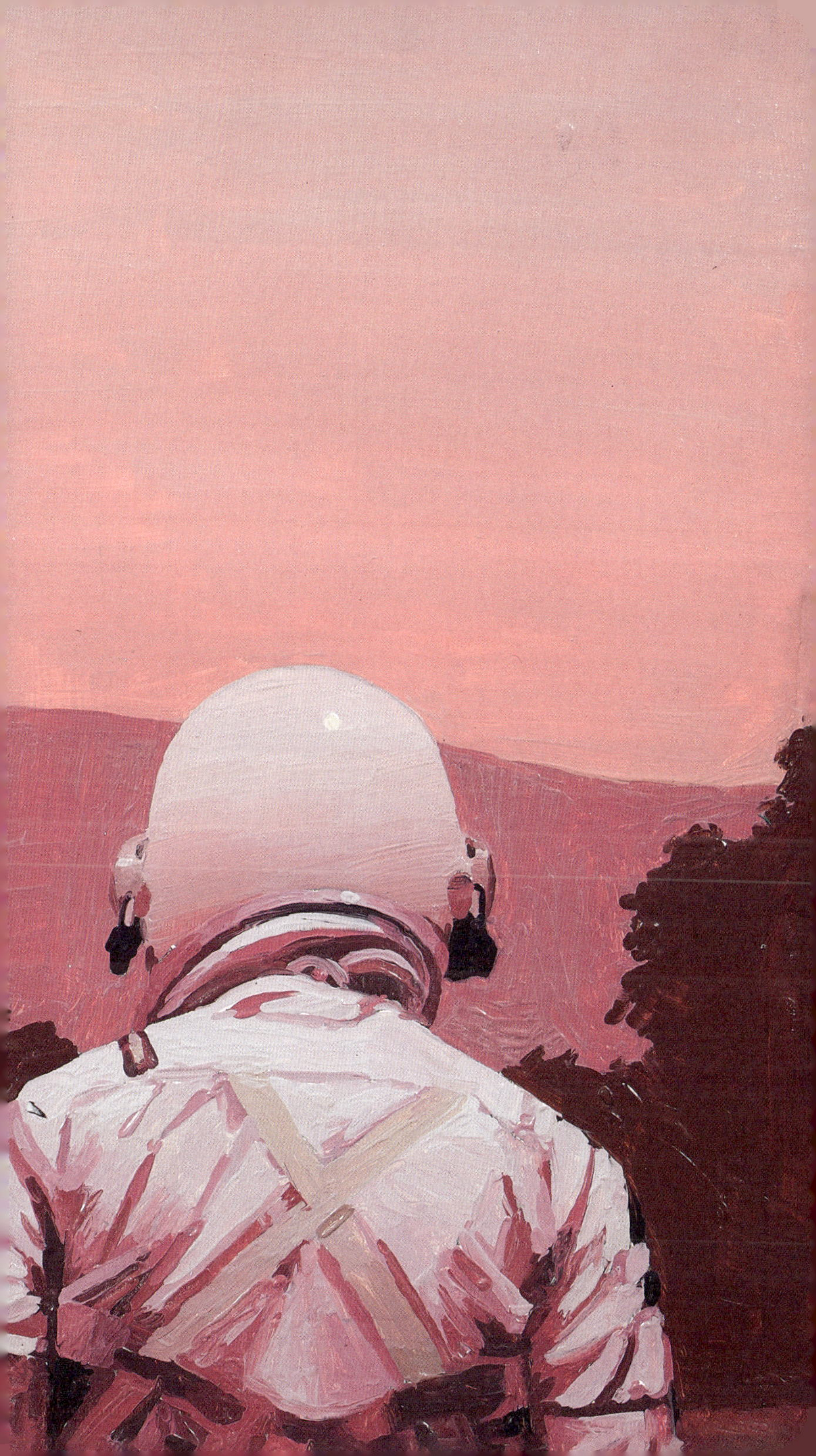

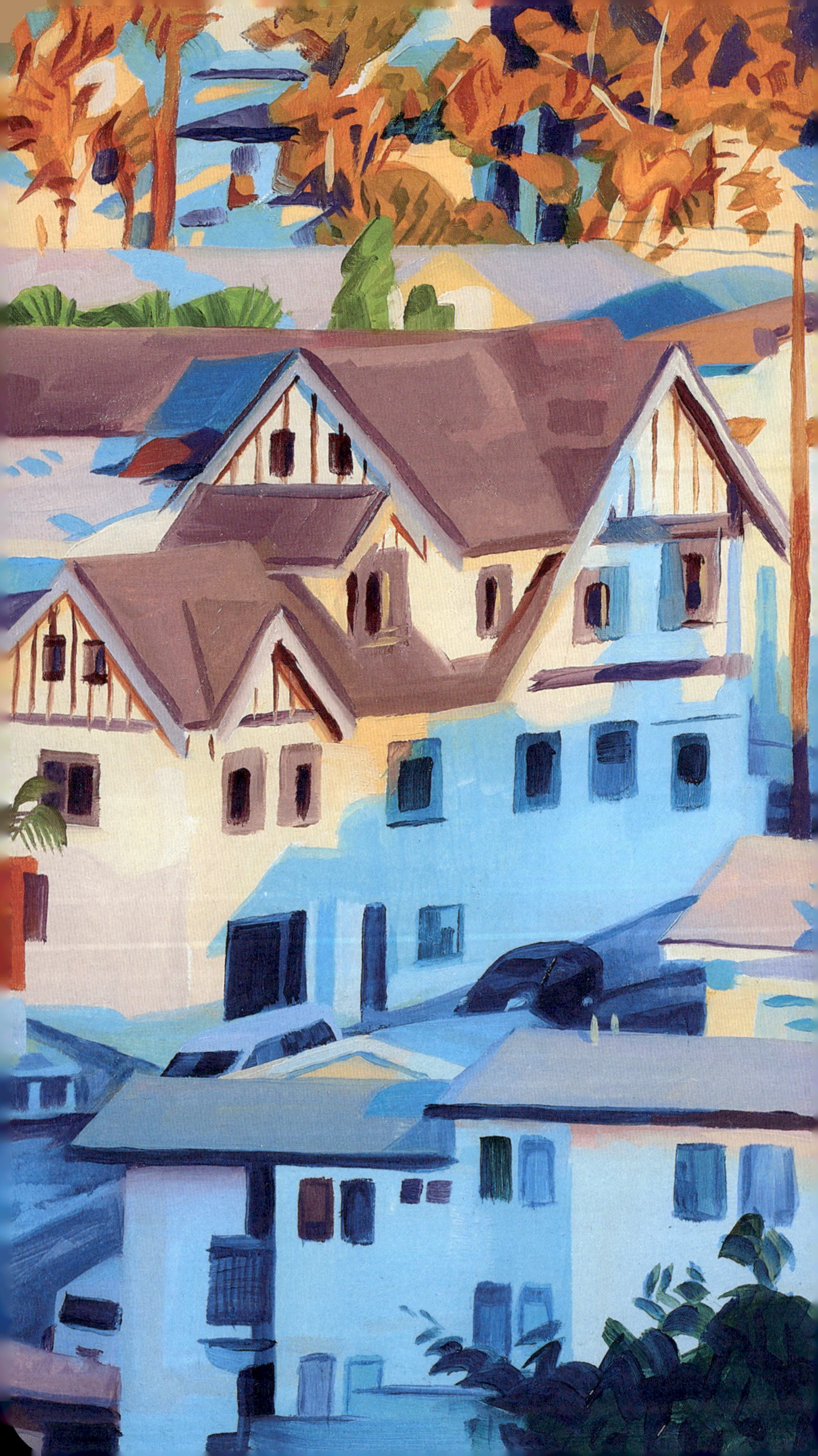

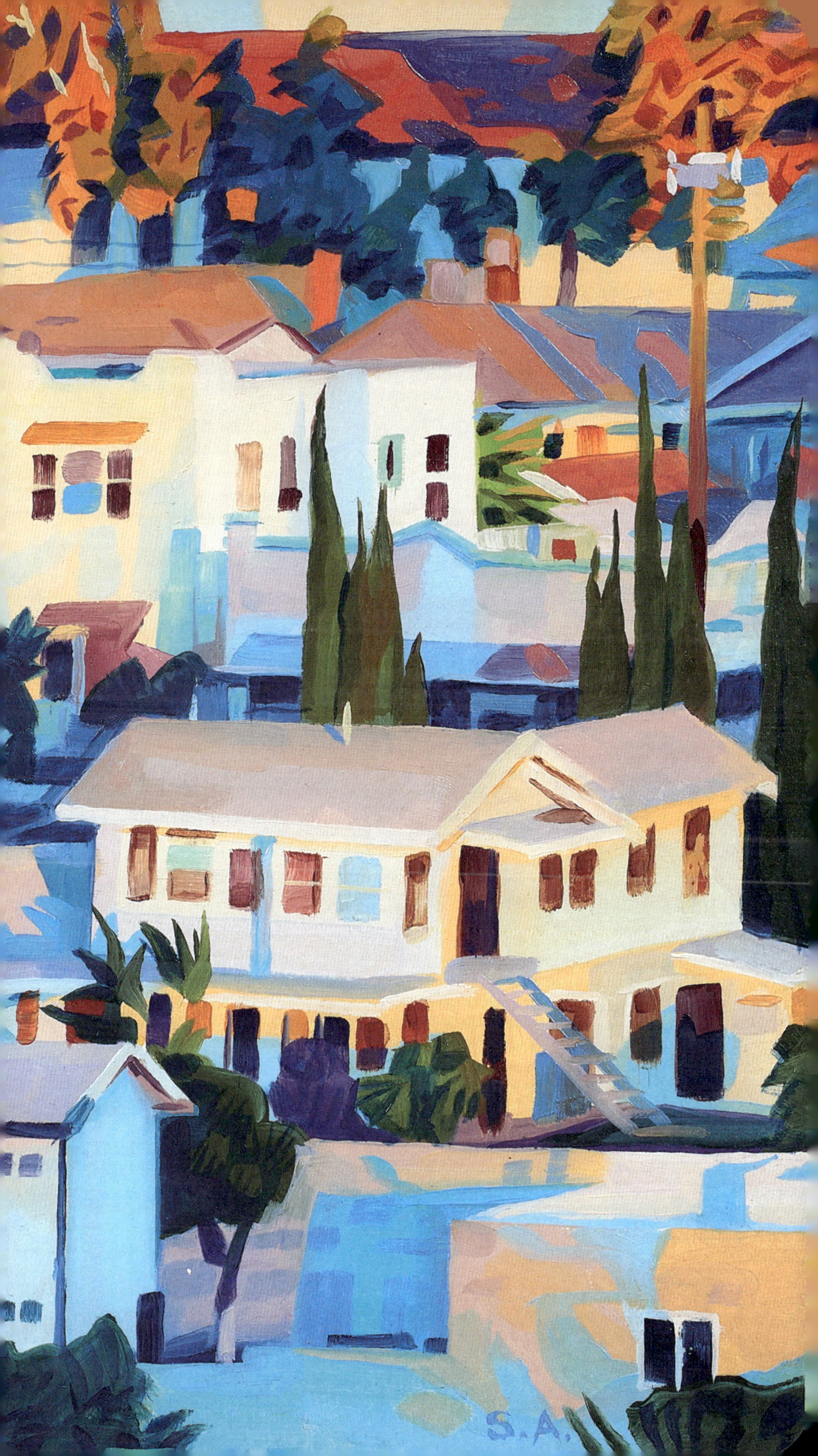
S. A.

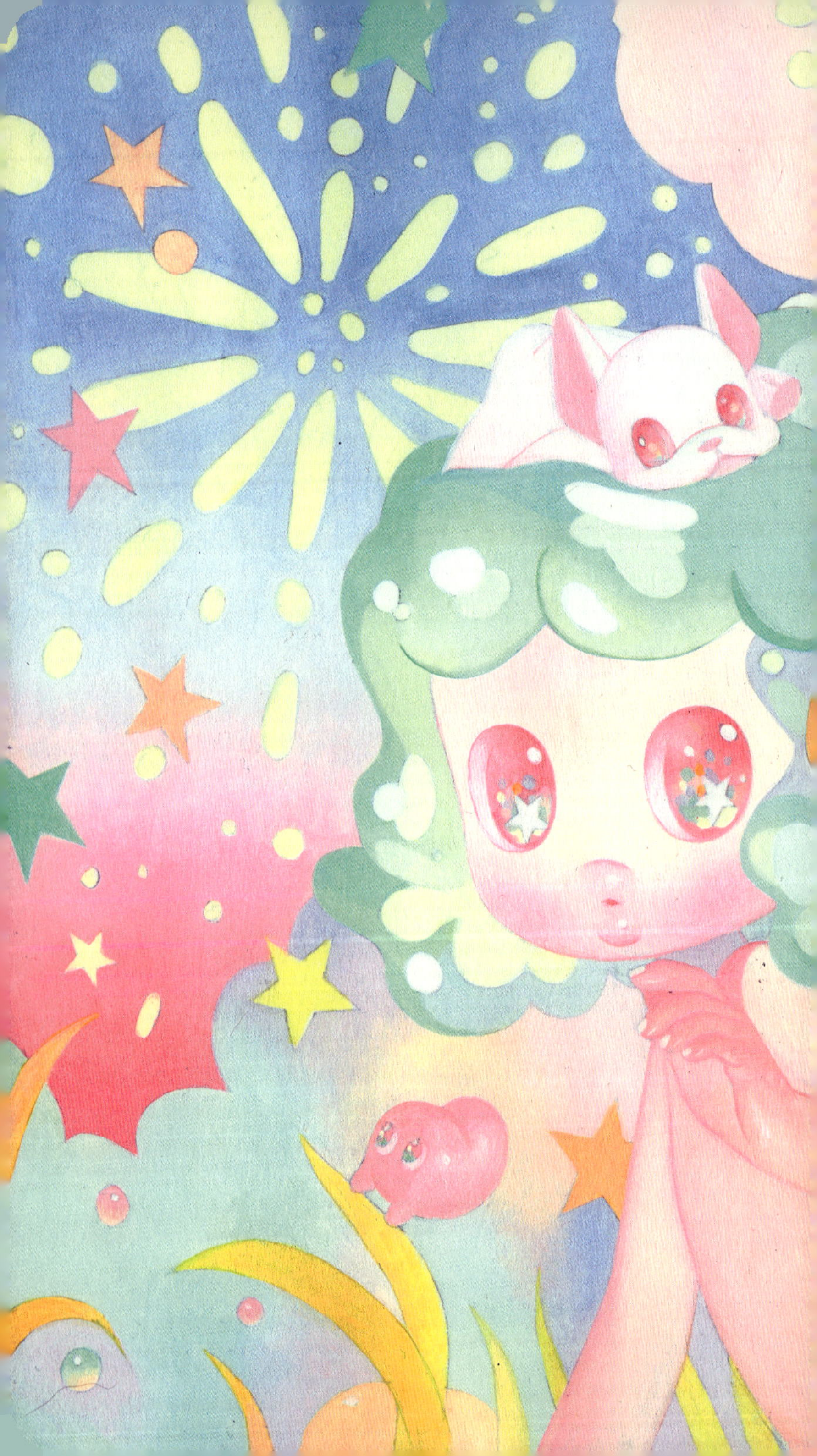

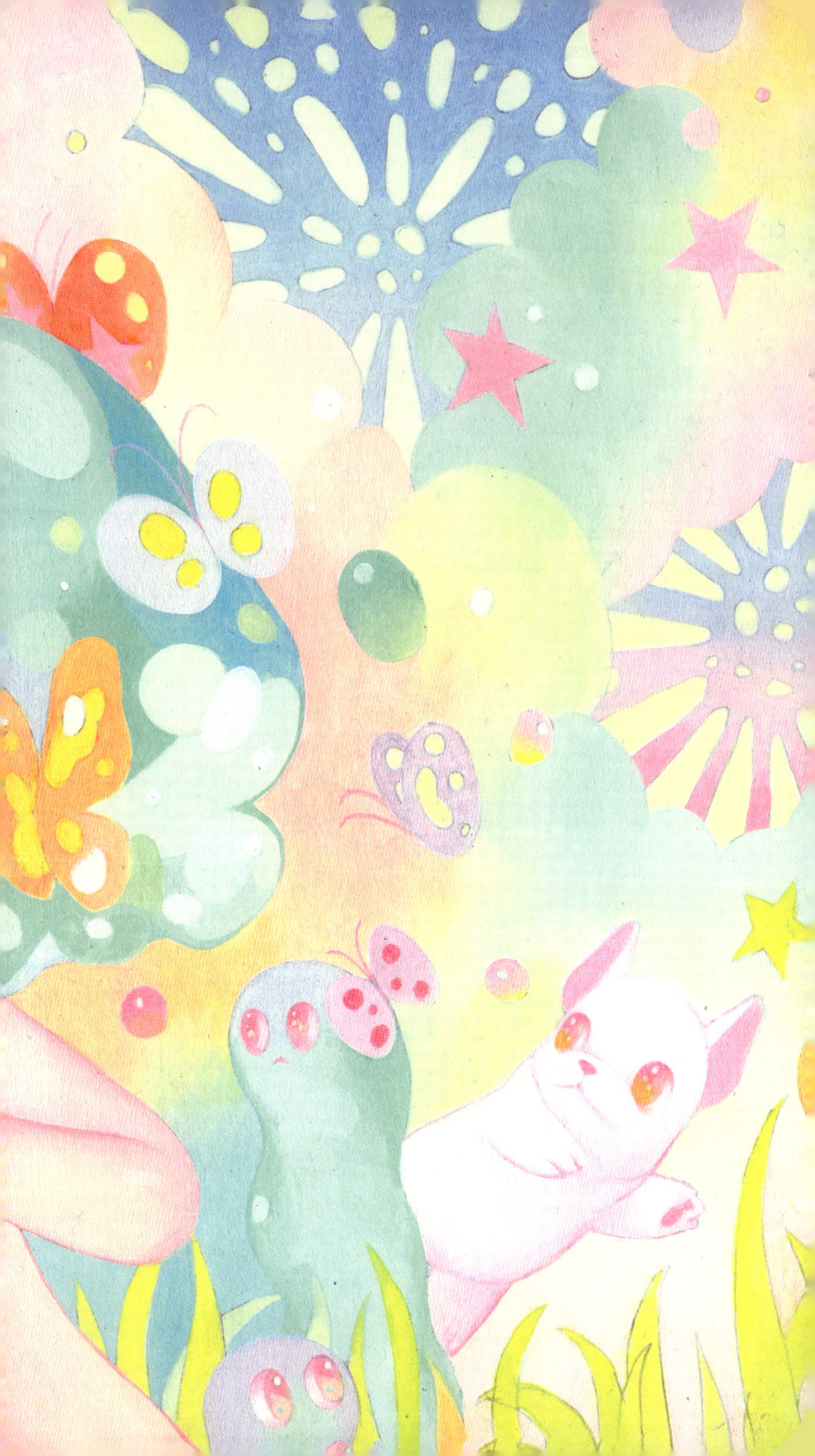

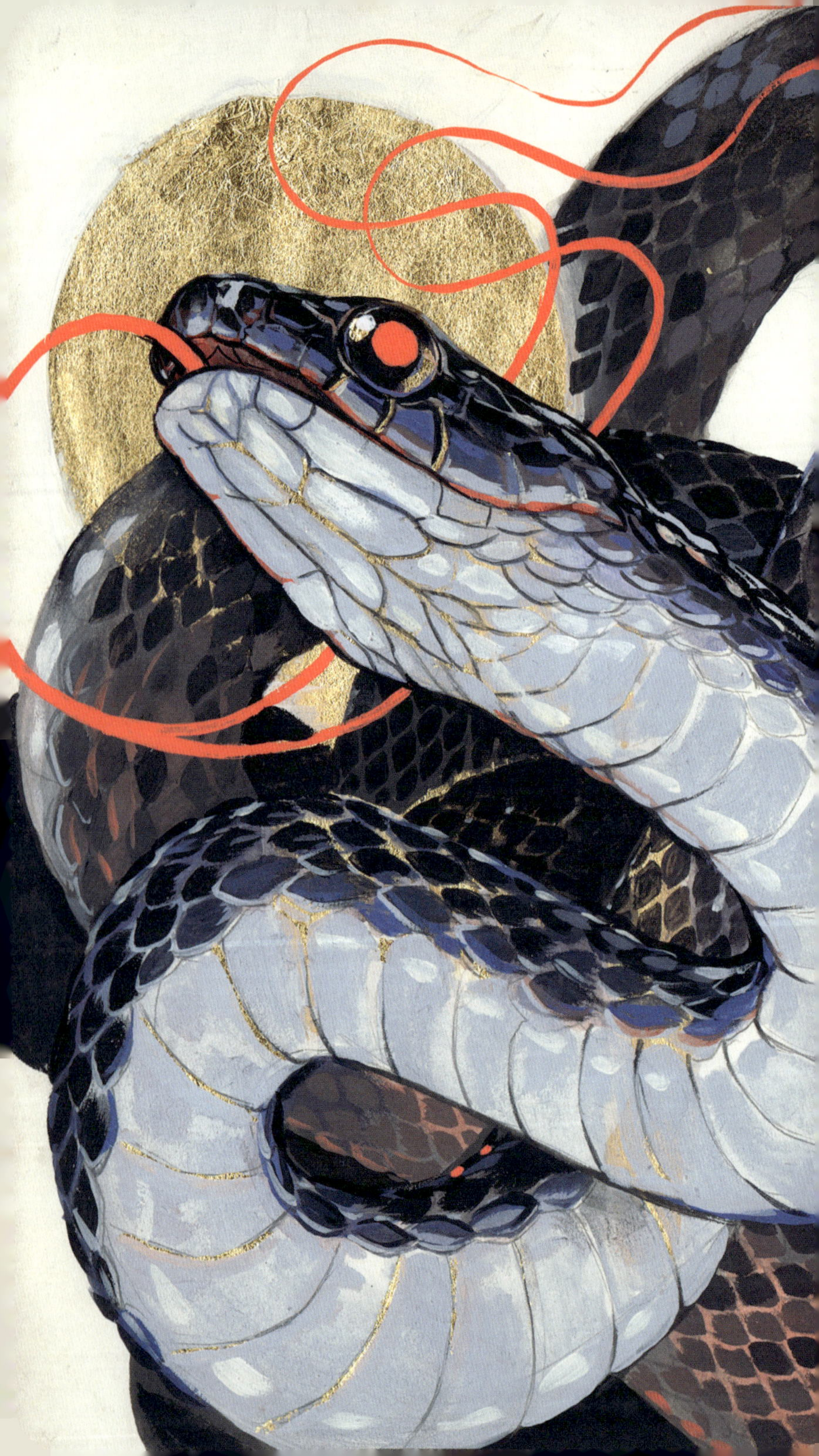

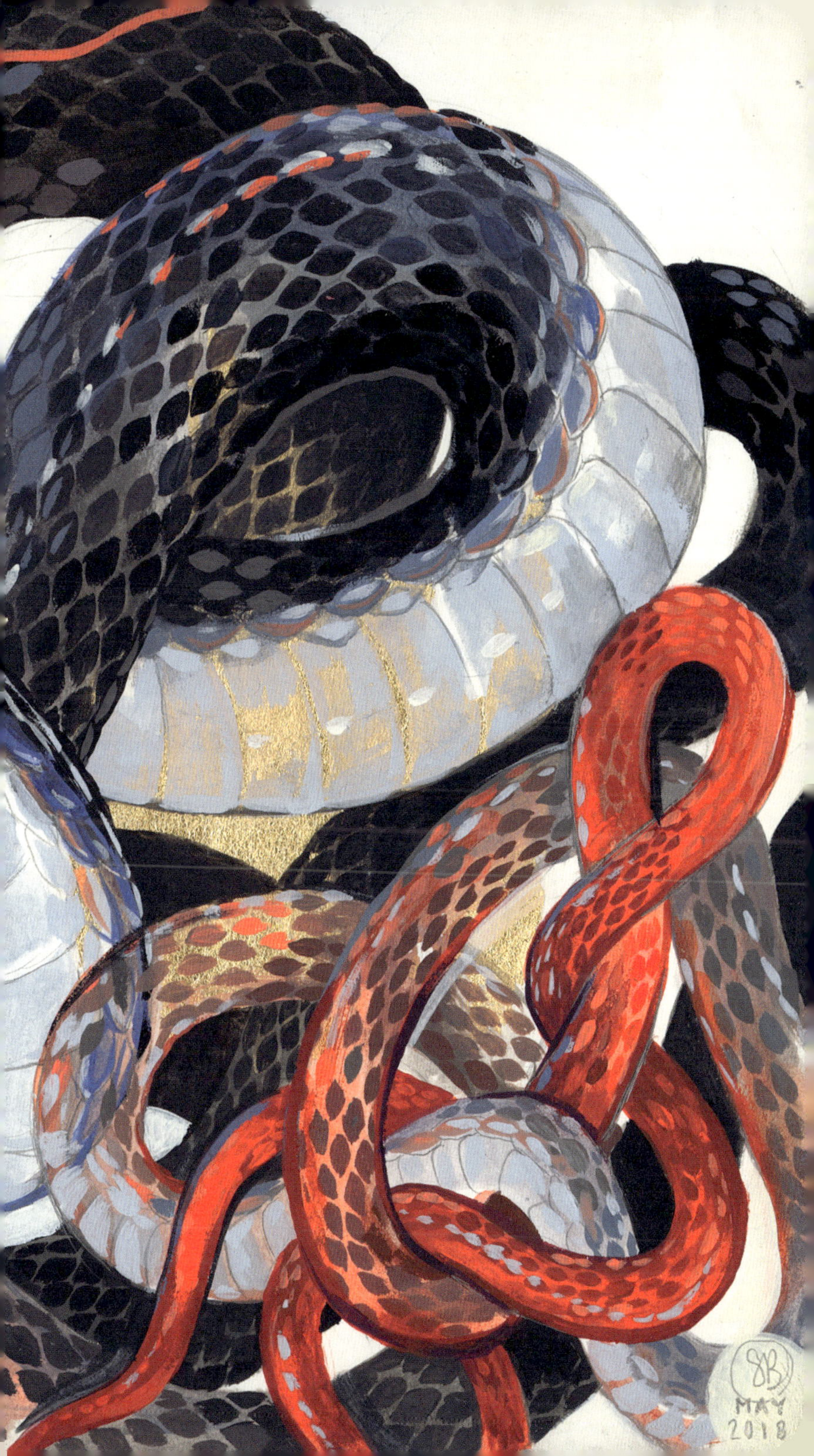

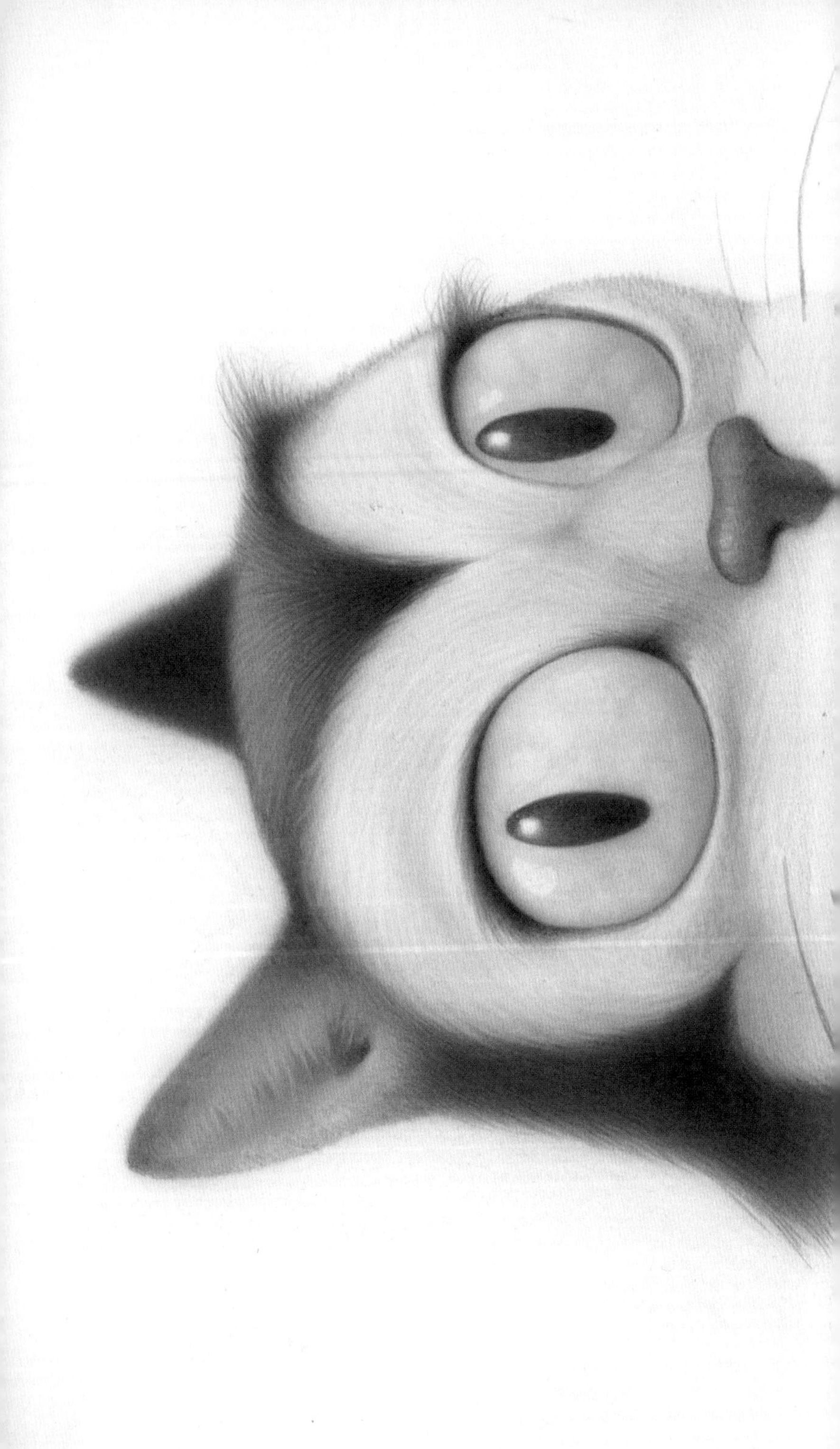

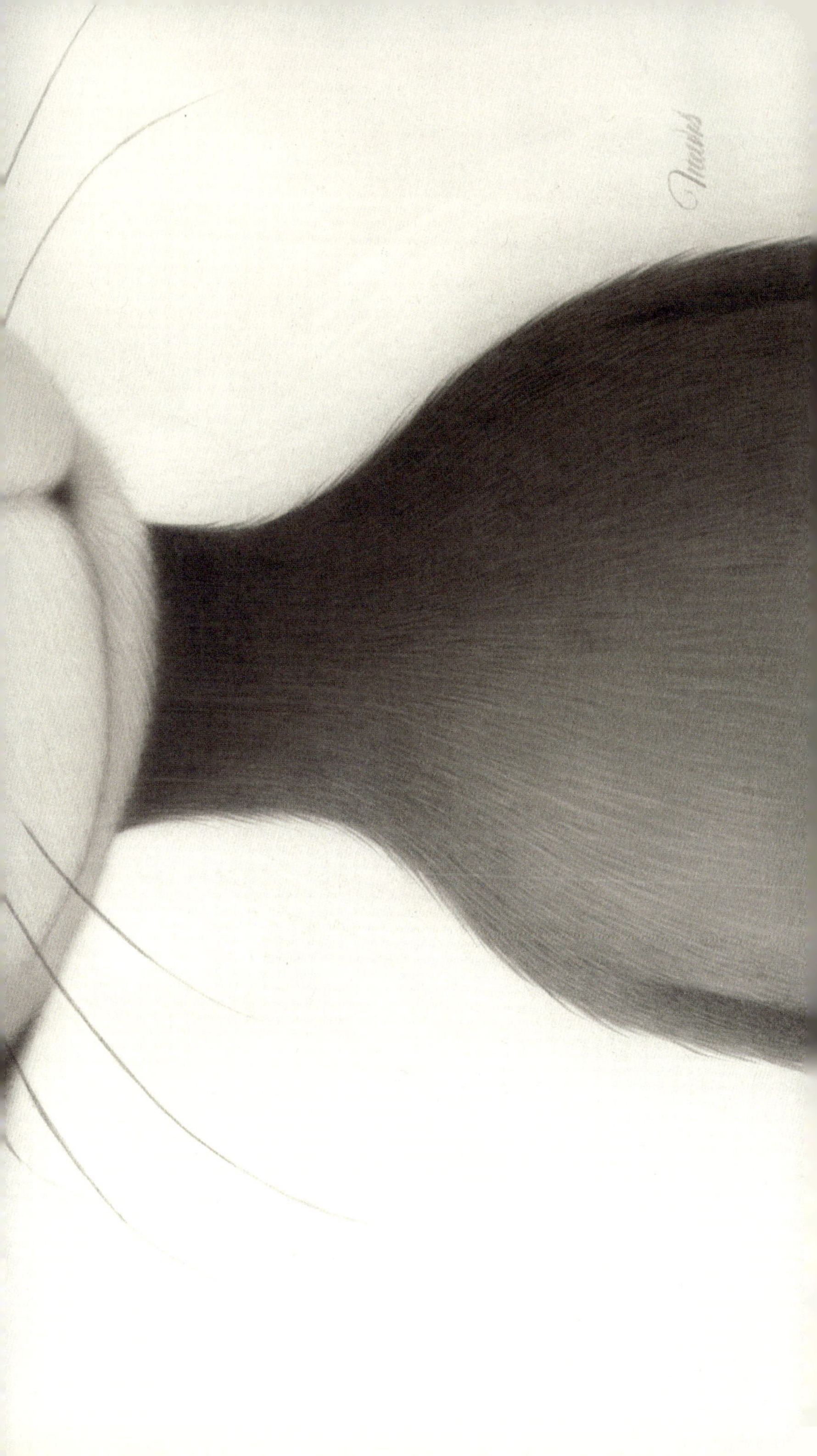

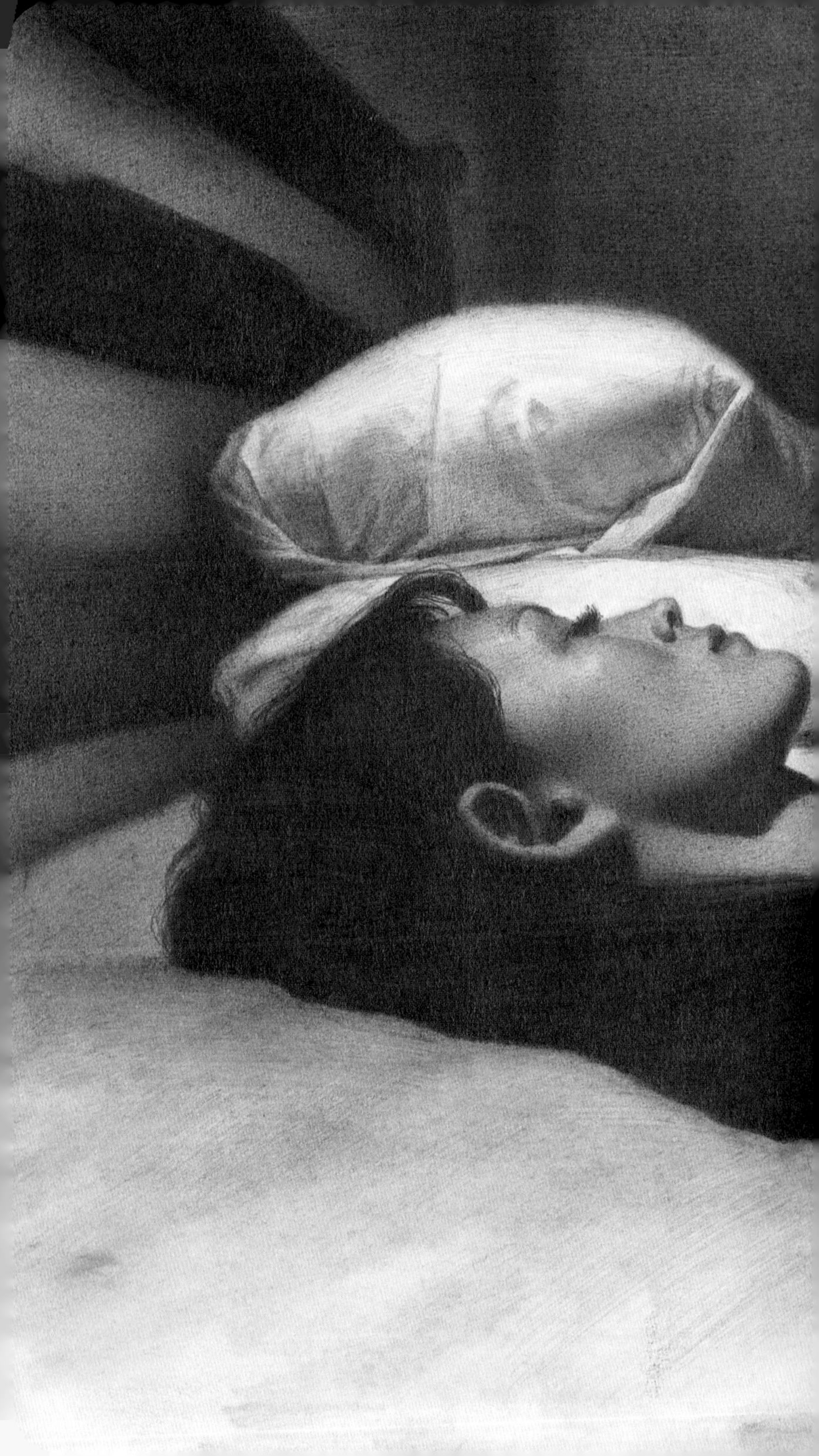

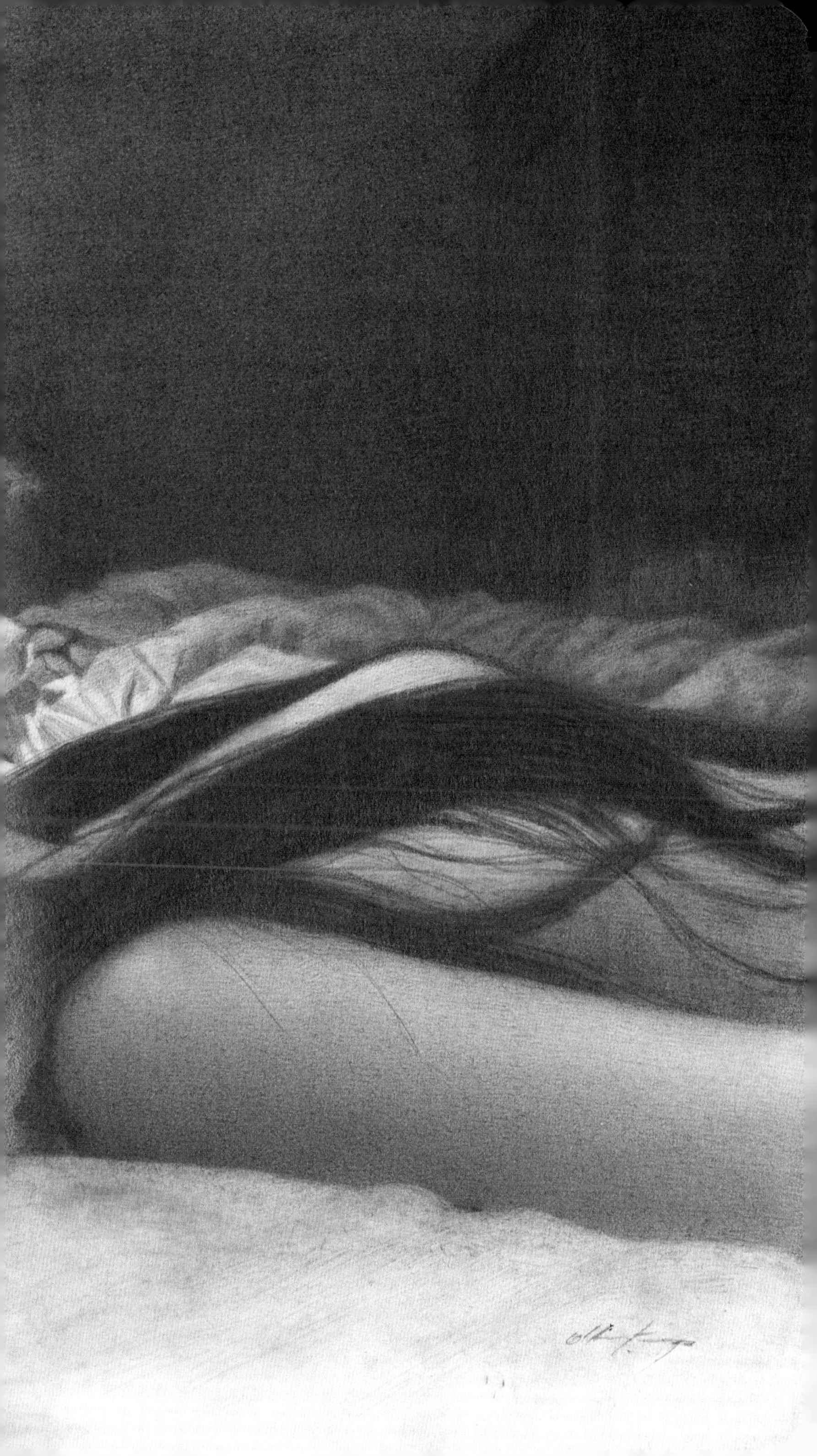

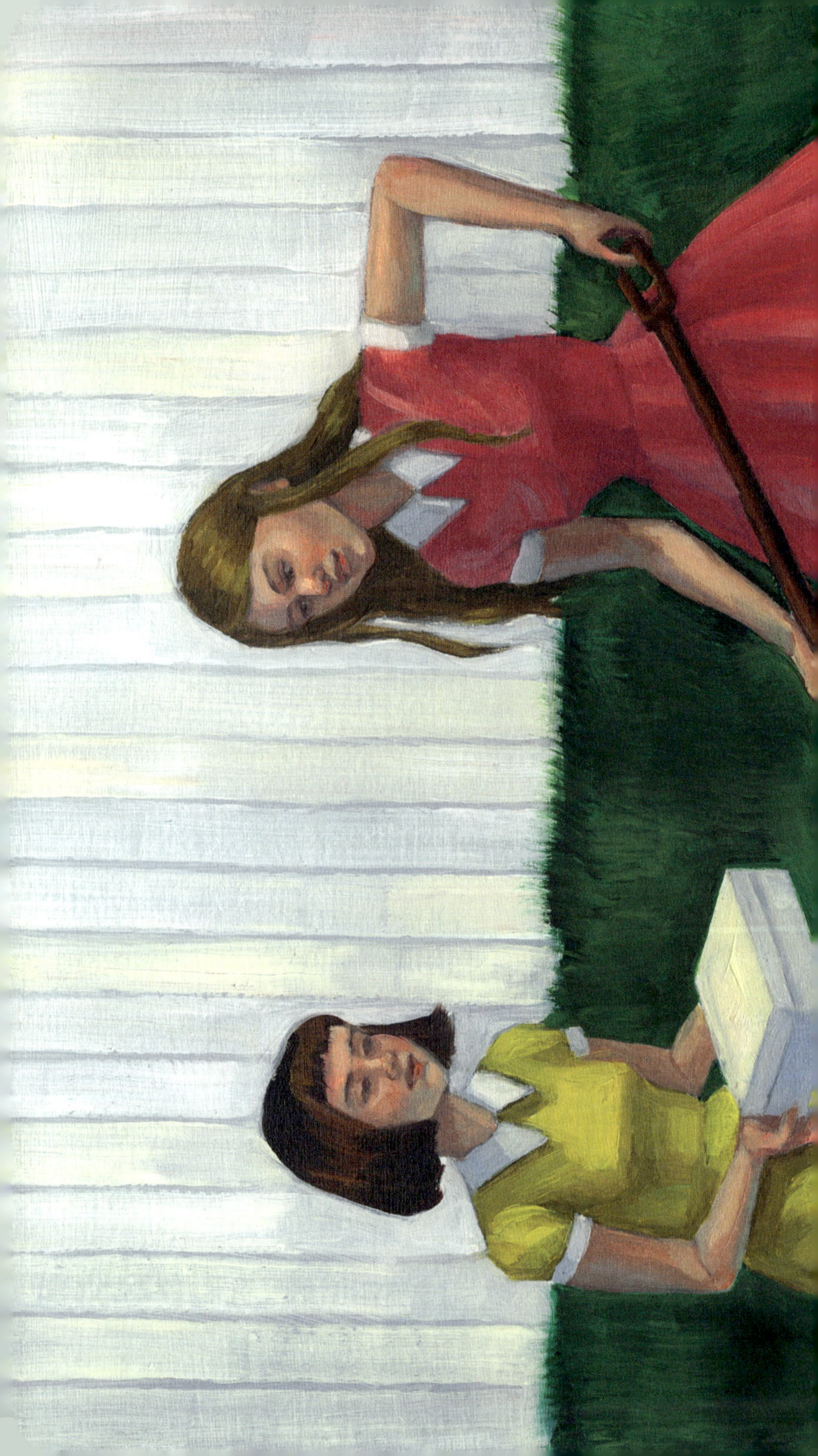

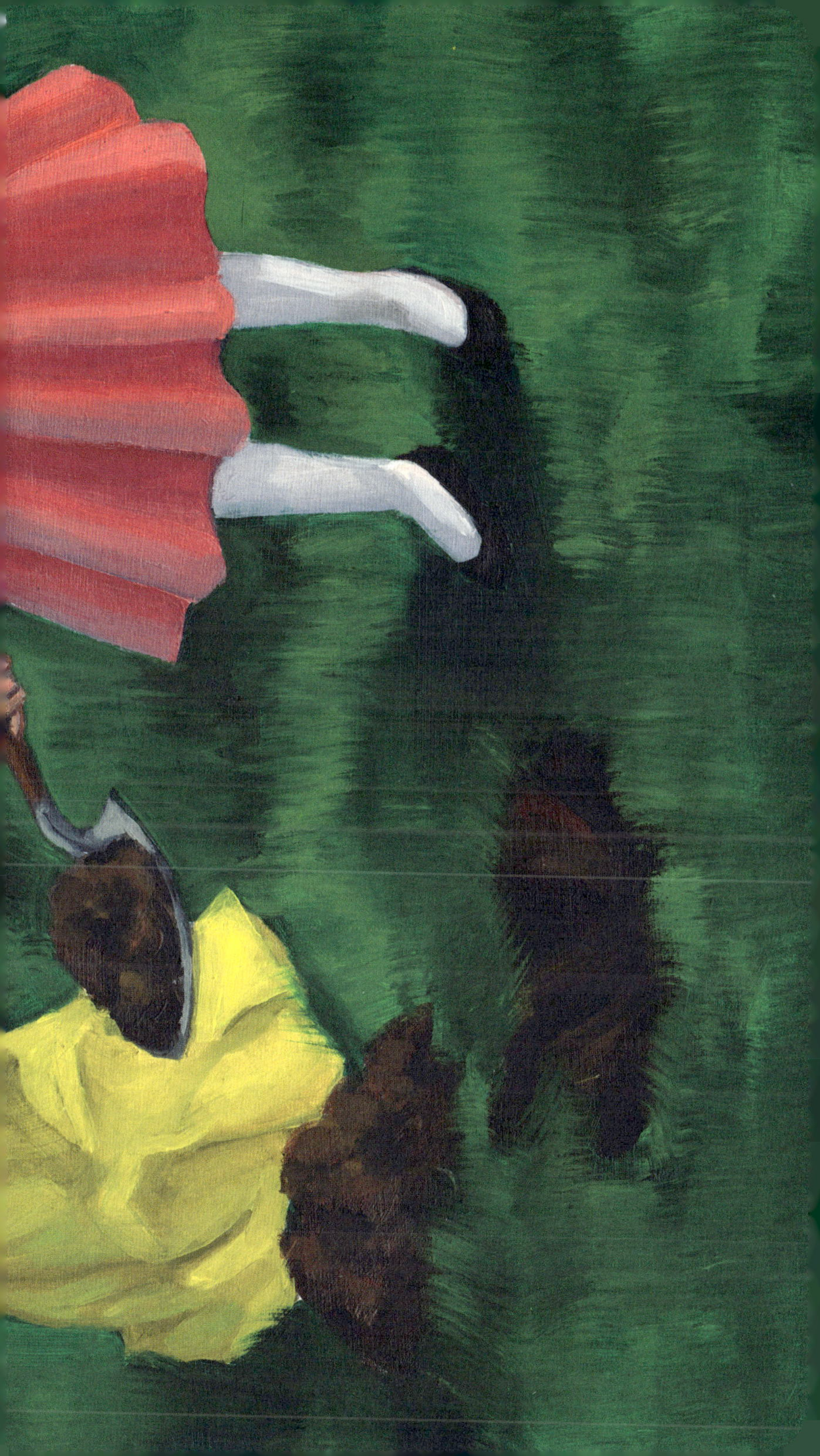

———

[**INDEX**
of
ARTISTS]

———

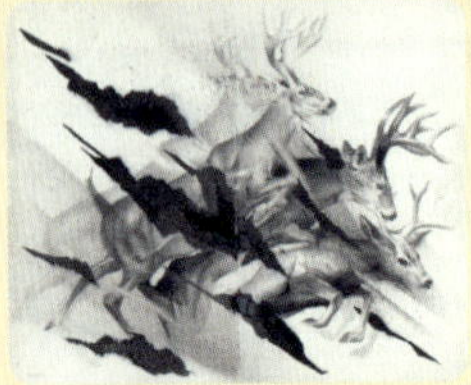

Aaron Li-Hill

Wild Fires

acrylic & aerosol on paper

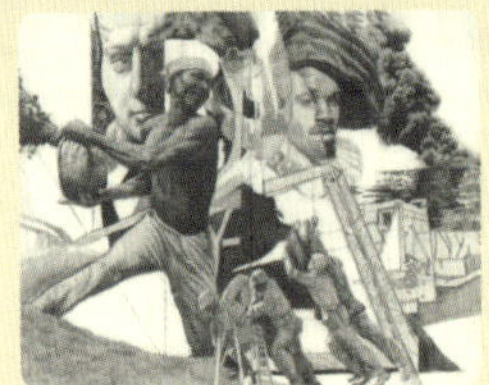

Adam Caldwell

Rare Earth Minerals

graphite on Moleskine

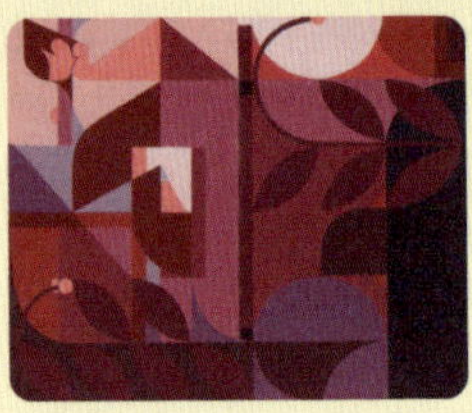

Adrian Kay Wong

Into the Living Room

oil & acrylic paint on Moleskine

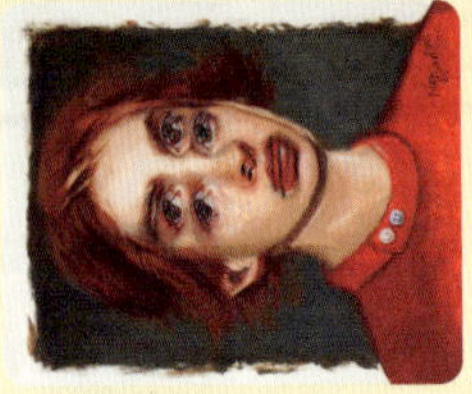

Alex Garant

1999

oil on Moleskine

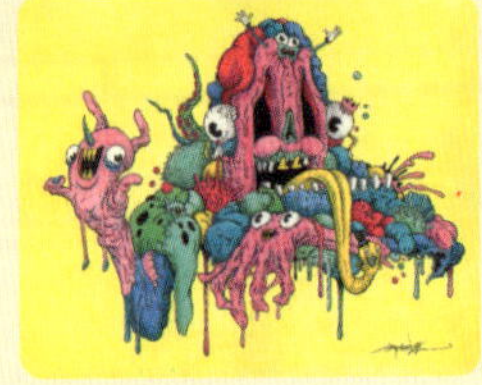

Alex Pardee

Sweathog

watercolor, marker & ink
on Moleskine

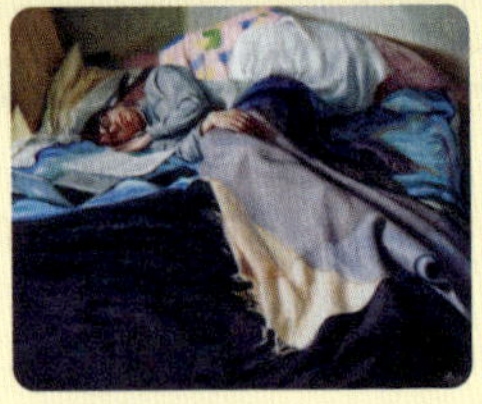

Alexandre Clair

Bedtime Story

oil on Moleskine

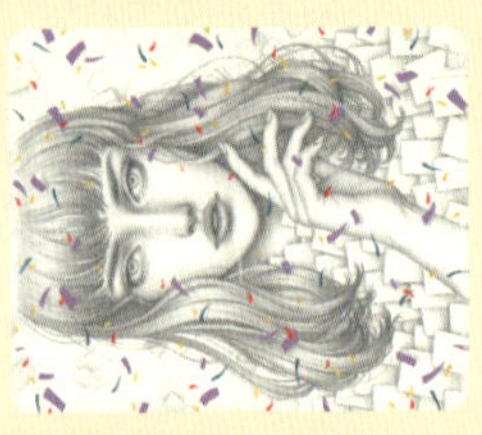

Allison Reimold

Kira

graphite & gouache on Moleskine

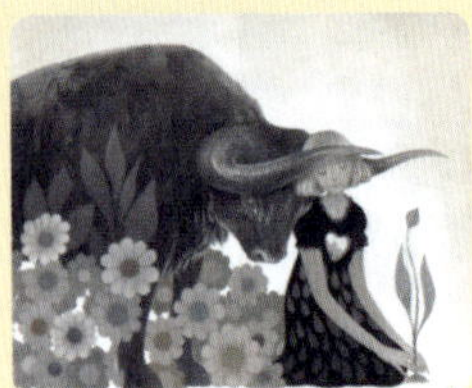

Amy Sol

The Year of the Ox

gouache & oil on Moleskine

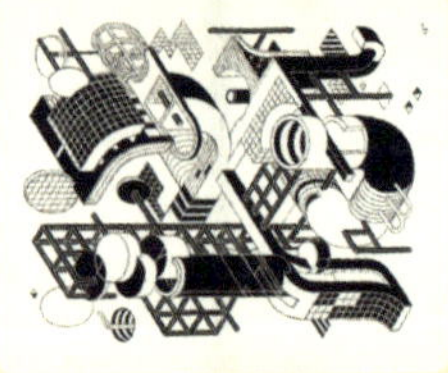

Andrew DeGraff

*Unfinished
Construction Site 30*

gouache on Moleskine

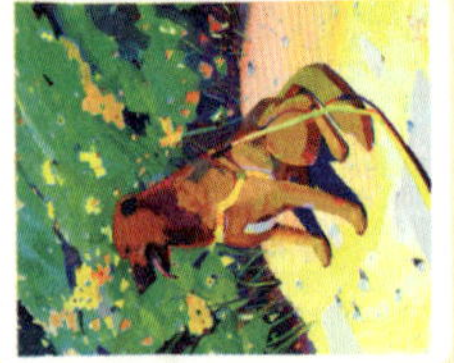

Angela Sung

Done with that Ruff Life

gouache on Moleskine

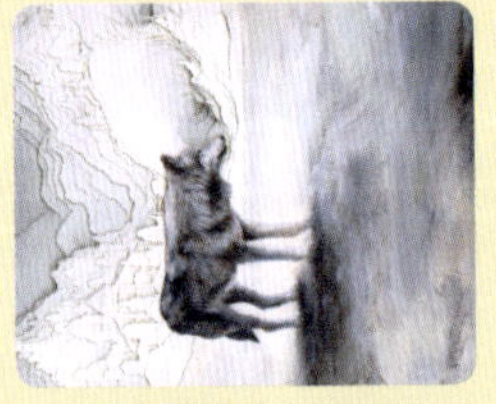

Brian Mashburn

Barred Owl

oil on Moleskine

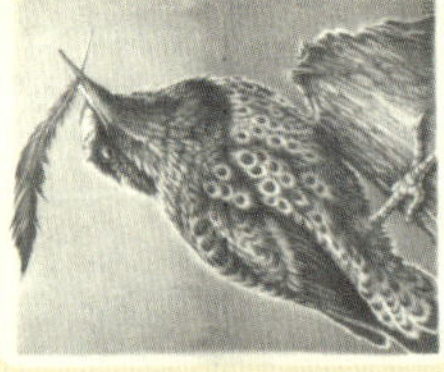

Brin Levinson

The Quill

gouache on Moleskine

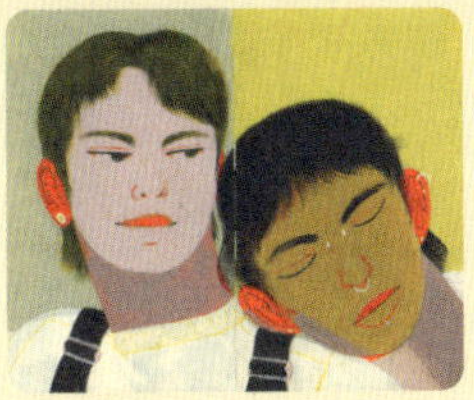

Celia Jacobs

Double Portrait

acrylic on Moleskine

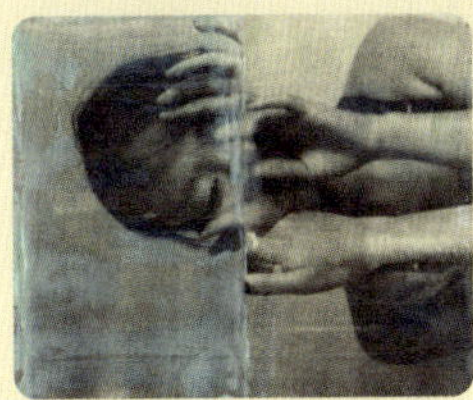

Christine Wu

When We Were Young

carbon, graphite, & wax
on Moleskine

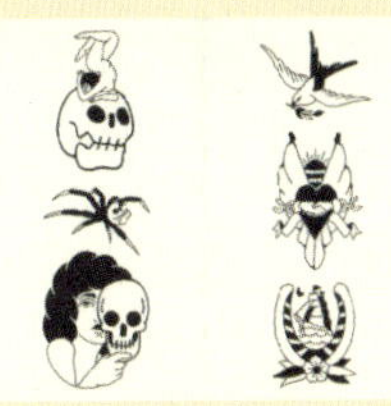

Christopher Martin

Skulls & Nautical Flash

pencil on Moleskine

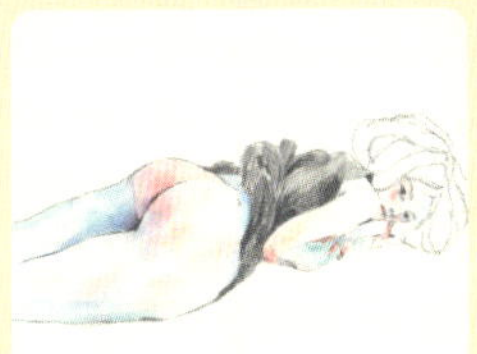

Conrad Roset

Untitled 1

colored pencil on Moleskine

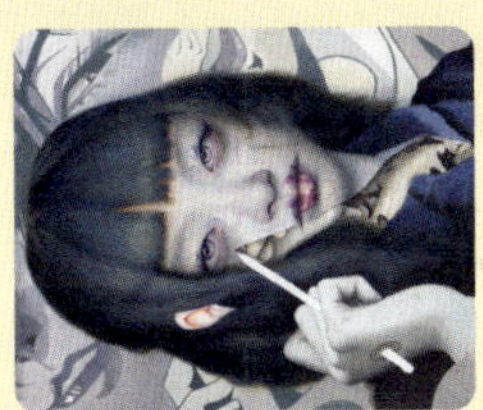

Dan Quintana

Plume

oil on Moleskine

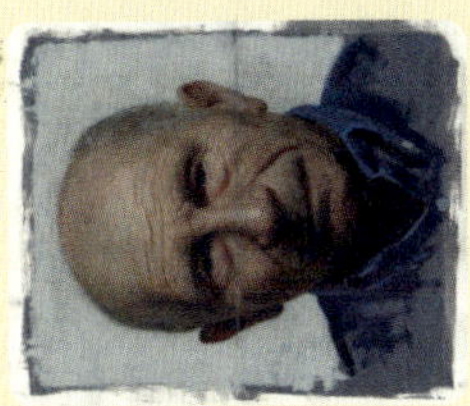

David Kassan

*Andrew Holten, Hidden
Child of the Holocaust*

oil on Moleskine

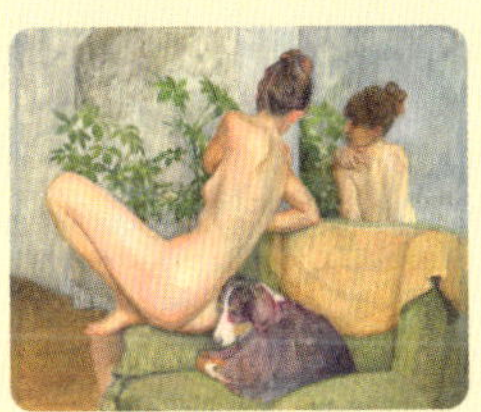

David Molesky

Skin Moles

oil & chalk medium over colored
pencil on Moleskine

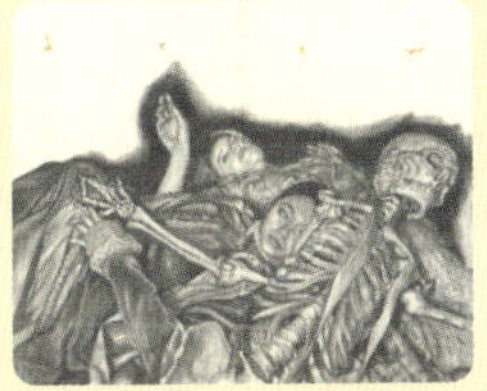

Drew Merrit

Oblivion

pencil & 24k gold on Moleskine

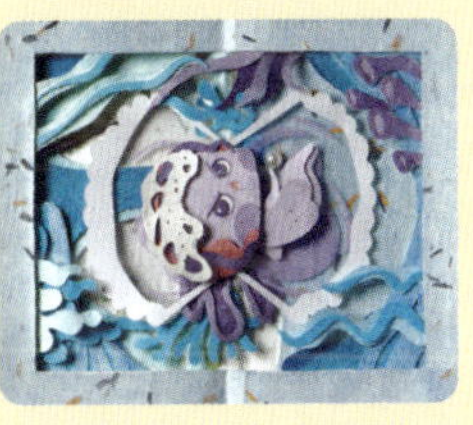

Fenway Fan

1001 Lonely Soul No.10

Mulberry paper, cardstocks &
gemstone on cut-out Moleskine

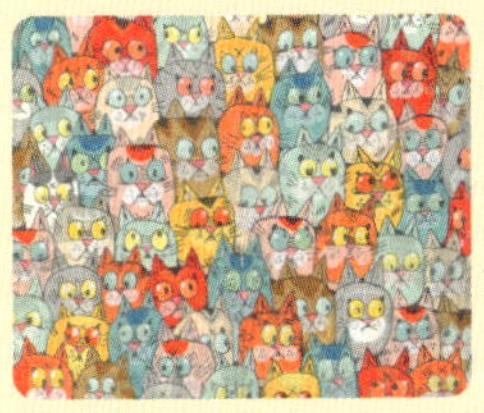

Ferris Plock

*Cats Upon Cats
Upon Cats*

gouache & pencil on Moleskine

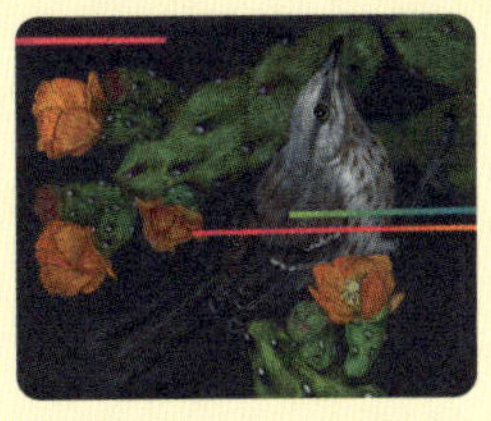

Frank Gonzales

Mockingbird & Nopalito

mixed media (acrylic, gouache &
aerosol) on Moleskine

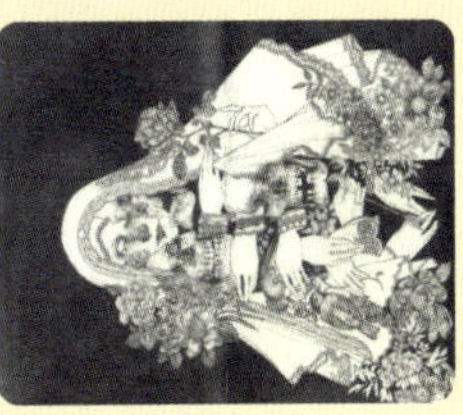

Fumi Mini Nakamura

*Keeping My Existence
Less Familiar*

graphite on Moleskine

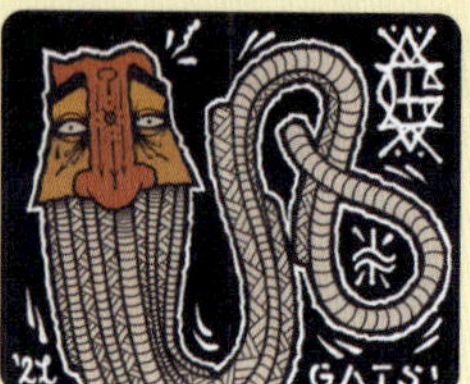

GATS

Unpopular Ideas

acrylic on Moleskine

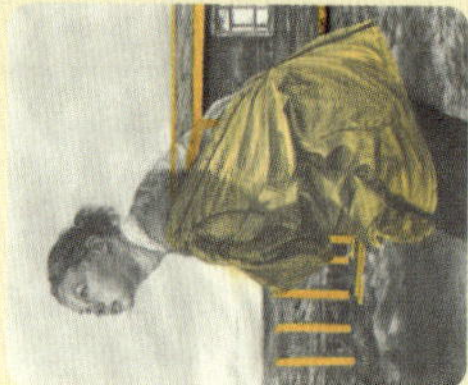

James Thistlethwaite

Valkyrie

graphite & acrylic on Moleskine

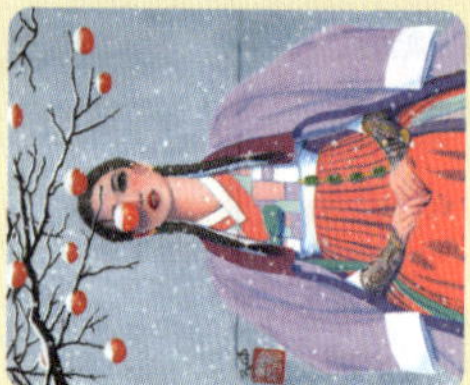

Jason Raish

Cultural Enlightenment

acrylic & ink on Moleskine

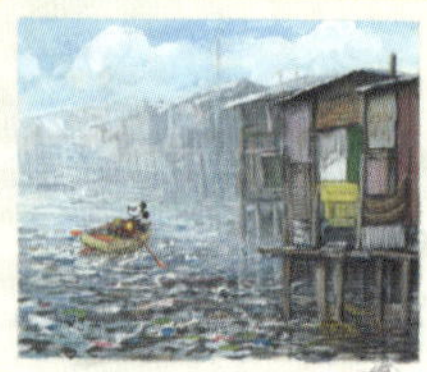

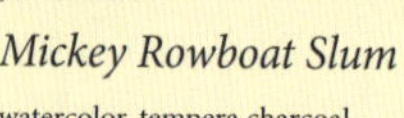

Jeff Gillette

Mickey Rowboat Slum

watercolor, tempera charcoal,
chalk, color pencil & collage
on Moleskine

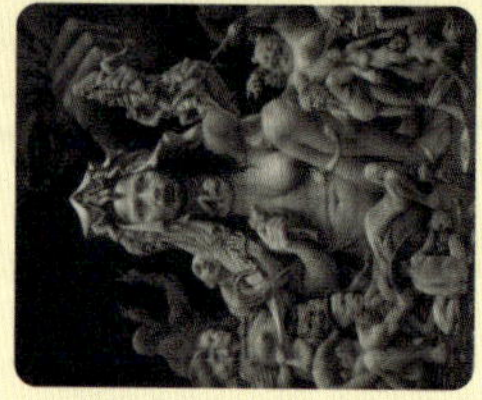

Jeremy Enecio

High Arch

graphite on Moleskine

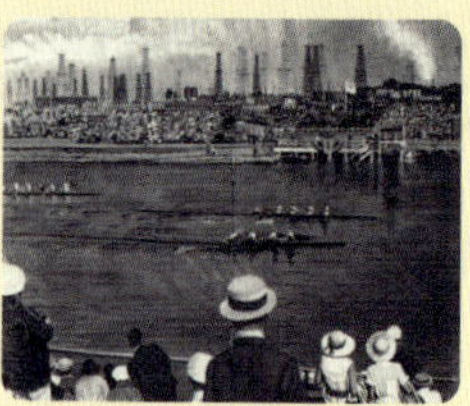

Joel Daniel Phillips

*The Area's Oil Richness
is Revealed*

charcoal, graphite, ink on Moleskine

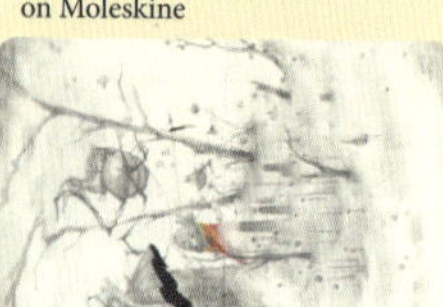

JP Neang

月の兎 *Usagi (On Earth)*

graphite & mixed media
on Moleskine

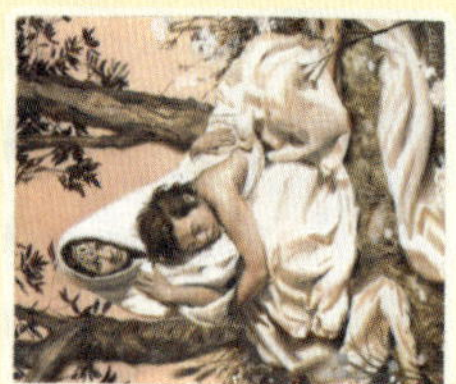

Karla Ortiz

Calm, Calm

oil on Moleskine

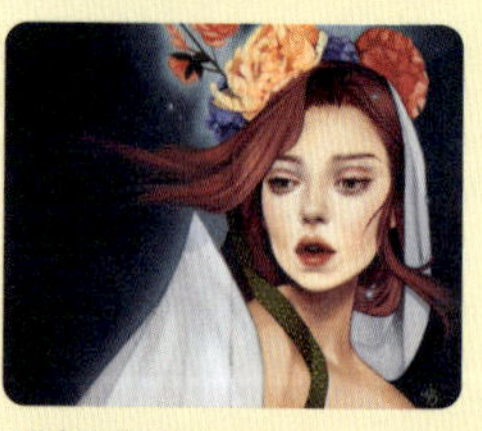

Kelsey Beckett

Soft & Dark

oil on Moleskine

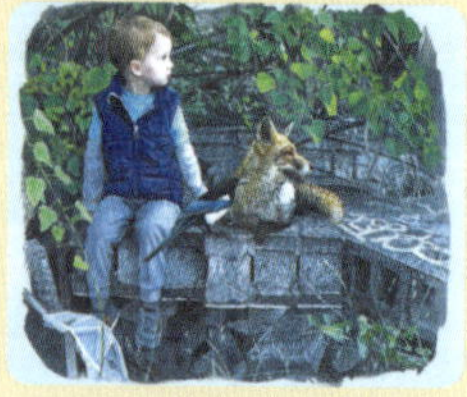

Kevin Peterson

Waiting (with Fox)

oil on Moleskine

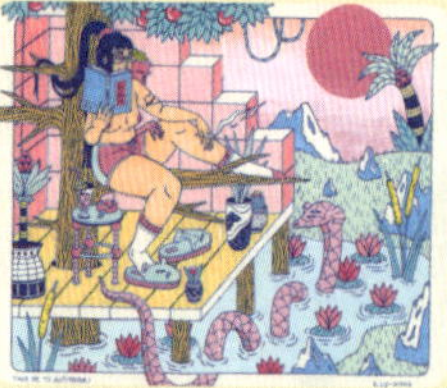

Kristen Liu-Wong

Take Me to Antiterra!

acrylic gouache, pen & mixed
media on Moleskine

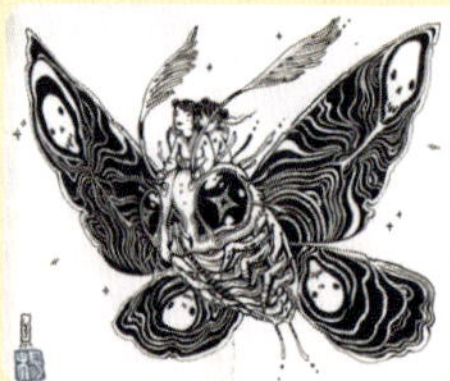

Lauren YS

Moth Riders

ink on Moleskine

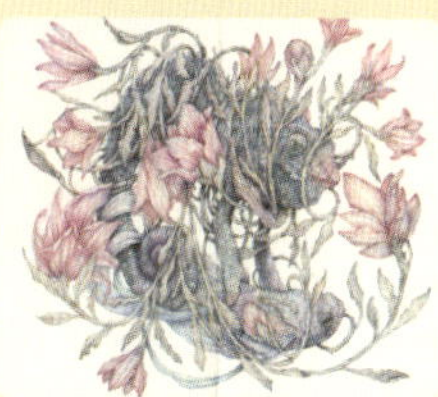

Marco Mazzoni

What We Become

colored pencil on Moleskine

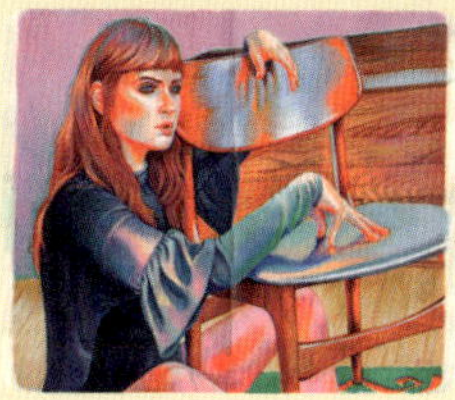

Martine Johanna

Untitled

acrylic on Moleskine

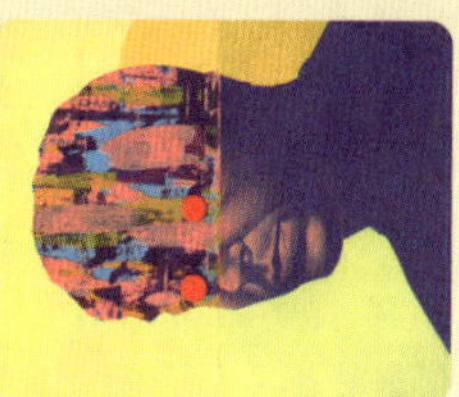

Michael Reeder

Diety 1

acrylic & spray paint on Moleskine

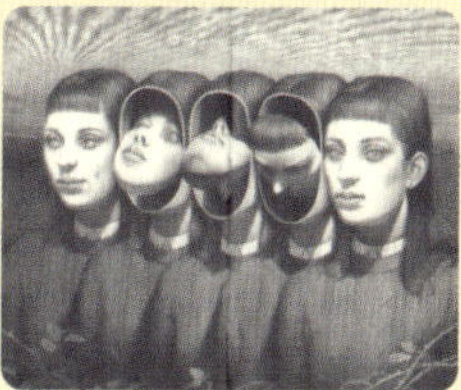

Miles Johnston

Persona Revolution

acrylic & spray paint on Moleskine

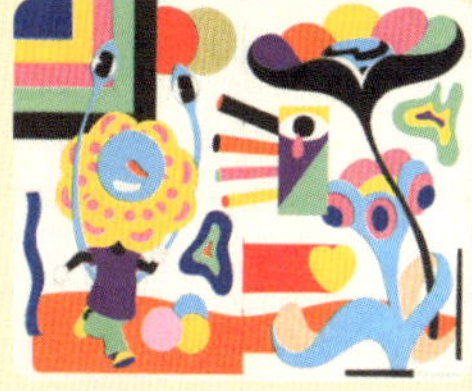

Murugiah

Play II

acrylic on Moleskine

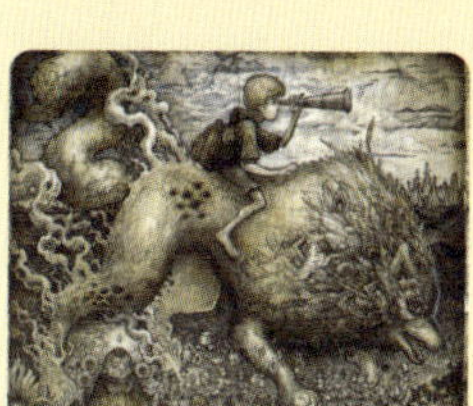

N.C. Winters

Voyager

pen/ink, acrylic on paper

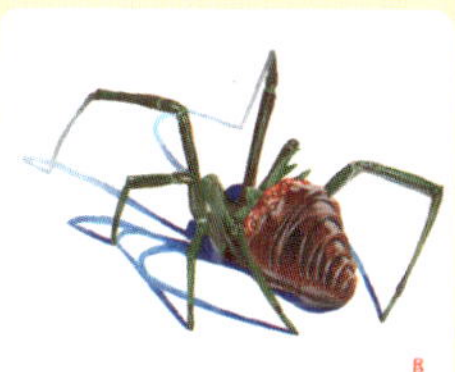

Robert Bowen

Strawberry Surprise

acrylic on Moleskine

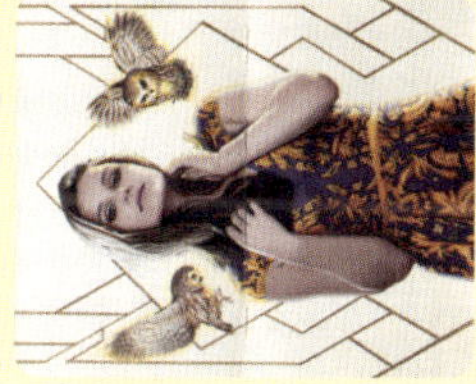

Rod Luff

Golden Dawn

oils & gold iridescent paint
on Moleskine

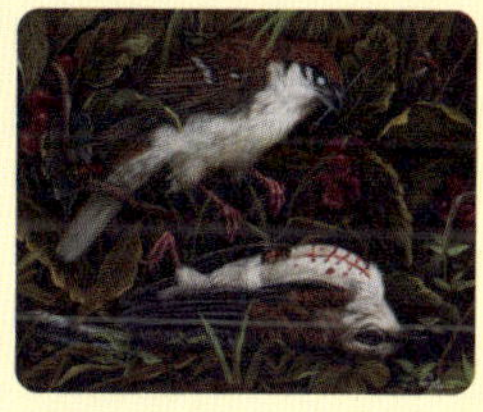

Sam Yong

Suture II

oil on Moleskine

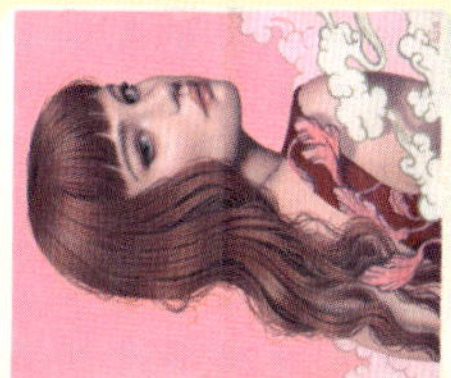

Sarah Joncas

Selina

oil & acrylic on Moleskine

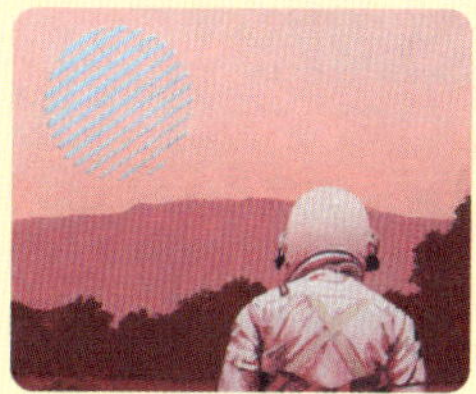

Scott Listfield

Pink Mountains

oil on Moleskine

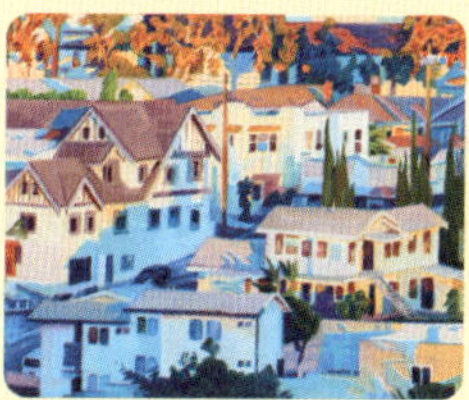

Seth Armstrong

Griffin Avenue Study

oil on Moleskine

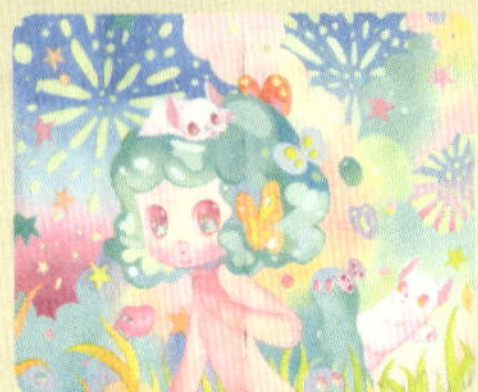

So Youn Lee

Spring

oil on Moleskine

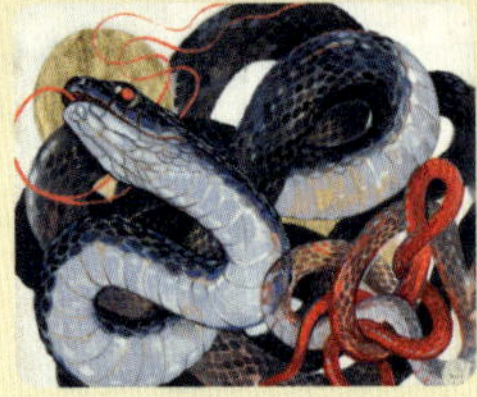

Stephanie Brown

Animus (study)

gouache & gold foil on Moleskine

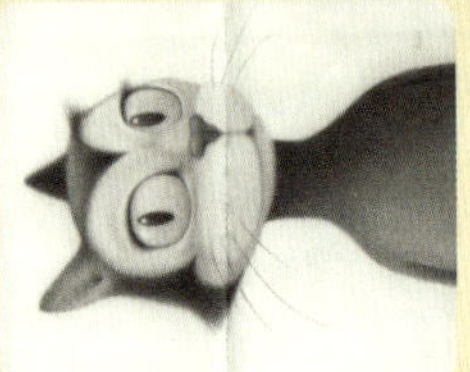

Travis Louie

Owner of a Bag of Tricks

graphite on Moleskine

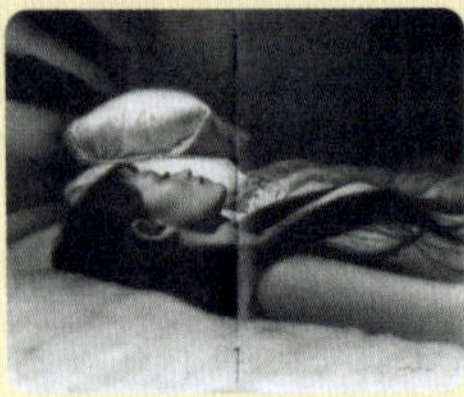

Zachary Oldenkamp

Turn & Disappear

graphite on Moleskine

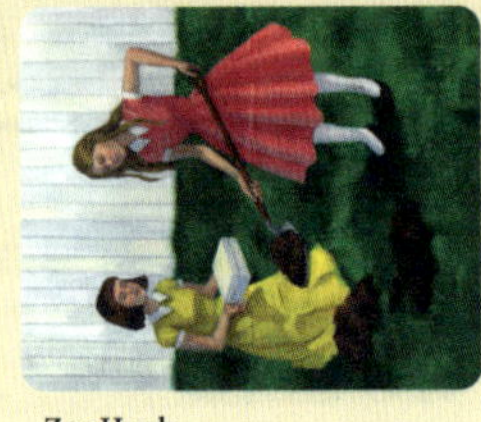

Zoe Hawk

Burial

oil on Moleskine

TMP III was produced by Ken Harman
Hashimoto & Rod Luff and designed
in Oakland, CA by Shaun Roberts.
The book was composed with
Minion Pro for body text and
Eidetic Neo for section titles.

ISBN: 978-1-952251-19-1

FIRST EDITION
2000 COPIES
OCTOBER, 2022

Publication © 2022 PARAGON BOOKS

Paragon Books
929 Camelia Street
Berkeley, CA 94710-1419

WWW.PARAGON-BOOKS.COM
WWW.SPOKE-ART.COM
WWW.RODLUFF.COM

Printed in China